INTERTEXTUALITY

Since Julia Kristeva first coined the term in the 1960s, intertextuality has been a dominant idea within literary and cultural studies, taken up by practically every theoretical movement. Yet intertextuality remains the subject of such a diversity of interpretations and is defined so variously, that it is anything but a transparent, commonly understood term.

This book, the first full-length study of intertextuality in English, follows all the major moves in the term's history and clearly explains how intertextuality is employed in structuralist, post-structuralist, semiotic, deconstructive, postcolonial, Marxist, feminist and psychoanalytic theories. With a wealth of illuminating examples from literary and cultural texts, including special examination of the World Wide Web, this book will prove invaluable for any student of literature and culture.

Graham Allen lectures on eighteenth-century literature, Romantic and Victorian literature, and literary theory at University College, Cork. He is author of *Harold Bloom: A Poetics of Conflict*.

THE NEW CRITICAL IDIOM

SERIES EDITOR: JOHN DRAKAKIS, UNIVERSITY OF STIRLING

The New Critical Idiom is an invaluable series of introductory guides to today's critical terminology. Each book:

- provides a handy, explanatory guide to the use (and abuse) of the term
- offers an original and distinctive overview by a leading literary and cultural critic
- relates the term to the larger field of cultural representation.

With a strong emphasis on clarity, lively debate and the widest possible breadth of examples, *The New Critical Idiom* is an indispensable approach to key topics in literary studies.

- Other books in this series:

INTERTEXTUALITY

Graham Allen

LONDON AND NEW YORK

First published 2000
by Routledge
11 New Fetter Lane, London EC4P 4EE

Simultaneously published in the USA and Canada
by Routledge
29 West 35th Street, New York, NY 10001

Routledge is an imprint of the Taylor & Francis Group

Typeset in Adobe Garamond and Scala Sans by Taylor & Francis
Books Ltd
Printed and bound in Great Britain by Clays Ltd, St Ives plc

British Library Cataloguing in Publication Data
A catalogue record for this book is available from the British Library

Library of Congress Cataloging-in-Publication Data
Allen, Graham
Intertextuality / Graham Allen.
p. cm.
Includes bibliographical references and index.
1. Intertextuality.
I. Title.
PN98.I58   A45   2000
809–dc21   99-055504

ISBN 0–415–17474–0 (hbk)
ISBN 0–415–17475–9 (pbk)

To my father, Arthur George Allen

In your retirement year, Dad, I'm very proud to be your son

CONTENTS

SERIES EDITOR'S PREFACE

The New Critical Idiom is a series of introductory books which seeks to extend the lexicon of literary terms, in order to address the radical changes which have taken place in the study of literature during the last decades of the twentieth century. The aim is to provide clear, well-illustrated accounts of the full range of terminology currently in use, and to evolve histories of its changing usage.

The current state of the discipline of literary studies is one where there is considerable debate concerning basic questions of terminology. This involves, among other things, the boundaries which distinguish the literary from the non-literary; the position of literature within the larger sphere of culture; the relationship between literatures of different cultures; and questions concerning the relation of literary to other cultural forms within the context of interdisciplinary studies.

It is clear that the field of literary criticism and theory is a dynamic and heterogeneous one. The present need is for individual volumes on terms which combine clarity of exposition with an adventurousness of perspective and a breadth of application. Each volume will contain as part of its apparatus some indication of the direction in which the definition of particular terms is likely to move, as well as expanding the disciplinary boundaries within which some of these terms have been traditionally contained. This will involve some re-situation of terms within the larger field of cultural representation, and will introduce examples from the area of film and the modern media in addition to examples from a variety of literary texts.

ACKNOWLEDGEMENTS

In writing this book I have benefited from the advice, support and example of a number of people: Ellen Beardsley, Padraig Bambury, Michael Brown, Liz Brown, Margaret Connolly, David Coughlan, Pat Coughlan, Alex Davis, Gail Davis, John Drakakis, David Duff, Anne Fitzgerald, Paul Hegarty, Lee Jenkins, Colbert Kearney, Pam Morris, Samantha Mullaney, Sinéad Murphy, Michele O'Connor, Talia Rodgers. Many friends have helped me over the period of writing this book and, apart from the above, I would like also to express my gratitude to the following: Deborah Amberson, Gary Baker, Jackie Clarke, Bernie Cronin, David Pickles, Catherine Twomey, Wendy Stewart, and, certainly not least, my mother, Daphne Allen. Thanks to Gail Davis for the quotation of Elizabeth Gaskell on p. 55. To Dani and Chrissie I would just say: thank you for being who you are.

I am grateful for the following permissions to quote copyright material:

Faber and Faber Ltd for 'Mary's Song' from Sylvia Plath, *Collected Poems*, ed. Ted Hughes (Faber and Faber: 1981), and HarperCollins Publishers, Inc. for 'Mary's Song' from *Ariel* by Sylvia Plath, copyright © 1963 by Ted Hughes; Carcanet Press Limited for 'The Red Wheelbarrow' from William Carlos Williams, *Collected Poems*, ed. A. Walton Litz and Christopher MacGowan (Carcanet: 1987) and New Directions Publishing Corporation for 'The Red Wheelbarrow' by William Carlos Williams from *Collected Poems: 1909–1939*, volume 1, ed. Christopher MacGowan (New Directions: 1938), copyright © 1938 by New Directions Publishing Corp.

INTRODUCTION

The idea that when we read a work of literature we are seeking to find a meaning which lies inside that work seems completely commonsensical. Literary texts possess meaning; readers extract that meaning from them. We call the process of extracting meaning from texts reading or interpretation. Despite their apparent obviousness, such ideas have been radically challenged in contemporary literary and cultural theory. Works of literature, after all, are built from systems, codes and traditions established by previous works of literature. The systems, codes and traditions of other art forms and of culture in general are also crucial to the meaning of a work of literature. Texts, whether they be literary or non-literary, are viewed by modern theorists as lacking in any kind of independent meaning. They are what theorists now call intertextual. The act of reading, theorists claim, plunges us into a network of textual relations. To interpret a text, to discover its meaning, or meanings, is to trace those relations. Reading thus becomes a process of moving between texts. Meaning becomes something which exists between a text and all the other texts to which it refers and relates, moving out from the independent text into a network of textual relations. The text becomes the intertext.

Intertextuality is one of the most commonly used and misused terms in contemporary critical vocabulary. 'An Intertextual Study of ... ' or 'Intertextuality and ... ' are such commonplace constructions in the titles of critical works that one might be forgiven for assuming that intertextuality is a term that is generally understood and provides a stable set of critical procedures for interpretation. Nothing, in fact, could be further from the truth. The term is defined so variously that it is, currently, akin to such terms as 'the Imagination', 'history', or 'Postmodernism': terms which are, to employ a phrase from the work of the US critic Harold Bloom, underdetermined in meaning and overdetermined in figuration. Intertextuality, one of the central ideas in contemporary literary theory, is not a transparent term and so, despite its confident utilization by many theorists and critics, cannot be evoked in an uncomplicated manner. Such a term is in danger of meaning nothing more than whatever each particular critic wishes it to mean.

This book does not seek to rectify this confusion by uncovering a fundamental definition of the term. Such a project would be doomed to failure. What is required is for us to return to the term's history and to remind ourselves of how and why it has taken on its current meanings and applications. The need to engage in such a project is a pressing one for literary critics and theorists as well as those wishing to learn about the term for the first time. The project which is undertaken by this book can thus be described as both a theoretical intervention and an introduction to a crucial area of theoretical debate.

Intertextuality, like modern literary and cultural theory itself, can be said to have its origins in twentieth-century linguistics, particularly in the seminal work of the Swiss linguist Ferdinand de Saussure. The first chapter of this study, therefore, will explain the ways in which Saussurean linguistics promotes notions of intertextuality. For readers unfamiliar with the field, beginning with the linguistic theories of Saussure has the added advantage of establishing some of the basic principles of modern literary theory. As we will see, Saussure's emphasis on the systematic features of language establishes the relational nature of meaning and thus of texts. However, intertextuality also emerges from theories which are more concerned than Saussure seems to be with the existence of language within specific social situations. The work of the Russian literary theorist M. M. Bakhtin is crucial here, and we will also explore Bakhtin's influential theories of literature and language. As readers move through this book they will find that Bakhtin's theories continually return to inform different theories of intertextuality. Julia Kristeva's attempt to combine Saussurean and Bakhtinian theories of language and literature produced the first articulation of intertextual theory, in the late 1960s, and an examination of her work in this area forms a necessary part in our survey of the origins of the term.

Kristeva's work on Bakhtin occurred during a transitional period in modern literary and cultural theory. This transition is usually described in terms of a move from structuralism to poststructuralism. What this move involves will form part of the analysis of Kristeva's work in Chapter 1. This transition is often characterized as one in which assertions of objectivity, scientific rigour, methodological stability and other highly rationalistic-sounding terms are replaced by an emphasis on uncertainty, indeterminacy, incommunicability, subjectivity, desire, pleasure and play. If structuralist literary critics believe that Saussurean linguistics can help criticism become objective, even scientific in nature, then poststructuralist critics of the 1960s and beyond have argued that criticism, like literature itself, is inherently unstable, the product of subjective desires and drives. The term intertextuality was initially employed by poststructuralist theorists and critics in their attempt to disrupt notions of stable meaning and objective interpretation. The second chapter of this study will move from Kristeva to one of the most famous exponents of poststructuralist theory, the French theorist Roland Barthes.

As Chapter 2 will demonstrate, Barthes employs intertextual theory to challenge long-held assumptions concerning the role of the author in the production of meaning and the very nature of literary meaning itself. For Barthes, literary meaning can never be fully stabilized by the reader, since the literary work's intertextual nature always leads readers on to new textual relations. Authors, therefore, cannot be held responsible for the multiple meanings readers can discover within literary texts. Barthes views such a situation as a liberation for readers; a liberation from the traditional power and authority of the figure of the 'author', who is now 'dead'. By the end of Chapter 2 readers unfamiliar with modern literary theory should have a much firmer grasp of the part intertextuality plays in poststructuralism, and indeed a much firmer grasp of what characterizes poststructuralism itself.

Barthes's deployment of intertextuality, his celebration of plurality and the freedom from constraint of all readers, is characteristically poststructuralist. There has, however, been another strand within theories of intertextuality which has taken a very different approach to the relationship between readers and the literary texts they read. Grouping such critics and theorists under the broad heading of 'Structuralist Approaches', Chapter 3 explores how intertextuality can be used to argue for critical positions at times diametrically opposed to those of Kristeva and Barthes. Despite differences between them, the French literary critics Gérard Genette and Michael Riffaterre both employ intertextual theory to argue for critical certainty, or at least for the possibility of saying definite, stable and incontrovertible things about literary texts.

That poststructuralist critics employ the term intertexuality to disrupt notions of meaning, whilst structuralist critics employ the same term to locate and even fix literary meaning, is proof enough of its flexibility as a concept. Chapter 4, however, will demonstrate that the different ways in which intertextuality has been used often stem from specific social and ideological agendas and perspectives. Harold Bloom's interest in the motivations behind poetic production directs him towards intertextual theory, but to a version of it which seems far from Barthes's celebration of the 'death of the Author'. As we will discover, other theorists and critics, working from feminist and postcolonial positions, have also attempted to deploy intertextual theory without necessarily embracing the celebration of plurality and the 'death of the Author' that poststructuralism would associate with that term. To feminist and postcolonial critics, concerned with marginalized and oppressed communities and individuals, the 'death of the Author' and the celebration of interpretive uncertainty are not as obviously liberatory as they appear to be to critics such as Barthes.

As we move through the various critical positions which intertextuality has inspired we will frequently observe that it is a term by no means exclusively related to literary works, or even simply to written communication. Chapter 5 will explore ways in which intertextuality has been adapted by critics of non-literary art forms such as painting, music and architecture. Having reached this chapter, readers will be aware of the manner in which accounts of intertextuality reflect visions of society and human relations. A concept such as this can be employed to make comments on, or even capture the characteristics of, a section of society or even a period of history. Many theorists style our current historical period in terms of the concept of Postmodernism. As a cultural and historical term, this is often associated with notions of pastiche, imitation and the mixing of already established styles and practices. Anyone aware of contemporary cultural trends will be familiar with discussions of the derivativeness of modern music, or the manner in which the film industry seems so dependent upon classic literary texts such as those by Shakespeare, or Jane Austen. Contemporary painting seems constantly to rely on recognizable images from past classic paintings; even contemporary literature seems concerned with echoing and playing with previous stories, classic texts and long-established genres such as the romance and the detective story. Intertextuality, as the discussion of Postmodern theory in Chapter 5 will demonstrate, is a major concept within discussions of contemporary culture.

Intertextuality seems such a useful term because it foregrounds notions of relationality, interconnectedness and interdependence in modern cultural life. In the Postmodern epoch, theorists often claim, it is not possible any longer to speak of originality or the uniqueness of the artistic object, be it a painting or a novel, since every artistic object is so clearly assembled from bits and pieces of already existent art. Intertextuality, as a term, stands at the centre of such contemporary conceptions of art and cultural production generally. As Barthes reminds us, the very word 'text' is, if we remember its original meanings, 'a tissue, a woven fabric' (Barthes, 1977a: 159). The idea of the text, and thus of intertextuality, depends, as Barthes argues, on the figure of the web, the weave, the garment (text) woven from the threads of the 'already written' and the 'already read'. Every text has its meaning, therefore, in relation to other texts. As we shall see throughout this study, this relationality can itself be figured in various ways: it can involve the radical plurality of the sign, the relation between signs and texts and the cultural text, the relation between a text and the literary system, or the transformative relation between one text and another text. However it is used, the term intertextuality promotes a new vision of meaning, and thus of authorship and reading: a vision resistant to ingrained notions of originality, uniqueness, singularity and autonomy. That such a turn of vision, when first articulated, looked forward to a world that in the 1960s and 1970s did not yet quite exist, as well as to a world that did, can be registered simply by switching our attention to the realm of the World Wide Web.

This study, then, follows intertextuality through its major theoretical contexts, from its origins in Kristeva's blending of Saussure and Bakhtin, through its poststructuralist articulation in the work of Barthes and its structuralist articulation in Genette and Riffaterre, on to feminist and postcolonial adaptations of the term, and finally to its application within the non-literary arts, the current cultural epoch and modern computer technologies. The study mounts a coherent history of the term and demonstrates links between the various approaches as well as the differences between them. Readers of this study will probably decide, therefore, to read it from beginning to end. Other readers, who may already have a knowledge of particular theories, may decide to begin with the chapters in which those approaches are discussed before circling backwards to the beginning. Readers unfamiliar with complex theoretical issues might find it more useful to skip the most densely argued theories – principally, those of Kristeva and Riffaterre – and to concentrate on the more accessible aspects of the issue, returning later to those less immediately accessible sections. Readers with a particular concern with one of the theoretical fields discussed might find that the best reading strategy is to read the sections on Saussure and Bakhtin and then to move directly to their specific area of interest. Intertextual reading encourages us to resist a passive reading of texts from cover to cover. There is never a single or correct way to read a text, since every reader brings with him or her different expectations, interests, viewpoints and prior reading experiences. Each reader of this study is encouraged to read it in whatever order best suits his or her purpose.

This book is designed for those studying at undergraduate levels, but also for those who have already passed through such a course of study. Most of the chapters which make up this book attempt to express the principal points involved in any particular area in the simplest way possible, before moving on to more subtle and sometimes technical issues. This movement from simplicity to complexity is particularly evident in Chapters 1, 2 and 3. Readers unfamiliar with modern theoretical debates might therefore help themselves by bearing this fact in mind as they read those initial chapters. To assist such readers a Glossary is included. A Bibliography has also been included to assist further reading in the field.

This study is written from a conviction that intertextuality is and will remain a crucial element in the attempt to understand literature and culture in general. Without a working knowledge of intertextual theory and practice, readers are likely to retain traditional notions of writing and reading, notions which have been radically challenged since the 1960s. The term intertextuality, however, emerges from the complex history of modern literary theory. Its very meaning contains this history, and cannot be grasped unless we have some knowledge of that history. To begin our study of the term, therefore, we must return to its origins, the linguistic theories of Saussure and Bakhtin.

1

ORIGINS: SAUSSURE, BAKHTIN, KRISTEVA

THE RELATIONAL WORD: SAUSSURE

Literary and cultural theory is often viewed as taking its origins from the birth of modern linguistics: a discipline which can be said to emerge in the work of Ferdinand de Saussure. In his *Course in General Linguistics*, a collection of his lectures first published in 1915, Saussure looked again at the fundamental question: what is a linguistic sign? Dividing the sign into parts, Saussure produced a definition in which a sign can be imagined as a two-sided coin combining a *signified* (concept) and a *signifier* (sound-image). This notion of the linguistic sign emphasizes that its meaning is non-referential: a sign is not a word's reference to some object in the world but the combination, conveniently sanctioned, between a signifier and a signified. In the English language we employ the word 'tree' not because it literally points to certain tree-like objects in the world but because the signifier 'tree' is associated with a certain concept. In Latin we would employ the signifier *'arbor'* to refer to the same concept; in Saussure's original French it would be designated by the word *'arbre'*. Signs are arbitrary, possessing meaning not because of a referential function but because of their function within a linguistic system as it exists at any one moment of time. Language as it exists at any moment of time is referred to as the *synchronic* system of language, rather than the *diachronic* element of language, which evolves through time. When humans write or speak they may believe they are being referential, but in fact they are producing specific acts of linguistic communication (*parole*) out of the available synchronic system of language (*langue*). The reference of the sign is to the system, not directly to the world.

Such a recognition of the arbitrary or non-referential nature of linguistic communication has many implications for traditional ideas about what it means to employ language. If traditional notions present us with a vision of a human speaker originating the meanings contained in his or her chosen words, then Saussure's linguistics replaces that vision with the recognition that all acts of communication stem from choices made within a system which pre-exists any speaker. As Barthes writes, clarifying the idea of *la langue*:

> It [*la langue*] is the social part of language, the individual cannot himself either create or modify it; it is essentially a collective constraint which one must accept in its entirety if one wishes to communicate.
>
> (Barthes, 1984: 82)

For Saussure, the linguistic sign is not simply arbitrary, it is also *differential*. The sign 'tree' has its place in the system of language (*la langue*) because of its position with regard to sets of related sounds and words. To write the sentence 'The tree is green' is to select the word 'tree' out of a set of related sounds – 'sea' or 'bee' – and related words – 'bush', 'trunk', 'branch' and all the particular names of trees, like oak or ash. The placing of words together in sentences involves what is termed the *syntagmatic* (combinatory) axis of language; the selection of certain words out of sets of possible words involves what is termed the *paradigmatic* (selection) axis of language. Any piece of language (*parole*) is produced by processes of combination along the syntagmatic axis and of selection along the paradigmatic axis.

The meanings we produce and find within language, then, are

relational; they depend upon processes of combination and association within the differential system of language itself. This relational aspect of language cannot be avoided or overcome. Saussure, in the *Course*, writes the following:

> in language there are only differences. Even more important: a difference generally implies positive terms between which the difference is set up; but in language there are only differences *without positive terms*. Whether we take the signified or the signifier, language has neither ideas nor sounds that existed before the linguistic system, but only conceptual and phonic differences that have issued from the system.
>
> (Saussure, 1974: 120)

Signs are not 'positive terms'; they are not referential, they only possess what meaning they do possess because of their combinatory and associative relation to other signs. No sign has a meaning of its own. Signs exist within a system and produce meaning through their similarity to and difference from other signs. The implications of such a vision of the sign, and of language generally, can be said to have affected all areas of the human sciences in the twentieth century. Saussure, in the *Course*, imagines a new science which would study 'the life of signs within society' which he calls *semiology* (Saussure, 1974: 16). Structuralism, a critical, philosophical and cultural movement based on the notions of Saussurean semiology sought, from the 1950s onwards, to produce a revolutionary redescription of human culture in terms of sign-systems modelled on Saussure's redefinitions of sign and linguistic structure. This revolution in thought, which has been styled the 'linguistic turn' in the human sciences, can be understood as one origin of the theory of intertextuality.

To cite Saussure as the origin of ideas concerning intertextuality is a move not without its problems, however. It is as viable to cite the Russian literary theorist M. M. Bakhtin as the originator, if not of the term 'intertextuality', then at least of the specific view of language which helped others articulate theories of intertextuality. Bakhtin, as we will see, takes a very different approach to language and is far more concerned than Saussure with the social contexts within which words are exchanged. If the relational nature of the word for Saussure stems from a vision of language seen as a generalized and abstract system, for Bakhtin it stems from the word's existence within specific social sites, specific social registers and specific moments of utterance and reception. Since neither Saussure nor Bakhtin actually employs the term, most people would wish to credit Julia Kristeva with being the inventor of 'intertextuality'. Kristeva, as we shall observe, is influenced by both Bakhtinian and Saussurean models and attempts to combine their insights and major theories.

Despite the above points, it is true enough to say that the basis upon which many of the major theories of intertextuality are developed takes us back to Saussure's notion of the differential sign. If all signs are in some way differential, they can be understood not only as non-referential in nature but also as shadowed by a vast number of possible relations. The linguistic sign is, after Saussure, a non-unitary, non-stable, relational unit, the understanding of which leads us out into the vast network of relations, of similarity and difference, which constitutes the synchronic system of language. If this is true of linguistic signs in general, then, as many after Saussure have argued, it is doubly true of the literary sign. Authors of literary works do not just select words from a language system, they select plots, generic features, aspects of character, images, ways of narrating, even phrases and sentences from previous literary texts and from the literary tradition. If we imagine the literary tradition as itself a synchronic system, then the literary author becomes a figure working with at least two systems, those of language in general and of the literary system in particular. Such a point reinforces Saussure's stress on the non-referential nature of signs, since in reading literature we become intensely aware that the signs deployed in any particular text have their reference not to objects in the world but to the literary system out of which the text is produced. If a modern author, for example, presents a characterization of Satan in their text they are far more likely to have in mind John Milton's representation of

Satan in his epic poem *Paradise Lost* than any literal notion of the Christian Devil. Similarly, if we read a novel in which a young heroine is pursued by supernatural forces before being imprisoned by an evil uncle in a ruined castle, our thoughts will be less of what actually happens in the world than of the tradition of the Gothic novel, popular since the eighteenth century. As Barthes and others have argued, even apparently 'realist' texts generate their meaning out of their relation to literary and cultural systems, rather than out of any direct representation of the physical world.

Such recognitions about the linguistic and the literary sign force us to reconsider the nature of literary works themselves. No longer the product of an author's original thoughts, and no longer perceived as referential in function, the literary work is viewed not as the container of meaning but as a space in which a potentially vast number of relations coalesce. A site of words and sentences shadowed by multiple potentialities of meaning, the literary work can now only be understood in a comparative way, the reader moving outwards from the work's apparent structure into the relations it possesses with other works and other linguistic structures. Comparison is, perhaps, the wrong word here, since we are talking not so much of the placing of one work in relation to others as of the registering of the relational position of signs and works within systems of meaning.

Perhaps the most famous expression of such a view of the literary work, now called a *text*, comes in Roland Barthes's essay of 1968, 'The Death of the Author'. The title of this short essay articulates neatly what the emergence of the concept of intertextuality frequently does to the concept of the author. At the beginning of his essay Barthes quotes a line from Balzac's short story *Sarrasine* in which we find this description of a 'castrato disguised as a woman': 'This was woman herself, with her sudden fears, her irrational whims, her instinctive worries, her impetuous boldness, her fussings and her delicious sensibility'. Barthes, in discussing the line, foregrounds the fact that its reader remains uncertain of who is speaking: is the speaker the hero of the story?

or Balzac as author? or some notion of general cultural wisdom? These questions also highlight the fact that in such a sentence we do not know precisely what *kind* of language is being used. Barthes here is also concerned with the notion of *discourse*, the idea that within society at any one time there are many different ways of speaking or writing. In the sentence, for example, Barthes lists various possible ways of speaking, various discourses: a universal wisdom concerning women? the personal experience of the author? a brand of Romantic psychology? literary conventions about gender difference? and so on (Barthes, 1977a: 142). Balzac's sentence does not express a single meaning stemming from an originary author; rather, it leads its reader into a network of possible discourses and seems to emanate from a number of possible perspectives. Certain single signs within the sentence, for example the word 'sensibility', have a potentially vast array of cultural and literary resonances. In French and in English, though differences between the two languages complicate things even further, sensibility can relate to psychology, eighteenth-century medical discourses, notions of Romantic love, of ethical and social concerns, ideological commitments and conflicts, literary conventions such as the novel of sentiment and sensibility and so on. Sensibility, as a single word within just one sentence of Balzac's short story, has an intertextual dimension far beyond any possible authorial intention. In that same essay, Barthes writes:

> We know now that a text is not a line of words releasing a single 'theological' meaning (the 'message' of the Author-God) but a multidimensional space in which a variety of writings, none of them original, blend and clash. The text is a tissue of quotations drawn from the innumerable centres of culture ... the writer can only imitate a gesture that is always anterior, never original. His only power is to mix writings, to counter the ones with the others, in such a way as never to rest on any one of them. Did he wish to *express himself*, he ought at least to know that the inner 'thing' he thinks to 'translate' is only a ready-formed dictionary, its words only explainable through other words, and so on indefinitely.
>
> (Barthes, 1977a: 146–7)

Informed by Saussurean linguistics and its theoretical legacy, Barthes announces the death of the Author on the basis of a recognition of the relational nature of the word. Barthes refers to that traditional notion of the author in theological terms. We might remember here the opening of the Gospel of John: 'In the beginning was the Word, and the Word was with God, and the Word was God'. In the religious traditions of the West, God is viewed as the originary author of two books: the Bible and the Book of Nature. In a comparable manner, the human author has traditionally been seen as the origin of the meaning of the work. Saussure's work allows us to question the understanding of the Word, or the sign, implied by such traditions. The meaning of the author's words, Barthes suggests, does not originate from the author's own unique consciousness but from their place within linguistic-cultural systems. The author is placed in the role of a compiler or arranger of pre-existent possibilities within the language system. Each word the author employs, each sentence, paragraph or whole text s/he produces takes its origins from, and thus has its meaning in terms of, the language system out of which it was produced. The view of language expressed in these lines by Barthes is what theorists since the period in which his essay was produced have termed intertextual.

Although Barthes's examination of this single sentence from Balzac's *Sarrasine* is a good example of the influence of Saussurean notions on modern literary theory, Barthes is also employing perspectives which derive from Bakhtin, and particularly from Julia Kristeva's poststructuralist work on Bakhtin. To go any further in our understanding of intertextual theories, we need to examine Bakhtin's major theories, and also what Kristeva does with them in her work of the late 1960s and early 1970s.

THE SOCIAL WORD: BAKHTIN

The term intertextuality first enters into the French language in Julia Kristeva's early work of the middle to late 1960s. In essays such as 'The Bounded Text' (Kristeva, 1980: 36–63) and 'Word,

Dialogue, Novel' (*ibid.*: 64–91) Kristeva introduces the work of the Russian literary theorist M. M. Bakhtin to the French-speaking world. Bakhtin's work is, today, extraordinarily influential within the fields of literary theory and criticism, and in linguistics, political and social theory, philosophy and many other disciplines. However, in the 1960s his work was relatively unknown, much of it still unpublished. We have then, in the study of intertextuality, a highly charged moment of emergence connected directly to Kristeva's 'Word, Dialogue, and Novel' and the related essays she published during this period. Not only does Kristeva coin the term intertexuality, but in doing so she introduces a figure who has since been styled the most important literary theorist of the twentieth century. Intertextuality and the work of Bakhtin are not, that is to say, separable, and in understanding the former we clearly must understand something of the latter.

The history of the composition and publication of Bakhtin's work is complex, fascinating and at times frustrating. Certainly Bakhtin's life-long insistence that all linguistic communication occurs in specific social situations and between specific classes and groups of language-users is borne out by the impossible tangle of his still hotly debated philosophical and critical *oeuvre*. I do not intend to go into the disputes over whether Bakhtin authored, co-authored, or did not author the texts of the 1920s: *The Formal Method in Literary Scholarship*, *Freudianism*, *Marxism and the Philosophy of Language*. Nor will I suggest an answer to the thorny question of whether an adherence or resistance to Marxism characterizes his works of the 1930s and beyond. There are now a good number of critical accounts which discuss these topics directly (see Todorov, 1984; Clark and Holquist, 1984; Morris, 1994; Pearce, 1994; Dentith, 1995; Vice, 1997).

What we need to bear in mind is that Kristeva's initial discussions of Bakhtin occurred at a specific historical moment. In our Introduction we noted that the term intertextuality emerged during a period of transition. In the middle to late 1960s in France structuralism was being hotly debated, leading to the emergence of what subsequently has been styled poststructuralism.

Kristeva's work stands beside the work of many other seminal poststructuralist thinkers such as Jacques Lacan, Jacques Derrida, Roland Barthes, Michel Foucault and Louis Althusser. All these theorists worked and wrote in a context, the France of the late 1960s, which was dominated by a political and social crisis culminating in the revolutionary events of 1968. Paris, in 1968, saw a student uprising, temporarily combined with a worker's uprising, which for a brief time threatened the authority of the French government. In the Russia of the late 1960s and early 1970s the previous Stalinist censorship of certain formal brands of literary and cultural theory began to fade, and Bakhtin's works, though themselves fundamentally anti-formalist, were finally being rediscovered, republished or published for the first time. We come to Bakhtin in very different historical and political contexts, and confronting a great deal of work, by Bakhtin and on Bakhtin, unknown to Kristeva in the 1960s. Various languages (Russian, French, English) act as less than neutral channels for the transmission of these contexts and ideas. Our Bakhtin is not Kristeva's, though her early discussions of his work helped to forge what we now have. From our perspective, Bakhtin can seem less an author from whose works a notion of intertextuality can be derived than a major theorist of intertextuality itself.

The starting point for any understanding of Bakhtin and intertextuality must be found in the work of the 1920s. In the book on the Formalist school of Russian literary theory associated with Medvedev (Bakhtin/Medvedev, 1978), and in the books associated with Volosinov (Bakhtin/Volosinov, 1986 and 1987), we find an alternative to the Saussurean theory of language we have just discussed. Whilst Bakhtin/Medvedev recognize the importance of the formalist method in Russian literary theory and practice, they criticize its 'fear of meaning in art' (Bakhtin/Medvedev, 1978: 118). Whilst formalism seeks to explain the general 'literariness' of literary works, and Saussurean linguistics seeks to explain language as a synchronic system, what is missed by both approaches is that language exists in specific social situations and is thus bound up with specific social evaluations. Without such an attention to social specificity, argue Bakhtin/Volosinov, in *Marxism and the Philosophy of Language*, Saussurean linguistics remains something describable as 'abstract objectivism'. To produce an abstract account of literary language or any language is to forget that language is utilized by individuals in specific social contexts. The crucial word here is *utterance*, a word which captures the human-centred and socially specific aspect of language lacking in formalism and Saussurean linguistics. As Bakhtin/Medvedev write:

> Not only the meaning of the utterance but also the very fact of its performance is of historical and social significance, as, in general, is the fact of its realization in the here and now, in given circumstances, at a certain historical moment, under the conditions of the given social situation.
>
> The very presence of the utterance is historically and socially significant.
>
> (Bakhtin/Medvedev, 1978: 120)

Meaning, Bakhtin/Medvedev argue, is unique, to the extent that it belongs to the linguistic interaction of specific individuals or groups within specific social contexts. It was partly this uniqueness, or infinite potential, of spoken language which led Saussure to focus his analysis of language on *langue* at the expense of *parole* and of *langage*. *Langage*, a term taken from Saussure, is understood by Bakhtin/Volosinov as 'language-speech ... the sum total of all manifestations of the verbal faculty' (Bakhtin/Volosinov, 1986: 59). If *parole* concerns the act of utterance, then *langage* concerns every conceivable *parole* generatable from the system of language (*langue*). However, as Bakhtin/Volosinov write in *Marxism and the Philosophy of Language*:

> Linguistics, as Saussure conceives it, cannot have the utterance as its object of study. What constitutes the linguistic element in the utterance are the normatively identical forms of language present in it. Everything else is 'accessory and random' .... *language stands in opposition to utterance in the same way as does that which is social to*

> *that which is individual.* The utterance, therefore, is considered a
> thoroughly individual entity.
>
> (Bakhtin/Volosinov, 1986: 60–1)

Saussure, in other words, in order to find some generalizable
rules within the study of language, argues that only language in
its abstract sense, only the norms and conventions presumed to
structure a language at any moment of historical time, can become the object of linguistic study. Such a vision of language
(*langue*) is said by Saussure to provide the possibility for the potentially infinite amount of possible utterances (*parole*) within
that language. And yet, as Bakhtin/Volosinov argue, such an account actually loses sight of the social specificity of language and
confines it to something as abstract as a lexicon or dictionary. As
a recent scholar of Bakhtin, Simon Dentith, writes: 'Dictionaries
are the graveyards of language' (Dentith, 1995: 24).

Bakhtin/Volosinov argue against Saussure that 'there is no real
moment in time when a synchronic system of language could be
constructed' (1986: 66). This is because language is always in a
'ceaseless flow of becoming'. Language, seen in its social dimension, is constantly reflecting and transforming class, institutional,
national and group interests. No word or utterance, from this
perspective, is ever neutral. Though the meaning of utterances
may be unique, they still derive from already established patterns
of meaning recognizable by the addressee and adapted by the addresser. But these established patterns are not the abstract ones of
Saussure's *langue*, they are rather the manner in which language
embodies and reflects constantly changing social values and positions. As Bakhtin/Medvedev put it, the unique discursive event
connects to the class relations between addresser and addressee,
but also to 'the more immediate and brief phenomena of social
life and, finally, with the news of the day, hour, and minute'
(1978: 121). To say, for example, in 1994 'I agree with you completely, not!' would have seemed (to many) an intelligible sentence, given the popularity of the film *Wayne's World* and its
characters' tendency to negate fully articulated statements.
Whether such a sentence would be so intelligible in 2000 is less

certain. At times, as in the first days after the bombing in August 1998 of the high street in Omagh, Northern Ireland, an event can so dominate collective, social thought that it seems to shadow almost any possible utterance. Aspects of spoken language, like intonation, clearly become important in such dimensions of language-use. The single word 'well' or 'so', or sounds such as 'oohh', lacking in meaning for other varieties of linguistics, can possess many specific meanings when we look at the concrete situation between addresser and addressee in which they are uttered.

The most crucial aspect of language, from this perspective, is that all language responds to previous utterances and to pre-existent patterns of meaning and evaluation, but also promotes and seeks to promote further responses. One cannot understand an utterance or even a written work as if it were singular in meaning, unconnected to previous and future utterances or works. No utterance or work, as Bakhtin/Volosinov argue, is independent or what they term 'monumental' (1986: 72).

From the simplest utterance to the most complex work of scientific or literary discourse, no utterance exists alone. An utterance, such as a scholarly work, may present itself as an independent entity, as monologic (possessing singular meaning and logic), yet it emerges from a complex history of previous works and addresses itself to, seeks for active response from, a complex institutional and social context: peers, reviewers, students, promotion boards and so on. All utterances are *dialogic*, their meaning and logic dependent upon what has previously been said and on how they will be received by others. The abstract linguistics of Saussure strips language of its dialogic nature, which includes its social, ideological, subject-centred and subject-addressed nature. Bakhtin/Volosinov summarize as follows:

> Language acquires life and historically evolves ... in concrete verbal communication, and not in the abstract linguistic system of language, nor in the individual psyche of speakers.
>
> (Bakhtin/Volosinov, 1986: 95)

If words, for Bakhtin, Medvedev and Volosinov, are relational, it is not simply because of their place within an abstract system of language, but because of the nature of all language viewed in its concrete social situatedness. All utterances are responses to previous utterances and are addressed to specific addressees. It is this *addressivity* of the word and utterance, as Bakhtin will later term it, which must be the central focus of the study of language. As Bakhtin/Volosinov argue:

> Orientation of the word towards the addressee has an extremely high significance. In point of fact, *word is a two-sided act*. It is determined equally by *whose* word it is and for whom it is meant. As word, it is precisely *the product of the reciprocal relationship between speaker and listener, addresser and addressee*. Each and every word expresses 'one' in relation to the 'other'. I give myself verbal shape from another's point of view, ultimately, from the point of view of the community to which I belong. A word is a bridge thrown between myself and another. If one end of the bridge depends on me, then the other depends upon my addressee. A word is territory shared by both addresser and addressee, by the speaker and his interlocutor.
>
> (*ibid.*: 86)

Lynne Pearce's reference to telephone conversations is a useful example of this argument about language (Pearce, 1994: 1–6). In telephone conversations, which take place between speakers unable to interpret physical signs, the nature of the intonations used, or the kinds of words employed, is crucial in establishing the meaning of the communicative act. Overhearing someone else's telephone conversation is often such a confusing experience because the dialogic nature of the conversation involved can only fully be understood by those participants who in effect are creating it. The manner in which I address my lover, my colleague, my bank manager will vary immensely in intonation and in what Bakhtin would later call *speech genre*. I will employ different phrases when speaking or writing to such different addressees, partly because they will expect the use of appropriate speech genres. 'Re. your letter of the 14th' is a fine opening for a letter to one's bank manager, but hardly appropriate in a letter home to one's parents. 'Hello darling!' might be a perfectly acceptable way in which to greet a close friend; one would hardly employ it in a formal introduction to a local dignitary. The words we select in any specific situation have an 'otherness' about them: they belong to specific speech genres, they bear the traces of previous utterances. They are also directed towards specific 'others', specific addressees. As Bakhtin writes, in his essay on speech genres:

> The speaker is not the biblical Adam, dealing only with virgin and still unnamed objects, giving them names for the first time .... In reality .... any utterance, in addition to its own theme, always responds (in the broad sense of the word) in one form or another to others' utterances that precede it. The speaker is not Adam, and therefore the subject of his speech itself inevitably becomes the arena where his opinions meet those of his partners (in a conversation or dispute about some everyday event) or other viewpoints, world views, trends, theories, and so forth (in the sphere of cultural communication). World views, trends, viewpoints, and opinions always have verbal expression. All this is others' speech (in personal or impersonal form), and cannot but be reflected in the utterance. The utterance is addressed not only to its object, but also to others' speech about it.
>
> (Bakhtin, 1986: 93–4)

It is this sense of the otherness of language which explains Bakhtin's most important concept, *dialogism*, and begins to demonstrate that concept's intertextual nature.

Dialogism

Dialogism, for Bakhtin, is a constitutive element of all language. However, these radically social and interpersonal dimensions can be promoted or repressed. If the dialogic aspect of language foregrounds class, ideological and other conflicts, divisions and hierarchies within society, then society, manifested in state power and those elements of society which serve state power, will frequently attempt to put the lid on such aspects. In *Marxism and the Philosophy of Language*, for example, Bakhtin/Volosinov speak of the manner in which 'the ruling class strives to .... extinguish or drive inward the struggle between social value judgements which occurs [in the sign], to make the sign uniaccentual' (1986: 23). There is, as Bakhtin argues elsewhere, an on-going struggle between centripetal and centrifugal forces of language which can be symbolized by the opposition between monologic and dialogic utterance. Bakhtin's book on Rabelais (Bakhtin, 1984b), for example, examines the manner in which ancient traditions of the *carnival* act as a centrifugal force promoting 'unofficial' dimensions of society and human life and does so through a profane language and drama of 'the lower bodily stratum': images of huge bodies, bloated stomachs, orifices, debauchery, drunkenness and promiscuity are all 'carnivalesque' images. Carnival, through such images, celebrates the unofficial collective body of the people and stands against the official ideology and discourse of religious and state power. We see the carnivalesque most explicitly in the medieval and Renaissance holidays and feast days in which the dominant order of society is overturned, fools dressing as nobles, nobles dressing as fools and so on. The modern inheritor of this unofficial, highly satirical and parodic, dialogical tradition of the carnivalesque is found, Bakhtin argues, in the novel.

In *Problems of Dostoevsky's Poetics* (Bakhtin, 1984a), and the essays collected in *The Dialogic Imagination* (Bakhtin, 1981), the reader will find Bakhtin's most sustained arguments concerning the novel's dialogical character. Other concepts, such as 'polyphony', '*heteroglossia*', 'double-voiced discourse' and 'hybridization', emerge to complement the term, dialogism. Attention to these terms and to his arguments about the novel can extend our understanding of Bakhtin's view of language and of its essentially intertextual nature.

Polyphony, literally the simultaneous combination of parts or elements or, here, voices, is a term which dominates much of Bakhtin's analysis of the novels of Dostoevsky, who for Bakhtin represents the apotheosis of dialogic literary creation. As Bakhtin writes: 'Dostoevsky could hear dialogic relationships everywhere, in all manifestations of conscious and intelligent human life; where consciousness began, there dialogue began for him as well' (1984a: 40). This dialogic element of Dostoevsky's work is not simply to do with 'mere rejoinders in a dialogue, laid out compositionally in the text' (*ibid.*). Dialogism is not literally the dialogues between characters within a novel. Every character in the dialogic novel has a specific, in some senses unique, personality. This 'personality' involves that character's world-view, typical mode of speech, ideological and social positioning, all of which are expressed through the character's words. Bakhtin speaks of characters as expressing an *idea* or 'world-view' and of the *image of voice* associated with that character's consciousness. Each character in a Dostoevsky novel interprets the world for him- or herself and expresses this interpretation through his or her own specific discourse. But this means that the author, as Bakhtin states:

> constructs the hero [character] not out of words foreign to the hero, not out of neutral definitions; he constructs not a character, nor a type, nor a temperament, in fact he constructs no objectified image of the hero at all, but rather the hero's *discourse* about himself and his world.
>
> Dostoevsky's hero is not an objectified image but an autonomous discourse, *pure voice*; we do not see him, we hear him; everything that we see and know apart from his discourse is nonessential and is swallowed up by discourse as its raw material, or else remains outside it as something that stimulates and provokes.
>
> (Bakhtin, 1984a: 53)

In the polyphonic novel we find not an objective, authorial voice presenting the relations and dialogues between characters but a world in which all characters, and even the narrator him- or herself, are possessed of their own discursive consciousnesses. The polyphonic novel presents a world in which no individual discourse can stand objectively above any other discourse; all discourses are interpretations of the world, responses to and calls to other discourses. A novelist in the English tradition often compared in these senses to Dostoevsky is Charles Dickens. Dickens's *Bleak House*, to take one example, is concerned not to comment upon but to present each character's discursive position. There is no objective narratorial voice to guide us through the vast array of voices, interpretations, world-views, opinions and responses presented in the novel. Esther Summerson, the novel's first-person narrator, is clearly only another subjective voice. Even the third-person narrator, who might appear to some as acting in the position of objective narrator, has idiosyncratic opinions, gets angry, sides with some issues and rejects others, uses distinct images and turns of phrase. As in Bakhtin's account of Dostoevsky's polyphonic novel, Dickens's *Bleak House* presents us with a world crammed full of individual voices, sharing, competing and clashing over different ways of speaking; yet the novel presents no overall voice, no controlling and omnipotent narrator. The fact that the novel is itself split into the two dominant narrative modes of the novel tradition, first-person and third-person narratorial voice, merely serves to highlight its polyphonic quality in Bakhtin's sense of this term.

Bakhtin does not seek to announce the death of the Author. The author, for Bakhtin, we might say, still stands behind his or her novel, but s/he does not enter into it as a guiding authoritative voice. Bakhtin's author also cannot be said to spin his or her characters out of an original imagination. Much of Dostoevsky's speech, according to Bakhtin's description, exists as reiterations, parodies, transformations and other kinds of appropriation of existing speech genres, utterances and words associated with particular ideological, class and other distinct social and cultural positions.

Like the tradition of the carnival, the polyphonic novel fights against any view of the world which would valorize one 'official' point-of-view, one ideological position, and thus one discourse, above all others. The novel, in this sense, presents to us a world which is literally dialogic. And yet it is important to note that dialogism does not concern simply the clash between different character-centred discourses; dialogism is also a central feature of each character's own individual discourse. As Bakhtin states: 'dialogic relationships can permeate inside the utterance, even inside the individual word, as long as two voices collide within it dialogically' (1984a: 184). This is what Bakhtin means by *double-voiced discourse* and is what he eventually studies in terms of the concepts of *heteroglossia* and hybridization. Bakhtin employs the opening passages of Dostoevsky's *Notes from the Underground* in which the character-narrator's opening comments gradually begin to display an 'internal polemic with the other' (*ibid.*: 228). Dostoevsky's character's speech increasingly shows marks of its addressivity – anticipating the comments of 'other' speakers, arguing, criticizing, refuting words – which increasingly demonstrate the dependence of his own discourse on other people's utterances.

The fact that the dialogic address with the other can occur within the utterance of a single speaker, is perhaps nowhere better demonstrated than in the Modernist 'stream-of-consciousness' technique of novelists such as Virginia Woolf and James Joyce. In the following paragraph from the 'Hades' section of Joyce's *Ulysses*, first published in 1922, Leopold Bloom's 'internal monologue' is thoroughly double-voiced in this sense. Not only does Bloom direct his utterance towards different addressees here, he also includes within his thoughts sections from texts he has previously read, along with the ritual discourses from religious contexts and other discursive snippets, clichés, recognizable sayings, opinions. The overall effect is to demonstrate how Bloom's thoughts comprise a network of utterances, texts and cultural commonplaces. His thoughts are not simply his own, they emerge from his dialogic place within spoken and written culture:

> One of those chaps would make short work of a fellow. Pick the bones clean no matter who it was. Ordinary meat for them. A corpse is meat gone bad. Well and what's cheese? Corpse of milk. I read in that *Voyages in China* that the Chinese say a white man smells like a corpse. Cremation better. Priests dead against it. Devilling for the other firm. Wholesale burners and Dutch oven dealers. Time of the plague. Quicklime fever pits to eat them. Lethal chamber. Ashes to ashes. Or bury at sea. Where is that Parsee tower of silence? Eaten by birds. Earth, fire, water. Drowning they say is the pleasantest. See your whole life in a flash. But being brought back to life no. Can't bury in

the air however. Out of a flying machine. Wonder does the news go about whenever a fresh one is let down. Underground communication. We learned that from them. Wouldn't be surprised. Regular square feed for them. Flies come before he's well dead. Got wind of Dingham. They wouldn't care about the smell of it. Saltwhite crumbling mush of corpse: smell, taste like raw white turnips.

(Joyce, 1971: 116)

Bakhtin tends to argue that poetic forms like the epic and kinds of lyric are essentially monologic, they enforce a singular, authoritative voice upon the world. Only the novel, and indeed only certain kinds of novel, are, according to Bakhtin, truly dialogic. This argument is on one level rather contradictory, since Bakhtin also discusses language in general in terms of dialogism. A simpler example of double-voiced discourse, which will also demonstrate the dialogic potentialities within lyric poetry, can be located in Robert Burns's famous love poem 'A Red, Red Rose', the first two stanzas of which run as follows:

O my Luve's like a red, red rose,
That's newly sprung in June;
O my Luve's like the melodie
That's sweetly play'd in tune.

As fair art thou, my bonie lass,
So deep in luve am I;
And I will love thee still, my Dear,
Till a' the seas gang dry.

(Burns, 1969: 582)

We have here only one lyric voice, which is why Bakhtin tends to style this kind of poetry monologic. And yet within that voice we discover a distinct clash between an official English language and a Scottish dialect. Certain lines or phrases bespeak the official, self-consciously literary language of Edinburgh society of the late eighteenth and early nineteenth centuries: 'As fair art thou', 'And I will love thee still, my dear'. Other lines and phrases pull against that official literary language, placing it alongside an alternative dialect: 'my bonie lass', 'Till a' the seas gang dry'. Burns's poem, seen from this perspective, stages the social tension within his native Scotland between an official society keen to classicize (others would say Englishify) Scottish literary tradition and a growing interest in local dialects and literary traditions pitted precisely against both English cultural and linguistic domination and any notion of a homogenous, monologic culture. Burns's words are double-voiced, all of them sound a clash between different ideological, class and literary positions.

With this notion of double-voiced discourse and its powerful place within the dialogic novel, and for us, in all dialogic texts, we begin to come close to what must appear a major theory of intertextuality. All utterances depend on or call to other utterances; no utterance itself is singular; all utterances are shot through with other, competing and conflicting voices. As Bakhtin writes:

> the word is not a material thing but rather the eternally mobile, eternally fickle medium of dialogic interaction. It never gravitates toward a single consciousness or a single voice. The life of the word is contained in its transfer from one mouth to another, from one context to another context, from one social collective to another, from one generation to another generation. In this process the word does not forget its own path and cannot completely free itself from the power of those concrete contexts into which it has entered.
>
> When a member of a speaking collective comes upon a word, it is not as a neutral word of language, not as a word free from the aspirations and evaluations of others, uninhabited by others' voices. No, he receives the word from another's voice and filled with that other voice. The word enters his context from another context, permeated with the interpretations of others. His own thought finds the word already inhabited.
>
> (Bakhtin, 1984a: 201)

Bakhtin's stress on otherness, like his stress on polyphony, double-voiced discourse, dialogism and a host of other concepts we have not touched on here, all stem from a recognition that language is never our own, that there is no single human subject who could possibly be the object of psychological investigation, that no interpretation is ever complete because every word is a response to previous words and elicits further responses. As Todorov writes: 'The most important feature of the utterance, or at least the most neglected, is its *dialogism*, that is, its intertextual dimension. After Adam, there are no nameless objects, nor any unused words' (Todorov, 1984: x). Bakhtin's vision of what Todorov rightly calls intertextuality is social, as is his vision of human beings, and thus, as we shall see, it can be somewhat distinguished from a poststructuralist vision which, if it has a notion of agency, of the origins of meaning, attributes it to language itself rather than to human authors. There is agency but no individual psychology in Bakhtin's work. Bakhtin's dialogic vision of human consciousness, subjectivity and communication is based, then, on a vision in which language embodies an on-going dialogic clash of ideologies, world-views, opinions and interpretations. In his crucial essay 'Discourse in the Novel' Bakhtin writes:

> any concrete discourse (utterance) finds the object at which it was directed already as it were overlain with qualification, open to dispute, charged with value, already enveloped in an obscuring mist – or, on the contrary, by the 'light' of alien words that have already been spoken about it. It is entangled, shot through with shared thoughts, points of view, alien value judgements and accents. The word, directed toward its object, enters a dialogically agitated and tension-filled environment of alien words, value-judgements and accents, and weaves in and out of complex interrelationships, merges with some, recoils from others, intersects with a third group: and all this may crucially shape discourse, may leave a trace in all its semantic layers, may complicate its expression and influence its entire stylistic profile.
>
> (Bakhtin, 1981: 276)

For Bakhtin, 'language for the individual consciousness, lies on the borderline between oneself and the other. The word in language is half someone else's' (*ibid.*: 293). The word becomes one's own through an act of 'appropriation', which means that it is never wholly one's own, is always already permeated with traces of other words, other uses. This vision of language is what Kristeva highlights in her new term, intertextuality, and it brings us back to the issues of double-voiced discourse and speech genres, an area which in essays such as 'Discourse in the Novel' is given a new definition through the concept of *heteroglossia*. Given that *hetero* stems from the Greek word meaning 'other' and that *glot* stems from the Greek for 'tongue' or 'voice', we can define *heteroglossia* as language's ability to contain within it many voices, one's own *and* other voices. As Bakhtin writes:

> at any given moment of its historical existence, language is heteroglot from top to bottom: it represents the co-existence of socio-ideological contradictions between the present and the past, between differing epochs of the past, between different socio-ideological groups in the present, between tendencies, schools, circles and so forth, all given a bodily form. These 'languages' of heteroglossia intersect each other in a variety of ways, forming new typifying 'languages'.
>
> (*ibid.*: 291)

The term *heteroglossia* again reminds us of the fact that this clash of ideologies and past utterances within language is not simply to do with a dialogic clash between distinct, separate 'languages' but often exists within individual utterances and even within the same word. In the polyphonic novel, for example, the speech of individual characters is always heteroglot, double-voiced, in that, as Bakhtin puts it: 'It serves two speakers at the same time and expresses simultaneously two different intentions: the direct intention of the character who is speaking, and the refracted intention of the author. In such discourse there are two voices, two meanings and two expressions' (1981: 324). The discourse of characters in a polyphonic novel, we might say, exemplifies the intertextual or dialogic nature of language by always serving two speakers, two intentions, two ideological positions, but always within the single utterance.

The attempt to understand and utilize such terms as *heteroglossia* is an example of the phenomenon to which I am referring. Bakhtin's terms are fluid and come to us through various interpretive translations; so that, for example, it is possible to retain *heteroglossia* for the recognition of the numerous different 'languages', of social and professional groups, of classes and literary movements, operating in society at any one time and to employ other terms, such as 'hybridity' and 'hybridization', to refer more specifically to a clash of 'languages' occurring within the same utterance (see also Clark and Holquist 1981: 428–9; Morris 1994: 248–9). *Heteroglossia* is at times in Bakhtin's work pitted against *monoglossia*, a term which brings us back to the recognition of the centrifugal and centripetal forces of language and to the fact that the dominant ideology within society frequently argues that there is only one unified and unifying language.

At the heart of Bakhtin's work is an argument that the dialogic, heteroglot aspects of language are essentially threatening to any unitary, authoritarian and hierarchical conception of society, art and life. If language is socially specific and thus embodies the stratifications, unfinalized interpretations, ideological positions and class conflicts at work in society in any epoch, and indeed at any specific moment, then no attempt to explain language or art through an abstract system of generalizable relations is viable for those wishing to understand language, art, even speech acts. It is this vision of human society and communication which stands behind the term 'intertextuality' which Kristeva coins as part of her account of Bakhtin's work, and it is this vision which she incorporates into the apparently methodologically rigorous and systematic field of structuralist theory.

TEL QUEL, PRODUCTION: KRISTEVA

The French intellectual scene into which Kristeva arrived in the mid-1960s was one in which an array of established positions within philosophy, political theory and psychoanalytic theory were being transformed by a structuralism dependent on Saussurean linguistics and, increasingly, by a critique of Saussurean linguistics which would become known, after the fact, as poststructuralism. The late 1960s in Paris can justifiably be styled, to employ Patrick Ffrench's term, 'the time of theory'. The political turmoil of 1968 and its aftermath brought the process of debate to a climax and can be said to have consolidated a poststructuralist critique of methodology, traditional notions of authorship and even the criterion of meaningfulness (see Kristeva, 1984b: 263–70).

An attention to the role of literature and literary language was crucial to the rise of poststructuralist theory, nowhere more so than in the journal *Tel Quel*. Most of the major theorists associated with the emergence of poststructuralism in France, including Jacques Derrida, Roland Barthes, Philippe Sollers and Michel Foucault, contributed to *Tel Quel*'s investigation of literature's radical relation to political and philosophical thought. If the theory of the text and of textuality can be said to be at the centre of these writers' work, then *Tel Quel* can be said to give that often divergent set of theories a common site, a place to perform 'writing-thinking', as Kristeva puts it (1998b: 7–11). Kristeva's position within this 'place' is, as Barthes wrote, paradoxically both that of 'l'étranger' (a woman, a literal foreigner) and of central theorist of textuality. Yet such a paradoxical position, as Barthes adds, is characteristic of the unsettling nature of Kristeva's work:

> Julia Kristeva changes the place of things: she always destroys the *last prejudice*, the one you thought you could be reassured by, could take pride in; what she displaces is the *already-said*, the *déjà-dit*, i.e., the instance of the signified, i.e., stupidity; what she subverts is authority – the authority of the monologic science, of filiation.
>
> (Barthes, 1986: 168)

Barthes chooses his words very carefully here, characterizing through them not merely the impact of Kristeva's work but more importantly its major theoretical tenets. The 'signified' Barthes refers to is the stable meaning or concept which any method of analysis requires if it is to present itself as scientific or objective. Kristeva's attack on notions of stable signification centred on the transformation of Saussure's idea of semiology, or what was increasingly called semiotics. Semiotics in mid-1960s France argued for its own objectivity by employing Saussurean concepts such as *langue* (the system) to stabilize the 'signifieds' it studied. Myths, oral cultural traditions, literary texts, indeed any cultural text, can be scientifically analysed, so structuralist semiotics argued, because at any one moment signifiers exist and function within a synchronic system which provides determinable signifieds for those signifiers. What such an approach needs to avoid, in order to maintain such an objectivity, is any attention to the human subject who performs the utterance under consideration. It must also evade the fact that signifiers are plural, replete with historical meaning, directed not so much to stable signifieds as to a host of other signifiers. These are the hidden spaces within which Kristeva works and from which emerges her theory of intertextuality.

Poststructuralist theory in general, and the key writers associated with the *Tel Quel* group in particular, view notions of a stable relationship between signifier and signified as the principal way in which dominant ideology maintains its power and represses revolutionary, or at least unorthodox, thought. Derrida, for example, argues that all major ideological discourses and apparently scientific or objective discourses rely on the illusion of the 'transcendental signified'. The transcendental signified would, as he remarks in an interview with Julia Kristeva, 'in and of itself, in its essence, ... refer to no signified, would exceed the chain of signs, and would no longer itself function as a signifier' (Derrida, 1987a: 19–20). God, for example, functions as a transcendental signified in most dominant religions; the role of this signifier is to refer only and always to itself, to the signified, the concept of the deity. To view the signified 'God' as a signifier in a chain of signifiers is highly unsettling for dominant religions. To ask the question 'to what does the sign "God" refer?', is to undermine the position of 'God' as a transcendental signified. Yet, religions inevitably do provide answers to such a question and so undermine the transcendental – central, single, ultimate, unquestionable – position of the sign 'God'. To answer the question is to set up a series of new signifieds which are themselves subject to questions concerning their reference and so to becoming signifiers for other signifieds. Creator, Father, Spirit, Supreme Being, Prime Mover and so on: all such answers to the initial question merely provide other signifieds which themselves become signifiers. The fact that signified concepts become, in the differential system of language, signifiers for other signifieds, which themselves become signifiers, must be erased if official, or what Bakhtin calls monological, discourse is to do its ideological work. Yet if we take almost any discourse which aspires to the condition of truthfulness or objectivity we find the same linguistic phenomenon. 'Justice' in legal institutions, 'equality' or 'the nation' in varieties of political discourse, 'truth' in scientific or educational institutions, all function in their specific contexts as 'transcendental signifieds'. Thus, almost all discourses attempt to stabilize the system of language by erasing the fact that language is always differential and cannot be stabilized or viewed as a coherent and ordered system (see Derrida, 1978: 278–93). And yet, in all these cases the movement from signified to signifier undermines the apparent centrality and transparency of meaning of the major signs which are meant to stabilize the discursive system in question.

In the work of the *Tel Quel* group the text becomes the site of a resistance to stable signification. There is an attack within *Tel Quel* theory on the very foundations of meaning and communication, a celebration and investigation of that which resists the stabilization of the signifier/signified relation. This is understood in Marxist terms as an attack on the commodification of thought and writing. As Barthes writes, placing Kristeva at the vanguard of such a movement:

> what Julia Kristeva produces is a critique of *communication* (the first, I believe, since that of psychoanalysis). Communication, she shows, the darling of the positive sciences (such as linguistics), of the philosophies and the politics of 'dialogue', of 'participation', and of 'exchange' – communication is *merchandise*.
>
> (Barthes, 1986: 170)

Communication and meaning, in other words, present knowledge and intellectual work as a product, a commodifiable and exchangeable object of value. Most people, it would be fair to say, believe that knowledge, if it exists, can be clearly communicated, and because of this it can be bought and sold in books, in educational courses and so on. The belief in the clear communication of ideas plugs intellectual work into a capitalist market system in which things are only of value if they can be bought and sold. In such a system, we might say, ideas are only valuable if they are consumable.

With this attack on notions of communication in her mind, Kristeva sets out to establish a new mode of semiotics, which she calls *semianalysis*. She attempts to capture in this approach a vision of texts as always in a state of *production*, rather than being products to be quickly consumed. This new semianalysis recognizes its productive role in constructing the 'object' of its study, and thus stresses its status as 'production' or 'productivity'. Combining a Marxist attention to production or 'work' with the Freudian analysis of (dream)-'work', Kristeva stresses that it is not merely the object of study that is 'in process', the process of being produced, but also the subject, the author, reader or analyst. Author, reader or analyst join a process of continual production, are 'in process/on trial' (*le sujet-en-procès*), over the text. Kristeva, in a move amplified within *Tel Quel* generally, posits literary Modernism, from Lautréamont, Mallarmé, Joyce, through Bataille and Artaud, on to Sollers himself, as the site of the emergence of a self-consciously textual production: 'a production that cannot be reduced to representation' (Kristeva, 1986: 86). In such work, Kristeva implies, ideas are not presented as finished, consumable products, but are presented in such a way as to encourage readers themselves to step into the production of meaning. It is, therefore, to this tradition that this new semiotics of productivity will most directly address itself. As Kristeva writes:

> Developed from and in relation to these modern texts the new semiotic models then turn to the *social text*, to those social practices of which 'literature' is only one unvalorized variant, in order to conceive of them as so many ongoing transformations and/or productions.
>
> (Kristeva, 1986: 87)

Literature cannot be the privileged site of this radical mode of semiotic production. Such a vision of literature would retain a hierarchy of discourses and at the same time bracket off the disturbing force of textual productivity to the field of the fictional and the imaginary. Such a move would also reinforce the traditional opposition between science (objective discourse) and fiction (creative, literary discourse), whereas for Kristeva the point is that communication and that which breaks communication apart – what Kristeva calls *signifiance* – are in a constantly antagonistic relationship with each other. The text is the site of this struggle, and Kristeva's new semiotics seeks to analyse it at the same time as being subjected to it. Kristeva, in this new semiotics, constantly places scientific and logical discourses within artistic and fictional contexts, thus self-consciously blurring the distinction and staging the struggle between science, or the logical, and the language or force of imagination and desire.

To understand how intertextuality emerges as a crucial concept within Kristeva's semiotic practice, and to understand this practice more fully, we must first examine her introduction of the writings of Bakhtin into Parisian theory. We must then chart the trajectory such a semiotics takes during the 'time of theory' which Ffrench dates between 1966 and 1975, or, in the case of Kristeva, between her earliest publications in the 1960s and her monumental study *Revolution in Poetic Language*, first published in 1974.

Dialogism to intertextuality

Two texts in the English translation of Kristeva's early work *Desire in Language* complement each other in demonstrating the influence of Bakhtin on Kristeva and the manner in which she transforms, revises and redirects his work: 'The Bounded Text' (Kristeva, 1980: 36–63) and 'Word, Dialogue, Novel' (*ibid*: 64–91). In 'The Bounded Text' Kristeva is concerned with establishing the manner in which a text is constructed out of already existent discourse. Authors do not create their texts from their own original minds, but rather compile them from pre-existent texts, so that, as Kristeva writes, a text is 'a permutation of texts, an intertextuality in the space of a given text', in which 'several utterances, taken from other texts, intersect and neutralize one another' (*ibid*: 36). Texts are made up of what is at times styled 'the cultural (or social) text', all the different discourses, ways of speaking and saying, institutionally sanctioned structures and systems which make up what we call culture. In this sense, the text is not an individual, isolated object but, rather, a compilation of cultural textuality. Individual text and the cultural text are made from the same textual material and cannot be separated from each other. We see here how the Bakhtinian notion of the dialogic has been rephrased within Kristeva's semiotic attention to text, textuality and their relation to ideological structures. Whilst Bakhtin's work centres on actual human subjects employing language in specific social situations, Kristeva's way of expressing these points seems to evade human subjects in favour of the more abstract terms, text and textuality. Bakhtin and Kristeva share, however, an insistence that texts cannot be separated from the larger cultural or social textuality out of which they are constructed. All texts, therefore, contain within them the ideological structures and struggles expressed in society through discourse. This means, for Kristeva, that the intertextual dimensions of a text cannot be studied as mere 'sources' or 'influences' stemming from what traditionally has been styled 'background' or 'context' (*ibid*: 36–7).

The text is a *practice* and a *productivity*, its intertextual status represents its structuration of words and utterances that existed before, will go on after the moment of utterance, and so are, in Bakhtin's terms, 'double-voiced'. If texts are made up of bits and pieces of the social text, then the on-going ideological struggles and tensions which characterize language and discourse in society will continue to reverberate in the text itself. This is what Kristeva means by the words 'practice' and 'productivity'. Texts do not present clear and stable meanings; they embody society's dialogic conflict over the meaning of words. If a novelist, for example, uses the words 'natural' or 'artificial' or 'God' or 'justice' they cannot help but incorporate into their novel society's conflict over the meanings of these words. Such words and utterances retain an 'otherness' within the text itself. Intertextuality, here, concerns a text's emergence from the 'social text' but also its continued existence within society and history. A text's structures and meanings are not specific to itself, and to emphasize this point Kristeva views the text, or at least each of its constituent parts, as an *ideologeme*. If we accept that words such as 'natural' or 'justice' are the subject of immense social conflicts and tensions, then their existence in a text will represent an *ideologeme*. One of the consequences of this way of describing texts is that we must give up the notion that texts present a unified meaning and begin to view them as the combination and compilation of sections of the social text. As such, texts have no unity or unified meaning on their own, they are thoroughly connected to on-going cultural and social processes. Kristeva writes:

> The concept of text as ideologeme determines the very procedure of a semiotics that, by studying the text as intertextuality, considers it as such within (the text of) society and history. The ideologeme of a text is the focus where knowing rationality grasps the transformation of *utterances* (to which the text is irreducible) into a totality (the text) as well as the insertions of this totality into the historical and social text.
> (Kristeva, 1980: 37)

Kristeva, in her characteristically complex mode of presentation, refers here to our tendency to presume that texts possess a meaning unique to themselves. Such an appearance of unity is illusory, however. The text's appearance of unity and independent existence is, in fact, part of its momentary arrangement of words and utterances which have complex social significance 'outside' the text in question. Kristeva's semiotic approach seeks to study the text as a textual arrangement of elements which possess a double meaning: a meaning in the text itself and a meaning in what she calls 'the historical and social text'. Such an approach blows apart notions of 'inside' and 'outside' with regard to the text. A text's meaning is understood as its temporary rearrangement of elements with socially pre-existent meanings. Meaning, we might say, is always at one and the same time 'inside' and 'outside' the text. One of the sentences which begins Mary Shelley's novel *The Last Man* (1826), for example, reads: 'England, seated far north in the turbid sea, now visits my dreams in the semblance of a vast and well-manned ship, which mastered the winds and rode proudly over the waves' (Shelley, 1994: 9). To gauge the meaning of this sentence 'inside' Shelley's text would involve establishing the position of the fictional speaker, of describing the manner in which the novel dramatizes a futuristic England which, on the verge of social and political perfection, is sucked into a global catastrophe in which a plague wipes out the human race save for the speaker of this sentence. Images concerned with dreams, mastery and the natural world also figure throughout the novel and might be said to help generate an internal meaning emanating from this sentence. However, it is impossible to remain 'inside' this novel when dealing with such a sentence. Ideas of England as a proud nation with mastery over the natural world and its own special destiny amongst the nations of the world is an *ideologeme* in the sentence, and the novel generally, which immediately takes readers 'outside' of the text to the ideological representations of England on the verge of the Victorian age. This proto-Imperialistic rhetoric is hardly Mary Shelley's own invention; the sentence's reference is to a discourse very much part of nineteenth-century English culture and society. A relatively simple sentence such as this one is enough to demonstrate the manner in which the meaning of texts is always at one and the same time 'inside' and yet 'outside' that text.

Kristeva's analysis moves on to the Bakhtinian theory of the novel, as that form of text which most expressly embodies these intertextual processes of appropriation and restructuration; a move enlarged upon in the essay, 'Word, Dialogue, Novel'. Kristeva is, in fact, interested less in the genre of the novel than in what she calls *poetic language*, something found by Bakhtin in the novel but which can be equally discovered in poetic genres and, as she will argue in later work, in other kinds of texts. What distinguishes Bakhtin's novel or Kristeva's poetic language is the dynamic conception of the '"literary word" as an *intersection of textual surfaces* rather than a point (a fixed meaning), as a dialogue among several writings: that of the writer, the addressee (or the character), and the contemporary or earlier cultural context' (Kristeva, 1980: 65). Kristeva incorporates Bakhtin's dialogism, his insistence on the social and double-voiced nature of language, into her new semiotics. She defines the dynamic literary word in terms of a *horizontal dimension* and a *vertical dimension*. In the horizontal dimension 'the word in the text belongs to both writing subject and addressee'; in the vertical dimension 'the word in the text is oriented toward an anterior or synchronic literary corpus' (*ibid.*: 66). The communication between author and reader is always partnered by a communication or intertextual relation between poetic words and their prior existence in past poetic texts. Authors communicate to readers at the same moment as their words or texts communicate the existence of past texts within them. This recognition, that the horizontal and vertical axis of the text coincide *within* the work's textual space, leads on to a major redescription of Bakhtin's theory of the dialogic text which culminates in the new term, intertextuality:

> horizontal axis (subject–addressee) and vertical axis (text–context) coincide, bringing to light an important fact: each word (text) is an intersection of word (texts) where at least one other word (text) can be read. In Bakhtin's work, these two axes, which he calls *dialogue* and *ambivalence*, are not clearly distinguished. Yet, what appears as a lack of rigour is in fact an insight first introduced into literary theory by Bakhtin: any text is constructed as a mosaic of quotations; any text is the absorption and transformation of another. The notion of *intertextuality* replaces that of intersubjectivity, and poetic language is read as at least *double*.
>
> (Kristeva, 1980: 66)

Kristeva brings into play here a focus on subject position, that is the position of author, of character and of the pronouns – 'I', 'we', 'they' – by which subjects (human speakers) refer to themselves and to those they address. Influenced by the French linguist Émile Benveniste, along with Roman Jakobson's theory of *shifters*, Kristeva introduces the concepts of *subject of enunciation* and *subject of utterance* to clarify and extend Bakhtinian theory. Jeremy Hawthorne gives the following definition of these terms:

> What is central ... is a distinction between the particular, time-bound *act* of making a statement, and the *verbal result* of that act, a result which escapes from the moment of time and from the possession of

the person responsible for the act. We can note that the important distinction between *utterance* and [enunciation] is that the former term links that uttered to its human originator, whereas the latter term concentrates attention on to the verbal entity itself ... [utterance] calls to mind the *act* of producing a form of words which involves a human subject ... [enunciation] is used when the intention is normally to consider a form of words independently from their association with a human subject.

(Hawthorne, 1992: 57)

If the 'subject of utterance' is best conceived of as a character speaking or thinking, then the 'subject of enunciation' is the subject of a narrative act. When I speak directly to someone else my words are, apparently, linked to me as a subject (of utterance); when I write those words down and they are read, perhaps years later, by someone else my position as a subject is no longer directly involved. 'I' have become merely a subject of enunciation. The subject, as poststructuralists like Kristeva and Barthes are fond of declaring, is *lost* in writing.

Poststructuralists go further than this, however, and refer to a loss of the subject in language generally. This concerns the 'apersonal' nature of language in general; a feature highlighted if we attend to the pronouns we are forced to employ when referring to ourselves and to others. As J. A. Cuddon writes:

[Benveniste] distinguishes between the 'personal' and 'apersonal' aspects of language. In one sense 'I' is personal; in another, apersonal. When apersonal, 'I' is nothing other than 'the person who utters the present instance of discourse containing the linguistic instance 'I''.

(Cuddon, 1992: 928)

When a dignitary utters the words 'I name this ship so-and-so', they may believe that it matters that it is they themselves that are speaking. However, the reality is that, so long as someone of appropriate social stature says these words, then the words will have the same effect upon reality. The meaning and effect of the 'I' in that sentence is not dependent upon the particular subject who utters them. What matters is that the clichéd phrase has been spoken, as it has many times before, and the fact that it is addressed to an audience, who are taking up a position of witnesses to an event (naming a ship) which has occurred many times previously and will occur countless times in the future. If a member of the audience with sufficient social standing were to change places with the specific speaker of the sentence, it would not at all affect the act of naming the ship.

The example of naming a ship might appear to involve a rather uncommon event, and thus not to be of particular relevance to language in its everyday use. However, poststructuralists argue that a similar substitutability occurs in all language use. Whenever subjects enter language they enter into situations in which their personal subjectivity is lost. Perhaps the reason we tend to say 'I *really* love you' or 'I *really do* like your shoes' is that even these common phrases are haunted by the same kind of substitutability as the sentence in which someone names a ship. 'I love you' is a cliché, said millions of times before, and we cannot perhaps but be nervous about a loss of the very subjectivity we would express by these words when we utter them. The 'I' in the sentence 'I love you' is rather less expressive of our own personal feelings and subjecthood than we would like to believe.

What is clear is that when we are dealing with literary forms of writing we cannot presume that the language we are dealing with gives us direct access to the subject who wrote it. Even in confessional modes of writing, the 'I' of the text cannot be identical to the authorial 'I', as we are dealing with a subject of enunciation rather than a subject of utterance. Authors can write narratives using the first person pronoun '*I,*' or the 'nonperson pronoun' (Kristeva, 1980: 87) '*he/she,*' or in a collective '*we*', or through their own or another proper name. Roland Barthes, in his critical memoir *Roland Barthes by Roland Barthes*, exploits these points by referring to himself throughout the text in the third-person 'he'. Such a technique foregrounds the point that the person who speaks or acts and the person who writes are never identical. The subject, 'he', represented in *Roland Barthes by Roland Barthes*, cannot, linguistically, be identical to the subject (Roland Barthes) who performs the act of representation in that text. The very title of the text, 'doubling' the name of the author/subject, makes this point. We might believe that our name always refers to the individual, unique person that we are, but the pronouns we use to refer to ourselves frequently shift our positions, from personal ('I') to collective ('we') to third-person ('he' or 'she'). In language, our subject positions shift; in writing, the subject is lost.

In the above senses then, the word but also the subject-position of the person who speaks in literary language is double-voiced. The pronominal 'I' is always directed towards an 'other', and employs words that are themselves directed towards and contain within themselves 'other words' and 'other utterances'. It is also itself double, the product of a subject 'outside' the text and the pronominal subject of the text itself. For Kristeva, the 'outside' subject is not at issue, since in writing all we can know is the apersonal, constantly shifting, pronominal subject. The subject in writing is always double because the words that subject utters are intertextual (clichéd, already written), and the pronominal signifiers which refer to that subject are always changing and have no stable signified ('outside' subject) to which they can be referred.

Kristeva's use of the word 'ambivalence' represents one of the many intertextual revisions to be found in her reading of Bakhtin. The Bakhtinian terms standing behind Kristeva's new term are '*heteroglossia*' and 'hybridity', and yet the new terminology implies a refocusing on logical criteria. Kristeva writes:

> Dialogue and ambivalence lead me to conclude that, within the interior space of the text as well as within the space of *texts*, poetic language is a 'double'. Saussure's poetic *paragram* ('Anagrams') extends from *zero* to *two*: the unit 'one' (definition, 'truth') does not exist in this field. Consequently, the notions of definition, determination, the sign '=' and the very concept of the sign, which presupposes a vertical (hierarchical) division between signifier and signified, cannot be applied to poetic language – by definition an infinity of pairings and combinations.

> (Kristeva, 1980: 69)

Kristeva thus employs Bakhtin's emphasis on the doubleness or dialogic quality of words and utterances to attack notions of unity, which she associates with claims to authoritativeness, unquestionable truth, unproblematic communication and society's desire to repress plurality. Kristeva's attack, in other words, is against the foundations of Western logic. Such a logic, stemming from Aristotle, works on the principle of non-contradiction. As Aristotle asserts, something cannot at one and the same time be something (A) and something else (not-A). If A, for example, represents 'here', and if not-A represents 'there', then, such logic would argue, a person cannot at one and the same time occupy space A and space not-A. Kristeva's point is that, with Bakhtin's view of the word or utterance, we find a fundamental challenge to Aristotelian logic and its notions of singularity. The dialogic word or utterance is double-voiced, heteroglot, and possesses a meaning (A) at the same moment that it possesses an alternative meaning or meanings (not-A). Mary Shelley's sentence about England, for example, refers to a fictional narrative at the same moment as it refers to an actual country's ideological representations of itself; it is at once her own utterance and the utterance of a fictional character. As such, the meaning of Shelley's sentence defies Aristotelian logic, since it at one and the same time has an 'inside' and an 'outside' referent, and is the utterance of at least two linguistic subjects. It is, in this sense, 'A' and 'not-A'.

Saussure's work on anagrams marks a fascinatingly undiscussed element in the development of poststructuralist theories of textuality and intertextuality. The unfinished work remained in manuscript form until it began to be rediscovered by certain theorists, the French theorist Jean Starobinski in particular. Starobinski's research on the project was published in *Mercure de France* in 1964 and in *Tel Quel* (37, spring 1969), finally emerging as a partial translation and commentary (see Starobinski, 1979). Julia Kristeva first used Saussure's theory in an article in *Tel Quel* in 1967 (see Kristeva, 1998a). Working on mainly Greek and Latin poetry, Saussure argued – but never finally proved to his own satisfaction – that these texts worked on non-representational levels in which groups of letters and phonemes (sounds), such as the first and last letters of consecutive lines, arranged themselves into deep textual units, often the names of Gods or heroes. So that, for example, in studying the arrangement of phonemes within a piece of poetry mentioned by the Roman poet Livy, Saussure discovers the name of the Greek and Roman sungod Apollo, despite the fact that Apollo is never literally (directly through the signifier 'Apollo') mentioned in the text. Saussure, as he discovered more and more varieties of such coded patterns, coined more and more cognate terms to capture such processes. As Kristeva and Derrida both recognize, Saussure's work on the 'gram' foreshadows their own work on the manner in which signifiers in the text exist in relation to chains of further signifiers, rather than in relation to transparent and stable signifieds. Saussure's work on anagrams is seen by Kristeva and Derrida as foreshadowing their own focus on how the signifier resists notions of direct or logical communication and thus meaning.

It may well seem perverse on Kristeva's part to conduct a reading of Bakhtinian notions 'insofar as they are congruent with the conceptions of Ferdinand de Saussure as related to his "anagrams"' (1980: 90). Kristeva rewrites Bakhtin's work, however, directing it towards a language conceived as beyond logic. If logic is based on Aristotle's assertion that something is either 'A' or 'not-A', then we might say that logic presumes that things cannot be more than one thing at a time. Something is what it is, or it is nothing. Kristeva's way of expressing this is to use the numerical expression (0 - 1): '0' here equals 'nothing', '1' here equals a singular element. On this basis, Kristeva sees a similarity between Bakhtin's view of language and Saussure's work on anagrams, a similarity which for her connects them to Freud's work on the non-logical language of dreams, or what Freud calls dream-work. Saussure's theory of anagrams functions as one more apparently scientifically-oriented discursive practice that can be strategically addressed to a kind of language which remains unassimilable within any science or logic; a kind of language that is ambivalent. Poetic language, as Kristeva stresses, works on the principal of 0 - 2, it is 'double', both 'A' and 'not-A'. Here, '0' equals 'nothing', whilst '2' equals an element which is at least 'double'; that which equals a single element, '1', has been omitted. Kristeva writes:

> the minimal unit of poetic language is at least *double*, not in the sense of the signifier/signified dyad, but rather, in terms of *one and other* .... The *double* would be the minimal sequence of a paragrammatic semiotics to be worked out starting from the work of Saussure ... and Bakhtin.
>
> (Kristeva, 1980: 69)

Poetic language, Kristeva argues, foregrounds the 'inability of any logical system based on a zero-one sequence (true-false, nothingness-notation)' (1980: 70). A whole host of additional vocabularies, linguistic, psychoanalytic and mathematical, allows Kristeva to appropriate Bakhtinian dialogism and to re-establish it upon the opposition between the monologic (0 - 1) and the dialogic (0 - 2). As she writes: 'Within this "power of the continuum" from 0 to a specifically poetic double, the linguistic, psychic, and social "prohibition" is 1 (God, Law, Definition). The only linguistic practice to "escape" this prohibition is poetic discourse' (*ibid.*: 70). If we accept Bakhtin's vision of society as always exhibiting a conflict between monologic and dialogic forces, then the monologic forces will argue for what it takes to be logical (0 - 1), whilst dialogic forces, for Kristeva 'poetic language', will constantly struggle to express the non-logical (0 - 2). Notions of unquestionable authority and singularity – 'God, Law, Definition' always work on the side of monologic power.

If intertextuality stands as the ultimate term for the kind of poetic language Kristeva is attempting to describe, then we can see that from its beginning the concept of intertextuality is meant to designate a kind of language which, because of its embodiment of otherness, is against, beyond and resistant to (mono)logic. Such language is socially disruptive, revolutionary even. Intertextuality encompasses that aspect of literary and other kinds of texts which struggles against and subverts reason, the belief in unity of meaning or of the human subject, and which is therefore subversive to all ideas of the logical and the unquestionable. We can register how far Kristeva's version of dialogism pushes this attack on unity and reason by referring to her reading of Bakhtin in relation to dialectics, an idea associated with the German Romantic philosopher G. W. F. Hegel. Hegelian dialectics depends upon the production of a synthesis out of the clash between a thesis and an antithesis. The synthesis is a 'third term', which not only resolves the clash between thesis and antithesis but takes us to a new, 'higher' position or state of consciousness or knowledge. Dialectics, therefore, implies that human thought and society can transcend or leap to a totality of knowledge, a third position, which resolves prior conflicts and ambivalences. In less totalized fashion, it at least suggests that the kind of 'doubleness' Kristeva finds in Bakhtin's work and in what she calls 'poetic language', can be resolved by a 'progression' to a new, resolved, position. In Hegelian dialectics, we might say, following Kristeva's arguments, since the clash between thesis and antithesis is resolved by the emergence of a synthesis, the notion of the monologic, of the restoration of singularity and unity is restored. What Bakhtin calls the dialogic is cancelled in dialectics by the move to a new, transcendent monological position. Marx famously adapted dialectics to argue that the clash of the proletariat and the owners of capital would bring a revolutionary third position, a social order beyond the power-struggles between workers and capitalists. It should be noted, as a fact not without interest to Kristeva's arguments, that Marx gradually incorporated a notion of counter-revolution, of the revolutionary transcendence of conflict leading to renewed conflict, within his political theories. When Kristeva directs her Bakhtin-inspired semiotics against Hegel, as in the following passage, she is, then, also attacking a much debated feature of Marxist thought:

> The notion of dialogism, which owes much to Hegel, must not be confused with Hegelian dialectics, based on a triad and thus on struggle and projection (a movement of transcendence), which does not transgress the Aristotelian tradition founded on substance and causality. Dialogism replaces these concepts by absorbing them within the concept of relation. It does not strive towards transcen-

dence but rather toward harmony, all the while implying an idea of
rupture (of opposition and analogy) as a modality of transformation.

(Kristeva, 1980: 88–9)

Kristeva's vision is not of transcendence but of production.
The language of logic, reason and Law (0 - 1) is constantly rup-
tured, transformed and repositioned by that which cannot be con-
fined within the logical, the meaningful or the literally
communicable (0 - 2). As she writes elsewhere, paraphrasing
Bakhtin on the polyphonic novel: 'Dostoevsky's "model" lacks
unity of speaker and of meaning; it is plural, anti-totalitarian and
anti-theological. It thus exemplifies permanent contradiction,
and could never have anything in common with Hegelian dialec-
tic' (Kristeva, 1973: 110; see also Todorov, 1984: 104). To understand further what Kristeva does with such a position, and what
implications it has for her account of the text and of intertextuality, we need to move away from her engagement with Bakhtin towards her development of semianalysis, a practice increasingly
dependent on a psychoanalytical theory of the subject in language.

Transposition

In their introduction to the collection of essays on intertextuality
Michael Worton and Judith Still remind us that for Kristeva 'intertextual relations are passionate ones' (Worton and Still, 1990:
18). Intertextuality has to do, for Kristeva, with desire and with
the psychological drives of the *split subject*. For Kristeva, the subject is split between the conscious and the unconscious, reason
and desire, the rational and the irrational, the social and the pre-
social, the communicable and the incommunicable. This aspect of
Kristeva's work signals more than any other the fruitful process of
influence which existed, during the 'moment of theory', between
Kristeva and Roland Barthes. In her essay on Barthes, for example (see Kristeva, 1980: 92–123), she praises his placing of desire
at the centre of critical language, and writes: 'The network to be
deciphered seems to be split in half. *Desire*, where the subject is

implicated (body and history), and *symbolic order*, reason, intelligibility' (1980: 116).

The 'symbolic order' here refers to the work of the influential theorist of psychoanalysis, Jacques Lacan and the distinction he makes between *the Imaginary* and *the Symbolic*. The 'Imaginary' concerns the child's early fragmented and yet heavily symbolized sense or map of the body. Infants, at this early stage, do not make clear distinctions between themselves and those around them, principally the mother. The 'Symbolic' concerns the state, after the full acquisition of language, which Lacan calls the 'Symbolic order'. With the acquisition of language, the subject enters into all the social positions and rules and relations which underpin society: the acquisition of language is associated by Lacan with the Father, the Law and ideas of unity, since language is always trying, if always failing, to fix subjects in specific linguistic and social positions. Unlike the *infans* (child before speech), which cannot tell the difference between its own body and the mother's body, the subject *in* language is always being temporarily fixed and positioned as an 'I' or a 'you' or as part of a collective 'we'.

Kristeva is greatly influenced by Lacanian psychoanalytical theory, as are many other members of the *Tel Quel* group. As with all her theoretical influences, however, she takes a critical, revisionary attitude towards his model. In the place of Lacan's 'Imaginary' she returns to Freud's work on 'primary process' and the pre-symbolic stage of the *infans*. Kristeva, through these moves, develops the concept of *the semiotic*, a state characterized by pre-symbolic drives, impulses, bodily 'pulsions' (rhythms and movements) and an initial total identification with the mother's body which is finally shattered but not completely effaced in what she terms 'the thetic phase'. By the 'thetic phase' Kristeva means that point at which human subjects enter the social world, governed, as it is, by monological notions of language. It marks, then, a phase dominated by social norms in which language is presumed capable of presenting a thesis, a singular, unitary meaning.

As one of her editors, Leon S. Roudiez, reminds us, Kristeva's focus is double: 'Her concern does lie with the field of *la sémio-*

tique (i.e., "semiotics" as a general science of signs) but it involves a more specific domain that she calls *le sémiotique* ("the semiotic") seen as one of the two components of the signifying process – the other being "the symbolic"(Kristeva, 1984a: 4). The subject, for Kristeva, is thus split between two signifying fields. The symbolic field involves socially signifying language operating under the banners of reason, communication and the ideal of singularity and unity. The semiotic involves the 'language' of drives, erotic impulses, bodily rhythms and movements retained from the infant stage prior to the subject's splitting during the thetic phase. At the heart of the semiotic is the *chora*, a word Kristeva takes from Plato's *Timaeus* and which refers to a 'receptacle' associated with the maternal body. This receptacle or *chora* is 'unnameable, improbable, hybrid, anterior to naming, to the One, and to the father'. The semiotic *chora*, as Kristeva writes, 'designates that we are dealing with a disposition that is definitely heterogeneous to meaning but always in sight of it in either a negative or surplus relationship to it' (1980: 133). We do not, as adults, that is, lose completely our relation to the pre-speech infant fluidity of self. That fluidity of self, registered in Kristeva's notion of the *chora*, prior to language, logic and the fixing of identity and subject position, bubbles up in poetic language disturbing the monologic order of the symbolic field. Kristeva's concern is again with what disrupts and temporarily dismantles stable meaning, communication, notions of singularity, unity and order.

This new model of the split subject *in language* describes the tension between a socialized, symbolic discourse and an unassimilable, anti-rational and anti-social semiotic language of instinctual and sexual drives. With this model Kristeva can rearticulate her account of 'poetic language', which is now viewed as existing in the symbolic whilst being shot through with traces of the semiotic. The language of logic and clear communication is disrupted by traces of the pre-logical and the uncommunicable. In her work on Bakhtin, Kristeva follows the general canon of the *Tel Quel* group by arguing that Dostoevsky, though responsible for a move to the polyphonic novel, remained within a 'representational', and thus essentially uncomplicatedly symbolic, discourse (1980: 71). For Kristeva, the moment in which Western art and literature begins to self-consciously unleash the force of the semiotic occurs at the end of the nineteenth century with the rise of Modernism. This break – Kristeva mentions Joyce, Proust, and Kafka – coincides with the rise of self-consciously intertextual art. She writes: 'Beginning with this break – not only literary but also social, political, and philosophical in nature – the problem of intertextuality (intertextual dialogue) appears as such' (*ibid.*: 71).

This association between intertextuality and a radical form of writing which unleashes the pre-logical force of the semiotic is important to register. It follows an observable trend among the theorists associated with the *Tel Quel* group to attempt to fix a moment in literary history in which a self-consciously intertextual writing first emerges. Kristeva's work on intertextuality focuses heavily on late nineteenth-century and early twentieth-century avant-garde writing. Barthes argues that explicitly intertextual writing comes to the fore in twentieth-century Modernism and avant-garde movements. Such explicitly intertextual forms of literature, Kristeva and Barthes argue, foreground the fact that they are not original works written by unique authors of great genius, but rather that they are the product of split subjects.

What is the relation between intertextuality and Kristeva's description of the subject split between the symbolic and the semiotic fields? The answer seems to be that texts follow the same split movement between logical and alogical, symbolic and semiotic forces. No text, however radical, is purely semiotic; the semiotic always manifests itself *within* the symbolic. To mark this split nature of texts, Kristeva introduces two new terms: the *phenotext* and the *genotext*. The 'phenotext' is that part of the text bound up with the language of communication, the 'thetic-thesis', which displays definable structure and appears to present the voice of a singular, unified subject (1984a: 87). The 'genotext' is that part of the text which stems from the 'drive energy' emanating from the unconscious and which is recognizable in terms of 'phonematic devices' such as rhythm and intonation, melody, repetition and even kinds of narrative arrangement (Kristeva, 1984a: 86). Remembering the etymological connection of the text to woven cloth, Roudiez remarks that a text can be woven of 'threads' from or 'within the semiotic disposition' (genotext) but also from threads 'that issue from societal, cultural, syntactical, and other grammatical constraints' (phenotext) (*ibid.*: 5). The genotext disturbs, ruptures and undercuts the phenotext and thus articulates the drives and desires of a pre-linguistic subjectivity. This pre-linguistic subjectivity, although it does not itself possess a language, uses the languages of the symbolic order (thetic language) to make itself heard and felt.

In some texts – rational, scientific or legalistic texts, for example – the traces of the genotext will be almost completely obliterated. In others, such as the Modernist writing of Mallarmé, Joyce, Artaud, Beckett and Sollers, the potential of the genotext is unleashed and the text reaches near the semiotic *chora*. The language of Joyce's Molly Bloom, at the end of his *Ulysses*, lacking in regular syntax, extraordinarily musical and so expressive of the body and bodily drives and desires of its speaker, provides us with a clear example of what Kristeva is describing:

> O that awful deep-down torrent O and the sea the sea crimson sometimes like fire and the glorious sunsets and the figtrees in the Alameda gardens yes and all the queer little streets and pink and blue and yellow houses and the rosegardens and the jessamine and geraniums and cactuses and Gibraltar as a girl where I was a Flower of the mountain yes when I put the rose in my hair like the Andalusian girls used or shall I wear a red yes and how he kissed me under the Moorish wall and I thought well as well him as another and then I asked him with my eyes to ask again yes and then he asked me would I yes to say yes my mountain flower and first I put my arms around him yes and drew him down to me so he could feel my breasts all perfume yes and his heart was going like mad and yes I said yes I will Yes.
>
> (Joyce, 1971: 704)

It is significant to note that Kristeva's semianalytical practice extends beyond the literary text and includes other art forms, such as music, painting and dance. Barthes's essay 'The Grain of the Voice' consolidates this point by employing phenotext and genotext in an analysis of musical performance (Barthes, 1977a: 179–89). There he contrasts the experience of hearing technically proficient professional singers with more individualistic, idiosyncratic or less technically proficient singers. The 'grain of the voice' of the latter kind of singer allows us, Barthes argues, to hear the *genotext* emerging.

Kristeva's approach is concerned, then, not with 'sense', or 'signification', but with what she calls '*signifiance*', the manner in which the text, in Roudiez's words, 'signif[ies] what representative and communicative speech does not say' (Kristeva, 1980: 18). What after all, we might ask, does Molly Bloom's 'poetic language' directly communicate (say)? As Barthes writes:

> 'Signifiance', unlike signification, cannot be reduced to communication, to representation, to expression: it puts the (writing or reading) subject into the text, not as a projection, not even as a fantasmatic one … but as a 'loss'.
>
> (Barthes, 1981a: 38)

The subject is 'lost' in the text in the manner in which, as I have discussed, the subject in writing is never identical to the subject itself. The linguistic subject is always split, determined (posited, constructed, structured) by the *signifying system* within which it speaks. In this sense Kristeva's work places a psychological dimension onto Bakhtin's analysis of double-voiced discourse, dialogism, *heteroglossia* and hybridity. However, as has been implied, the pre-symbolic subject, the subject of drives rather than of thetic language, constantly announces itself in poetic language by breaking apart, or restructuring, the signifying systems within which it speaks and writes. It is at this point that a theory of intertextuality is rearticulated in Kristeva's work.

Freud, in his analysis of dreams, argued that they tend to function through *condensation* and *displacement*. In condensation one sign collects into itself a host of meanings or signifiers; in displacement a sign from another area of signification stands in for the real content of the dream. A ring in a dream might symbolically condense ideas and desires concerning a host of aspects of life: marriage, religious faith, sexual desire, economic stability or instability. A surreal dream centring on a cake might be a symbolically displaced working-through of the dreamer's desires for a person associated in the unconscious with cakes. Condensation and displacement can, then, be seen as two operations in the semiotic process. Kristeva, in *Revolution in Poetic Language*, styles intertextuality as a third operation within the semiotic process. Intertextuality is thus understood as 'the passage from one sign system to another' which involves 'an altering of the thetic *position* – the destruction of the old position and the formation of a new one' (1984a: 59). Keen to avoid the reduction of intertextuality to the traditional notions of influence, source-study and simple 'context', Kristeva now drops the term intertextuality in favour of a new term, *transposition* (*ibid.*: 59–60).

Whether we use the term 'intertextuality' or 'transposition' would seem to be less important, however, than recognizing that texts do not just utilize previous textual units but that they transform them and give them what Kristeva terms new thetic positions. We might understand this by comparing Kristeva's own discussion of these issues with the attempt to explain Kristeva's work you are reading in this Chapter. The text you are reading attempts to be as clear as it can possibly be. However, the numerous signifying systems used by Kristeva – Bakhtin, other accounts of textuality, structuralism, psychoanalytical theory, Marxism, and so on – often pull against that attempt at communication and produce what we might call an 'otherness' within the text. The analysis you are reading attempts to transpose complex, often extremely difficult signifying systems into a communicable and logical structure: in this analysis, the phenotext dominates. Kristeva's own work represents a signifying practice which seeks not only to account for other texts but, in transposing them into her textual practice, also to unleash a semiotic force (the genotext) which disrupts communication, or more particularly over-monologic thought. The 'otherness' which pulls against this Chapter's attempt to communicate clearly, stems from Kristeva's far more radical attempt to unleash the genotext. My attempt to pull

Kristeva's work into the phenotext does not completely succeed, and an element of the *polysemy* (multiple meaning) of her texts remains in my description of her work. What Kristeva calls transposition directly concerns this struggle to employ pre-existent signifying practices for different purposes. Kristeva employs Freud's notion of 'representability' to explain this fundamental dimension of intertextual or transpositional practice:

> We shall call *transposition* the signifying process' ability to pass from one sign system to another, to exchange and permutate them; and *representability* the specific articulation of the semiotic and the thetic for a sign system. Transposition plays an essential role here inasmuch as it implies the abandonment of a former sign system, the passage to a second via an instinctual intermediary common to the two systems, and the articulation of the new system with its new representability.
>
> (Kristeva, 1984a: 60)

Although Kristeva has her eye on specifically poetic language here, her model can also be referred to the example of intertextual/transpositional practice I have just been outlining. This current analysis and Kristeva's texts share, naturally, some of the same sign systems: Marxist, Freudian, structuralist, Kristeva's own. However, the 'trans-position' (exchange and permutation, repositioning) of these sign systems is radically different in both cases, due to different representational objectives. Bakhtin's vision of the utterance or the dialogic word as stemming from and being filled with previous utterances and words and yet also directed towards an Other, an addressee, is still recognizable here. But what Kristeva's approach also emphasizes is the manner in which the speaking subject itself forms part of the transpositional practice we are discussing. The subject which speaks in a text is constructed in and by the specific transposition of signifying systems which make up the text. The 'I' that speaks in the study you are currently reading depends upon the transposition (arrangement, appropriation, structuring) of the threads of previous signifying systems which it weaves into this text, and it also depends on the manner in which the text of this study is oriented (re-presented) towards its addressees. The 'I' that speaks in this book is not the same 'I' that speaks in other texts by 'Graham Allen', such as research articles or scholarly reviews, nor is it the same 'I' which speaks in the many different signifying situations within which that subject finds himself: pub, classroom, family party, telephone conversation with a publisher. The subject position which any speaker or writer takes up is largely dependent upon the context in which that subject speaks or writes. Bakhtin's notion of speech genres is recognizable here. Kristeva's contribution is to focus far more than Bakhtin does on the changes and transpositions this involves for the subject who speaks or writes.

Kristeva argues that it is in Modernist texts that this transpositional aspect begins to be self-consciously exploited. However, a recognition that the subject is not identical to the 'I' which speaks, and that the same words can mean different things in the context of different signifying systems, can be found in writers of earlier periods. Elizabeth Gaskell, the Victorian realist novelist, writes, for example, of her many 'mes':

> for I have a great number and that's the plague. One of my mes is, I do believe, a true Christian – [only people call her socialist and communist], another of my mes is a wife and mother, and highly delighted at the delight of everyone else in the house .... Now that's my 'social' self I suppose. Then again I've another self with a full taste for beauty and convenience whh [sic] is pleased on its own account. How am I to reconcile all these warring members? I try to drown myself (my *first* self), by saying it's Wm [William Gaskell] who is to decide on all these things, and his feeling it right ought to be my rule. And so it is – only that it does not quite do.
>
> (Gaskell, 1966: 108)

Gaskell's remarks highlight the manner in which the 'I' is constructed and positioned by and within different signifying systems: Christianity, socialism, communism, the Victorian ideal of the female domestic sphere, the Romantic artist. However, her remarks also remind us of Kristeva's point that this positioning of the subject in language has to do with desire. Gaskell searches here for her authentic 'I' whilst recognizing its socially split existence, a quest which clearly relates to her production of realist novels and the psychological motives which, along with socio-cultural pressures, produced those novels. Modernist writers, according to Kristeva and other members of the *Tel Quel* group, celebrate the dissolution of the unitary 'I' in a signifying practice shot through with semiotic and intertextual forces. A realist writer such as Gaskell might bemoan her 'many mes'; Modernist writers, according to *Tel Quel* theory, exploit and celebrate the variety of subject positions into which writing forces them. This can reach a point in Modernism and avant-garde writing where the very notion of a singular self, of a coherent identity for the author, is abandoned. Intertextuality, or transposition, becomes that which foregrounds, celebrates and plays with the dissolution or abandonment of the single subject, a play which in the most radical texts reaches a stage or state styled by Kristeva and Barthes as *jouissance*. As the poststructuralist critic Robert Young puts it: '"Jouissance" means enjoyment in the sense of enjoyment of a right, of a pleasure, and, most of all, of sexual climax. "Jouissance" and "signifiance" invoke the sense of an ecstatic loss of the subject in a sexual or textual coming – a textasy' (Young, 1981: 32). What for Gaskell represents an anxiety-inducing lack of stable subject positioning becomes for *Tel Quel* theorists a liberatory release from the shackles of singular, monologic notions of identity and of meaning. Plurality, of self as well as of meaning, is seen as the source of liberation and joy.

BAKHTIN OR KRISTEVA?

The question of whether *jouissance* occurs only in work from the late nineteenth century onwards or can be found in earlier writers opens up the issue of how Kristeva's theorizing of the text relates to history and society. John Frow argues that in assimilating Bakhtinian dialogism into French semiotics Kristeva loses sight of the precise manner in which a literary text relates to social ideological structures: that is, by transforming the ideologically significant *norms* of the literary canon (Frow, 1986: 127–9). Frow's point is that to talk merely of the transposition of 'signifying practices' is insufficient, since in literature it is essentially the available literary genres and dominant formal practices, which new writers transpose and attempt to transform. Clayton and Rothstein also write of a 'vagueness' in Kristeva's work 'about the relation of the social text to the literary text' (Clayton and Rothstein, 1991: 20). David Duff has recently developed this critique by examining the manner in which attention to literary genre evaporates as we move from the work of Bakhtin to Kristeva's and other poststructuralists' work (Duff, 1997). Jill Felicity Durey also sees Kristeva's work as a misrepresentation of Bakhtin, particularly in its evaporation of the author-writer into purely linguistic and textual processes (Durey, 1991).

The ideological force in Dostoevsky's novels as read by Bakhtin, Frow argues, lies in their dialogic or intertextual transformation of dominant norms within the novel tradition. It also resides in their incorporation of residual literary conventions outside the current novelistic norm, such as the dialogic forms of Menippean satire and carnivalesque forms generally. Dostoevsky's transpositions are essentially of the dominant literary norms of his time, and the importance Bakhtin ascribes to his novels concerns their development of the novel as a specifically literary genre, his creation of a form of novel better suited to the ideological climate within which he lived. According to Frow Kristeva's semiotic focus, which views the whole of social and cultural life in terms of signifying systems, does not recognize this evolutionary 'interplay of norm and transformation, because the point of reference (the material which is to be transformed) lies outside the literary system' (Frow, 1986: 127). Kristeva is guilty, according to Frow, of describing literary transpositions in non-literary terms and therefore cannot do justice to the manner in which transformations of genres and forms within the 'literary system' reflect literature's response to society and history. Kristeva, that is, makes literature part of general cultural discourse and ends up unable to describe literature, its history and its response to ideological and cultural conflicts and debates.

These critiques of Kristeva's appropriation of Bakhtin centre, then, on the question of whether her semiotic approach erases the specific social situation, including specific literary situations, within which, Bakhtin argues, all dialogic utterance occurs. As Simon Dentith argues:

> Kristeva effectively deracinates the signifying process, tearing it out of the dialogic encounter which is its only imaginable context for Bakhtin ... the production of meaning happens as a result of purely textual operations independent of historical location; the multiplicity of possible meanings in a text spring from that text and not from the multiplicity of possible occasions in which the text can be read.

(Dentith, 1995: 98)

Dentith argues that the clash between Bakhtin and Kristeva has to do with two distinct notions of social liberation. Whilst Bakhtin's vision concerns a process of constant struggle, a constant unfinished dialogue *within* specific social situations, the vision of *Tel Quel* theorists such as Kristeva and Barthes, Dentith writes, is of 'a version of liberation which takes you out of the historical process altogether'. Bakhtin, unlike Kristeva and Barthes, he argues: 'is the philosopher, not of coming, but of becoming' (*ibid.*: 98). Yet we might object that we can find ways in which both of these apparent 'sides' are accurate representations of, and vital responses to, the specificities of social and historical forces and trends. The post-Revolutionary Russia of the 1920s, 1930s and beyond understandably produced different visions of liberation from that imagined in the heady days of communal revolt in late 1960s Paris. What Manfred Pfister styles as Bakhtin's revolt against 'the increasing rigidity of post-revolutionary Soviet cultural politics and the doctrinary canonization of Soviet Realism' is inevitably distinct from *Tel Quel's* 'struggle against the "bourgeois" ideology of the autonomy and unity of individual consciousness and the self-contained meaning of texts' (Pfister, 1991: 212). Intertextuality, as a concept, has a history of different articulations which reflect the distinct historical situations out of which it has emerged. The important task, at least for a study such as this, is not to choose between theorists of intertextuality. It is, rather, to understand that term in its specific historical and cultural manifestations, knowing that any application of it now will itself be an intertextual or transpositional event. We can make this point even clearer by recognizing that intertextuality as a concept with a complex history presents us with a series of oppositions between which we cannot simply decide. The oppositions offer us a series of questions:

Is intertextuality an historically informing term, or is it essentially ahistorical?

Does intertextuality open the text to history, or to yet more textuality?

Is intertextuality a manageable term, or is it essentially unmanageable, concerned with finite or infinite and overwhelming dimensions of meaning?

Does intertextuality provide us with a form of knowledge, or does it destroy what was previously considered to be knowledge?

Is the centre of intertextuality in the author, the reader or the text itself?

Does intertextuality aid the practice of interpretation, or resist notions of interpretation?

We could devise more questions than are contained in this list. It should be clear, however, that they all bear upon a fundamental distinction between knowledge, including socio-historical knowledge, and the rejection of the very idea of stable knowledge. A second dimension concerns the kind of frame we construct for the intertextual field; does intertextuality possess a definite frame of reference, or, in covering all signifying practices – what ultimately gets called 'the social or general text' – is it beyond any possible framework?

To study intertextuality and intertextual processes is to confront these and similar questions, which is perhaps why the term has spawned such a plethora of definitions and redefinitions. Each theorist comes to intertextuality hoping it will provide an informing tool or model for interpretation, but each theorist soon realizes that, as a concept, intertextuality plunges one into a series of oppositions and questions. Our task is to engage with it as a split, multiple concept, which poses questions and requires one to engage with them rather than forcing one to produce definite answers. No theorist of intertextuality accepts this challenge more completely than Roland Barthes.

2

THE TEXT UNBOUND: BARTHES

FROM WORK TO TEXT

A critic and theorist who, like Kristeva, has always attacked notions of the 'natural', stable meaning and unquestionable truth, Roland Barthes remains the most articulate of all writers on the concept of intertextuality. Bearing in mind our analysis of the work of Kristeva, we need to ask what Barthes means by the term 'text', and thus 'intertextuality'. In his essay 'Theory of the Text' (Barthes, 1981a: 31–47) he produces an answer to that question which begins by describing the traditional notions of *work* and *text* but ends by practically reversing the relations usually ascribed to them. In traditional terms, as Barthes explains, a text is 'the phenomenal surface of the literary work' (*ibid.*: 32). A textual scholar is still considered to be someone concerned with manuscript studies, with ascertaining a *true* text. The textual scholar searches for as complete a version as possible of the author's intended structure, individual sentences, paragraphing, and so forth. A text is the material inscription of a work. It is that which gives a work permanence, repeatability and thus readability. Barthes puts the case as follows:

> it [the text] is the fabric of the words which make up the work and which are arranged in such a way as to impose a meaning which is stable and as far as possible unique. In spite of the partial and modest character of the notion (it is, after all, only an object, perceptible to the visual sense), the text partakes of the spiritual glory of the work, of which it is the prosaic but necessary servant ... the text is, in the work, what secures the guarantee of the written object, bringing together its safe-guarding functions: on the one hand the stability and permanence of inscription, designed to correct the fragility and imprecision of the memory, and on the other hand the legality of the letter, that incontrovertible and indelible trace, supposedly, of the meaning which the author has intentionally placed in his work; the text is a weapon against time, oblivion and the trickery of speech, which is so easily taken back, altered, denied.
>
> (Barthes, 1981a: 32)

Barthes is setting up the traditional viewpoint in order to open it to a new semiotic approach which will dramatically challenge the entire set of premises it contains. The work of Jacques Derrida is just as vital as Kristeva's to Barthes's account and ironic strategy, and can be heard echoing through this account of the text and the work traditionally conceived.

The fundamental tension Barthes is referring to concerns notions of stability and security. This security, he goes on to assert, is based on the 'civilization of the sign'. That is to say, everything in Barthes's account appears commonsensical because of our long-standing Western understanding of the sign and of signification. Saussurean linguistics and the structuralism it engendered are the logical endpoint of this understanding. The text, as material writing, gives stability and security to the work, as intended meaning, because it stands in the relation of material signifier to the work as signified. As Barthes writes:

> The notion of text implies that the written message is articulated like the sign: on one side the signifier (the materiality of the letters and of their connection into words, sentences, paragraphs, chapters), and on the other side the signified, a meaning which is at once original,

univocal, and definitive, determined by the correctness of the signs
which carry it. The classical sign is a sealed unit, whose closure ar-
rests meaning, prevents it from trembling or becoming double, or
wandering. The same goes for the classical text: it closes the work,
chains it to its letter, rivets it to its signified.

(*ibid.*: 33)

The clash of verbs and of notions of action and hierarchy observable within these passages, alert us to a paradox explored
within Derrida's deconstructive writing. The paradox concerns
the relationship between speech and writing, the manner in
which the latter is supposed to be subservient to the former and
yet continually struggles free from such a subservient position.
Derrida articulates this in his *Of Grammatology*:

Writing in the common sense is the dead letter, it is the carrier of
death. It exhausts life. On the other hand, on the other face of the
same proposition, writing in the metaphoric sense, natural, divine,
and living writing, is venerated; it is equal in dignity to the origin of
value, to the voice of conscience as divine law, to the heart, to sentiment, and so forth.

(1976: 17)

We see this tension, for example, in Christian attitudes towards the Bible. The Bible is a material record of God's Word,
the *Logos*, and thus secondary. And yet, conceived as existing on a
par with nature itself (God's two Books being Nature and the
Bible) and not merely recording but constituting the Divine
Logos, the writing which constitutes the Bible is also viewed as
primary, Divine itself. Are the Ten Commandments, as presented
in Genesis, a record of Divine Law or Divine Law itself? Does
Moses merely inscribe God's commandments in the physical form
of writing, or does that writing itself contain God's commandments? Questions of the translation, or transcription, of thoughts
into writing become crucial here. Derrida's work is particularly
attentive to notions of loss, surplus force or value and the violence
of transforming the apparently spiritual into brute materiality

which revolve around traditional ideas concerning speech, thought and writing.

On the 'common' logic of the sign which Barthes invokes, the work is primary, the text secondary. The text exists to give stability to something which is presumed to come before it; writing merely helps the thought of the author to gain permanence. To call the text a 'servant' of the work's 'spiritual glory' is, no doubt intentionally, to portray the relationship between the two, and thus the relation of signified to signifier, in a manner reminiscent of the bourgeois household: writing here takes the position of the 'servant' whose primary function is 'correctness', whilst the signified of that writing, the work, takes the place of patriarch, 'original, univocal, and definitive'. The signified/work has priority, in the sense of firstness but also of authority and agency, over the signifier/text. Writing, home of the material signifier, is the signified's servant/slave; writing follows the orders and at the same time protects and preserves the 'transcendental signified', which Derrida and Barthes both gloss in terms of 'God, Law and Father'.

Throughout Western philosophical tradition, as Derrida argues in a series of ground-breaking works in the late 1960s, this hierarchical division of the sign has been affirmed. It constitutes the basis of notions of meaning, of communication, but also of the self-presence of the human subject. In a manner encapsulated in the seventeenth-century philosopher Descartes's famous phrase 'I think, therefore I am', the subject declares its existence, its self-presence, by proving that its thoughts and its speech occur simultaneously. In that phrase the subject combines the signifier (thought, speech) with the signified (the existence of the thinker) and by so doing proves its ability to produce meaning, and thus proves the uniqueness and the presence in the world of its meaning-making consciousness. Notions of unity, presence, autonomy, originality and Being, notions which can apply to the work, the sign and to the human speaker/thinker, all depend upon this hierarchy. Derrida studies this tradition particularly in terms of the hierarchy established between speech and writing. At the very beginning of *Of Grammatology*, he defines writing in terms of the 'signifier of the signifier'. Writing represents the fact which must be erased if the hierarchical division between work and text, speech and writing, signified and signifier is to be established. This fact is that all signifiers refer to signifieds which themselves function as signifiers within language conceived, after Saussure, as a system of differences without positive terms. If language is a differential system in which meaning is generated by the relationship of signifiers within that system, then writing, rather than speech (thought, intended meaning), is its appropriate and primary characteristic. Taking a phrase from the work of the eighteenth-century philosopher Rousseau, Derrida declares that writing, *écriture*, is that 'dangerous supplement' which appears secondary, and yet is in actual fact necessary for speech to exist at all, and is thus disturbingly primary.

Derrida coins the term *différance* to consolidate this point about speech and writing, signifier and signified (see Derrida, 1973: 129–60). As Christopher Norris writes, the sense of this neologism 'sets up a disturbance at the level of the signifier' since it 'remains suspended between the two French verbs "to differ" and "to defer"' (Norris, 1982: 32). The play of signifiers within *différance* opens it up to the force of writing, the play of signifiers leading to no stable signified. One cannot tell, when Derrida employs the term *différance*, whether he means 'difference' or 'deferral' or both. Even if Derrida were to speak his text we would not be able to decide between these meanings. *Différance* exhibits the fact that speech does not *come before*, have priority and authority over, writing. Like 'writing', then, *différance* is not a stable concept, cannot function as a stable signified and thus disrupts and deconstructs the hierarchy traditionally established between signified and signifier, speech and writing, work and text. Writing, in this sense, belongs to Kristeva's notion of 'productivity'. As Barthes writes: '*the Text is experienced only in an activity of production*' (1977a: 157). A process of *signifiance* rather than a medium within which meaning is secured and stabilized, writing opens the sign up to an explosive, infinite and yet always already deferred dimension of meaning. The meaning of the word *différance* is already deferred, lost amongst possible meanings, before it is used either in speech or in writing. The new vision of the text articulated in Barthes's essay is born out of this recognition of the disruptive, unstabilizable, playful dimension of writing.

In Barthes's account the traditional terms 'work' and 'text' are given new definitions. The term 'work' now stands where 'text' once stood, as the material book offering up the possibility of meaning, of closure and thus of interpretation. The term 'text' now stands for the play of the signifier within the work, its unleashing of the disruptive and yet playful force of writing. We should not confuse text and work, writes Barthes:

> A work is a finished object, something computable, which can occupy a physical space (take its place, for example, on the shelves of a library); the text is a methodological field. One cannot, therefore, count up texts, at least not in any regular way; all one can say is that in such-and-such a work, there is, or there isn't, some text. 'The work is held in the hand, the text in language'.
>
> (Barthes, 1981a: 39)

Barthes's distinction clearly relates to Kristeva's work on phenotext and genotext, only now the 'work' stands not only for the idea of stable meaning, communication and authorial intention, but also for a physical object; the 'text', on the other hand, stands for the force of writing which, although potentially unleashed in some works, is in no sense the property of those works. Barthes here combines various theories of language, including Derrida's account of writing and Kristeva's transposition of Bakhtinian dialogism. The text is radically plural because of the force of writing seen in its differential sense. That is, it is plural not in the sense of having 'several meanings' but in terms of its accomplishment of 'the very plural of meaning' (Barthes, 1977a: 159). To have several meanings is merely to exhibit an ambiguity which, because each meaning involved in the ambiguity remains identifiable, ultimately can be resolved. The plural meaning of the text involves the play of signifiers, always leading on to other signifiers, and the 'trace' (Derrida's term) of signifying chains which disrupt and infinitely defer the meaning of each signifier. Every text depends on a language within which is inscribed vast histories of meaning.

Meaning, in the text, according to Derrida's account of writing, is an 'explosion, a dissemination' of already existent meaning. Bakhtin's double-voiced discourse or dialogic word gives way here to a vision of the text in which no word means one thing alone, in which no signified stabilizes meaning, and in which the reader no longer 'discovers' meaning but follows the 'passage' of meaning as it flows, explodes, and/or regresses. Barthes writes:

> The plural of the Text depends ... not on the ambiguity of its contents but on what might be called the *stereographic plurality* of its weave of signifiers (etymologically, the text is a tissue, a woven fabric). The reader of the Text may be compared to someone at a loose end.
>
> (Barthes, 1977a: 159)

The theory of the text, therefore, involves a theory of intertextuality, since the text not only sets going a plurality of meanings but is also woven out of numerous discourses and spun from already existent meaning. The text's plurality is neither wholly an 'inside' nor an 'outside', since the text itself is not a unified, isolated object upon which an 'inside' and an 'outside' can be fixed. This point needs stressing, because without it Barthes's statements about the text can at times seem contradictory.

Following an account of literary history very much associated with the *Tel Quel* group, Barthes frequently confirms Kristeva's sense of a break in literature and other signifying practices at the end of the nineteenth century. In 'From Work to Text', for example, Barthes argues that although one can 'delight' in reading Proust, Flaubert, Balzac and even Alexandre Dumas, one cannot '*re-write* them ... and this knowledge, depressing enough, suffices to cut me off from the production of these works' (1977a: 163). It would appear that for Barthes, as for Kristeva, only Modernist and Postmodernist literature give us examples of the *text*; examples, that is, of texts which, because they self-consciously put into play the power of the signifier and of writing, can be re-written, rather than simply read, by the reader. Only literature after the emergence of Modernism allows the reader to become fully active in the production of meaning; a fundamental characteristic, it would appear, of what Barthes and Kristeva mean by the 'text'. However, near the beginning of the same essay, Barthes seemed to distance himself from this account of literary history:

> the tendency must be avoided to say that the work is classic, the text avant-garde; it is not a question of drawing up a crude honours list in the name of modernity and declaring certain literary productions 'in' and others 'out' by virtue of their chronological situation: there may be a 'text' in a very ancient work, while many products of contemporary literature are in no way texts.
>
> (Barthes, 1977a: 156)

Whilst many would see a tension between a theory of literary history and a theory of reading here, Barthes argues that the tension is generated by the text's and intertextuality's disturbance of apparently stable oppositions: reading and writing, author and critic, meaning and interpretation, inside and outside. As a recent commentator on Barthes, Michael Moriarty, stresses, readers of Barthes should not give in to the temptation to solidify the text, to imagine it as a determinate object: 'It [text] is used in a highly fluid fashion, both as a general term for the object of an act of reading and in particular contrast with the term "work"' (Moriarty, 1991: 143). Annette Lavers, another commentator, employing a terminology of *scriptible* (writerly) and *lisible* (readerly) that we shall presently examine, confirms this point:

> Strictly speaking, the *scriptible* text, when seen in terms of structuration, is not an object as such (although some texts contain more *scriptible* than others); it is '*ourselves writing*' ... Like the genotext, it has to be created anew in each reader, the observer being part of the observed.
>
> (Lavers, 1982: 202)

The 'text' is that which is potentially released within a 'work' and yet that which exists *between* that text and other texts. It is intertextual to the core and, in Barthes's hands, it foregrounds dramatically the productive role of the reader. Intertextuality, as Kristeva has asserted, has nothing to do with influence, sources, or even the stabilized model favoured in historical work of 'text' and 'context'. In this model, 'context' might explain 'text' but remains, ultimately, distinct from it. Since there is no end to the text's *signifiance*, inside and outside are merely products of any particular reading of the text, which itself can always proceed further, ceases arbitrarily, never comes to the end of the text's threads. Barthes describes the text as:

> woven entirely with citations, references, echoes, cultural languages (what language is not?) antecedent or contemporary, which cut across it through and through in a vast stereophony. The intertextual in which every text is held, it itself being the text-between of another text, is not to be confused with some origin of the text: to try to find the 'sources', the 'influences' of a work, is to fall in with the myth of filiation; the citations which go to make up a text are anonymous, untraceable, and yet *already read*: they are quotations without inverted commas.
>
> (Barthes, 1977a: 160)

Within Barthes's work we can hear Bakhtin's attack on monologism. The work, he writes, 'has nothing disturbing for any monistic philosophy', whilst the text, from a monological viewpoint, seems 'demoniacal' since it asserts the 'evil' of plurality. Barthes employs the words of the possessed man in Mark 5: 9 to encapsulate this aspect of the text, so threatening to monologic society: 'My name is Legion: for we are many' (*ibid.*: 160). As in the work of Kristeva, text and intertextuality function here as part of an attack on monological conceptions of meaning and communicability; an attack exhibiting Barthes's relation to the politics, theory and aesthetics of *Tel Quel*. Barthes's contribution to this poststructuralist project, however, is to emphasize explicitly the role of the reader in the production of the anti-monologic text.

Barthes distinguishes between two kinds of readers: 'consumers' who read the work for stable meaning, and 'readers' of the text who are productive in their reading, or, to put it in Barthes's terms, are themselves 'writers' of the text. Barthes styles this second kind of reading 'textual analysis' and contrasts it to more traditional 'criticism'. He writes: 'Textual analysis is pluralist', 'There are no more critics, only writers' (1981a: 43–4).

The theory of the text, as Barthes puts it in his 'From Work to Text', produces a disciplinary and even generic shift comparable to the shift from Newtonian to Einsteinian physics. Just as Einsteinian physics demands that *the relativity of the frames of reference* be included in the object studied', so the new theory of the text demands a wholesale 'relativization of the relations of writer, reader, and observer (critic)' (1977a: 156). If we are to understand what Barthes has in mind by this relativization we need to progress somewhat further in our understanding of the text and of its consequence for the traditional site of authority and origination of the superseded work, the author. We also need to look at the textual analysis Barthes creates and how this practice of reading conceived as re-writing depends upon the developing theory of intertextuality. Finally, we need to return to the questions posed at the end of our discussion of Kristeva: is Barthes's plural text, and thus also his account of intertextuality, capable of registering the historical and social situatedness of literary works?

THE DEATH OF THE AUTHOR

The fact that the theory of intertextuality propounded by Barthes causes what he, in an essay of 1968, famously styled 'the death of the Author' (Barthes, 1977a: 142–8) is perhaps one of the more widely known features of intertextual theory. As an event, if we can figure it as such, the death of the Author has been much bemoaned by those wishing to hold on to the idea that human beings retain a degree of agency, of choice, or at least rational thought in history and society. It is an event, however, which has frequently been misunderstood, and which needs to be understood within the context of Barthes's characteristic disturbance of apparently 'natural' ideas. In an argument bearing many similarities to the one made by Michel Foucault, also in 1968, in his

'What is an Author?' (Foucault, 1977: 113–38 and 1979: 141–60), Barthes demonstrates that the figure of the author is a modern one, in fact a capitalist one, which serves to commodify works by attaching them to a name. In pre-capitalist eras writing was not attached to the name of the author in the manner that it has been in the 'modern' period. The 'author function', to employ Foucault's phrase, has a history, and changes as one epoch follows another. The author might seem an unquestionable or even a 'natural' figure; Barthes, like Foucault, however, argues that the author is anything but unquestionable or natural.

In the modern market system, the name of the author allows the work to be an item of exchange value, but it also, Barthes argues, promotes a view of interpretation, and of the relationship between author, work and the reader-critic, in which reading is a form of consumption. The author places meaning in the work, so traditional accounts argue, and the reader-critic consumes that meaning; once this process has been accomplished the reader is free to move on to the next work. This process of interpretation as it is normally understood fosters the capitalist market system because it encourages us to view works as disposable, or at least finite, commodities. As Moriarty puts it, paraphrasing Barthes's arguments in *S/Z* (see Barthes, 1974: 15–16): 'a book reread is one fewer sold' (Moriarty, 1991: 127).

The author, or the name of the author, then, is what fosters the 'work' as opposed to the 'text'. As Barthes puts it: 'The *explanation* of a work is always sought in the man or woman who produced it, as if it were always in the end, through the more or less transparent allegory of the fiction, the voice of a single person, the *author* "confiding" in us' (1977a: 143).

The ideology of the author, that which argues that the author's dominance over the text is unquestionable, depends upon the same kind of logic which we have already seen Barthes attacking with regard to the idea of the 'work'. Notions of paternity, of authority, of filiation – fathership, ownership, giving birth, familial power – all attach themselves to the name of the author in order to endorse it at the same moment as they express through it dominant social structures of power. Barthes writes:

> The Author, when believed in, is always conceived of as the past of his own book: book and author stand automatically on a single line divided into a *before* and an *after*. The Author is thought to *nourish* the book, which is to say that he exists before it, thinks, suffers, lives for it, is in the same relation of antecedence to his work as a father to his child.
>
> (Barthes, 1977a: 145)

The author's *delivery* of the finished work is a commonplace in literature which can take us all the way from the epic poet's offering up of his poem to the Muse, an act which rhetorically transfers parentage from the author to a spiritual deity, to more psychologically complex and modern forms, such as Mary Shelley's offering to her readers of *Frankenstein*, in her 1831 preface, as if it were a deformed or disturbing baby, 'my hideous progeny'. Yet all such references to the rhetoric of filiation reinforce the illusion that a text possesses and conveys a meaning imparted to it by its author, and thus that the text has a unity which stems directly from the unified and original thought of its creator.

Against such a naturalized image of the author Barthes pits the theory of the text. Like his *Tel Quel* colleagues, Barthes constructs this theory out of a number of different discourses: psychoanalytic, linguistic, structural, deconstructive, Marxist. Like Kristeva, for example, he combines psychoanalytical and linguistic accounts of the subject to argue that the subject always suffers a loss when entering into writing: writing, as Barthes puts it, 'knows a "subject", not a person' (1977a: 145). Influenced by Kristeva's work on Bakhtin, Barthes develops this point into a recognition that the origin of the text is not a unified authorial consciousness but a plurality of voices, of other words, other utterances and other texts. If we were able to look inside the head of the author – something traditional literary criticism believes is possible by interpreting the literary work – then, Barthes's argument implies, we would not discover original thought or even uniquely intended meaning, but what he styles as the 'already-read', the 'already-written'. The French author La Rochefoucauld (1613–80) once argued that if there were no novels, no one would ever fall in love (see Barthes, 1974: ix). In *S/Z*, Barthes produces a modern paraphrase of La Rochefoucauld's maxim:

> Without the – always anterior – Book and Code, no desire, no jealousy: Pygmalion is in love with a link in the code of statuary; Paolo and Francesca love each other *according to* the passion of Lancelot and Guinevere (Dante, *Inferno*, V): itself a lost origin, writing becomes the origin of emotion.

(Barthes, 1974: 73–4)

There are, in Barthes's intertextual world, no emotions before the textual description of emotions, no thoughts before the textual representation of thoughts, no significant actions which do not signify outside of already textualized and encoded actions; we feel and think and act in codes, in the cultural space of the *déjà*, the already spoken, written, read (see Barthes, 1987: 47). The modern author, whom Barthes styles the 'modern *scriptor*', does not, in writing the book, release 'a single "theological" meaning (the "message" of the Author-God)' but rather arranges and compiles the always already written, spoken, and read into a 'multi-dimensional space in which a variety of writings, none of them original, blend and clash'. The text is, then, 'a tissue of quotations drawn from the innumerable centres of culture' (Barthes, 1977a: 146).

Let us be clear about this concept of the *déjà*, the 'always already written or read'. To recognize that the text's meaning does not spring from an author combining a signifier (writing) with a signified (concept), but springs in fact from the intertextual, does not mean we can simply move to the intertextual level to unite signifier and signified. To say that the text is constructed from a mosaic of quotations does not mean we can find the text's inter-texts and then view them as the signified of the text's signifiers. The inter-texts, other works of literature, other kinds of texts, are themselves intertextual constructs, are themselves able to offer us nothing more than signifiers. Although many subsequent users of intertextuality have employed the concept in this manner, a use which Barthes and Kristeva view as tied to traditional concepts of 'source' and 'influence', in Barthes the intertextual has less to do with specific inter-texts than with the entire cultural code, comprised, as it is, of discourses, stereotypes, clichés, ways of saying. Intertextuality, viewed in this way, means that for Barthes, as for Derrida, 'nothing exists outside the text' (Barthes, 1974: 6; 1975: 36); text here meaning the intertextual. For this reason Barthes, following Derrida's critique of the notion of 'origins', states that meaning is always 'anterior' and always 'deferred'. Meaning occurs because of the play of signifiers, not because a signified can be found to stabilize a signifier; the signified is always, as it were, over the horizon.

Barthes's use of textual and intertextual theory destroys, therefore, the 'myth of filiation': the idea that meaning *comes from* and is, metaphorically at least, the *property of* the individual authorial consciousness. The modern scriptor, when s/he writes, is always already in a process of reading and of re-writing. Meaning comes not from the author but from language viewed intertextually. As Barthes puts it in 'The Death of the Author':

> In France, Mallarmé was doubtless the first to see and to foresee in all its full extent the necessity to substitute language itself for the person who until then had been supposed to be its owner. For him, for us too, it is language which speaks, not the author; to write is, through a prerequisite impersonality (not at all to be confused with the castrating objectivity of the realistic novelist), to reach that point where only language acts, 'performs', and not 'me'.
>
> (Barthes, 1977a: 143)

Such pronouncements have caused many to argue against Barthes, believing it fatuous to transfer all agency to language itself (see Bloom, 1975a: 60). Yet such reactions do not recognize the tension we have noted within Barthes's work between an historical and a theoretical approach. Such theoretical statements as the above appear to give all agency to language viewed intertextually. Yet at the very moment that Barthes makes that move he is citing Mallarmé as an authorial point not of origin but at least of conscious determination. Mallarmé's writing, for Barthes, evinces a choice within that author to become a modern scriptor.

Likewise, as we have noted, Barthes recognizes that not every modern author chooses to become a scriptor.

Clearly the 'death of the Author' does not murder all forms of authorial agency, and Barthes in *The Pleasure of the Text* even writes of a certain desire *for* the author (1975: 27). The tension between theory and history is clearly a persistent one, and we will return to it at the end of this Chapter. Whatever we decide about that issue, however, it is indisputable that Barthes's account of the text and of intertextuality disturbs the previously hierarchized, filial relationship between author and reader. The intertextual nature of writing and of the text turns both terms of the traditional model, author and critic, into readers. As Barthes asserts at the conclusion of 'The Death of the Author':

> a text is made of multiple writings, drawn from many cultures and entering into mutual relations of dialogue, parody, contestation, but there is one place where this multiplicity is focused, and that place is the reader, not, as was hitherto said, the author. The reader is the space on which all the quotations that make up a writing are inscribed without any of them being lost; a text's unity lies not in its origin but in its destination. Yet this destination cannot any longer be personal: the reader is without history, biography, psychology; he is simply that *someone* who holds together in a single field all the traces by which the written text is constituted ... the birth of the reader must be at the cost of the death of the Author.
>
> (Barthes, 1977a: 148)

There are questions generated even here, however. If language viewed intertextually is 'infinite', as Barthes frequently states, and if this fact is part of the reason for the death of the Author, then does not Barthes here merely replace one figure of mythical authority with another? If the author dies as an authority for meaning because s/he cannot control the meaning s/he unleashes in the act of writing, then how can the reader be said to 'hold together' all the traces which make up the text? Whether we take 'reader' to refer to the subject traditionally designated by that term or whether we also now include the previously authoritative 'author' within that term, there seems to be a problem here with regard the new 'reader's' possession and recognition of 'all the [intertextual] traces by which the text is constituted'. The poststructuralism of Barthes, Kristeva and Derrida moves away from structuralism, with its belief in the possibility of a totalizing or scientific methodology, by privileging and promoting notions of difference. Is not the reader, lost amongst difference, writing, intertextuality, the figure which poststructuralism posits against earlier totalized visions of meaning? And, if so, is not Barthes's figuration of the reader here contrary to that approach, standing as a totalized figure possessing and containing all differences?

Barthes's writing might be said to generate the appearance of contradiction, or at least of tension, because he is prone to more programmatic and more strident statements than theorists such as Kristeva or Derrida. Yet, the tensions and contradictions stem from a recognition, shared by all three, of the never-resolved struggle between truth and its subversion, between myth and its critique, between what Kristeva calls the phenotext and the genotext and what Barthes calls the *doxa* and the *para-doxa*.

Barthes's texts explore, but also self-consciously embody, the constant struggle between *doxa* and *para-doxa*. To fully engage with his texts, it is insufficient to merely locate contradictions and tensions and then to make choices within them. These tensions and contradictions are confirmations of the struggle and clash between discourses and between ideological positions which Barthes's texts explore and embody. It is crucial for us, therefore, to understand intertextuality's place within the on-going clash between *doxa* and *para-doxa*. However, before we come on to that subject directly, we need to engage with the practice of textual analysis developed by Barthes.

READERLY AND WRITERLY TEXTS

The structural analysis of narrative articulated by Barthes and others during the 1960s sought to establish a model which could 'master' the 'numberless' narratives of the world (see Barthes, 1977a: 79–124). Taking Saussurean linguistics as its model, structural analysis proceeded to argue that all narratives function by employing 'elementary combinatory scheme[s]' (*ibid.*: 81). Each individual narrative, then, was seen as a *parole*, a particular act of narration produced by operating the *langue* of the narrative system itself. The task of structural analysis was to isolate the 'units and rules' which constitute the narrative *langue* and are set in motion by each individual narrative act. The theory of the text, however, caused Barthes and others to radically question the objectives and the methodology of structural analysis which, in searching for a common system, elided the 'difference' of the text, reducing it to a reiteration of a totalized system. Structural analysis did not, for Barthes, pay sufficient attention to the power of the signifier or to the plurality of meaning which the text unleashes. It also presumed a stable distinction between text and reader which the theory of text and of intertextuality shatters.

Structural analysis tends to dispense with the question of the meaning of texts in favour of an assessment of the text's relation to the system out of which it is presumed to have been produced. The theory of the text refocused attention on meaning. As opposed to the traditional search for a final meaning, however, Barthes's textual analysis seeks to trace the manner in which the text 'explodes and disperses' (1981b: 135).

Barthes's most important discussions of textual analysis were written during a period in which poststructuralism was emerging from within structuralism: the late 1960s and early 1970s. Thus textual analysis is often posited not as a critique of structuralism but as something new within the structuralist movement. The textual analysis Barthes developed retained a commitment to the exploration of the structure of the text, its fundamental elements and units of combination, but also put this structure within the context not of a closed narrative system but of the intertextual, within which no closure, no finite system, is available. The intertextual nature of the text means that its signifiers offer up the 'always already written/read'; texts produce meaning understood as always already anterior and always deferred. The text has a structure of definable elements, and yet, woven from the threads of the social text, its intertextual relations can never be stabilized, exhaustively located and listed. The text combines structure and an infinity of meaning.

Does this mean that textual analysis as developed by Barthes looks exclusively at 'texts' rather than 'works', at the productions of the 'modern scriptor' rather than those of the traditional author? The tension between an historical and a theoretical account of intertextuality immediately returns when we consider Barthes's textual analysis. Some of the most impressive examples of textual analysis produced by Barthes are based on readings of literary works which are, on the historical argument, very much classifiable as works rather than modern texts. In 'The Struggle with the Angel: Textual Analysis of Genesis 32: 22–32' Barthes looks at a section in Genesis in which Jacob, crossing the Jabbok, wrestles with 'a man' and receives through this both a spiritual blessing and his new name of 'Israel' but also a wound on his thigh. Employing the techniques of structural analysis upon this text Barthes's stated aim is not, by that method, to discover the text's singular meaning; it does not possess one single meaning. His aim, rather, is to see the text in its 'difference'. This difference does not concern any notion of the individuality of the text so much as the manner in which its employment of 'familiar codes' implicates it in 'the very infinity of language, itself structured without closure'. Textual analysis in this way: 'tries to say no longer *from where* the text comes (historical criticism), nor even *how* it is made (structural analysis), but how it is unmade, how it explodes, disseminates – by what coded paths it *goes off*' (1977a: 126–7). As Rick Rylance states, there is perhaps a certain 'impishness in Barthes's choice of the Bible to expose the way language undermines truth and authority' (Rylance, 1994: 73). It is also worthwhile considering Barthes's choice of text in two other instances of textual analysis: Poe's 'The Facts in the Case of M. Valdemar' (Poe, 1986: 350–9) and Balzac's short story *Sarrasine* (see Barthes, 1974: 221–54). We will look at these examples in more detail.

In his study of Balzac's *Sarrasine* Barthes employs a distinction between what he calls the *lisible* (readerly) and the *scriptible* (writerly) text. This distinction gives a more specific nomination to the opposition between 'work' and 'text'. The readerly text is oriented towards representation and, in Barthes's handling, is very much associated with the realist novel of the nineteenth century; Barthes frequently classifies it as the 'classic' as opposed to the 'modern' text. This readerly text leads the reader towards *a* meaning, it creates the illusion that it is produced by a singular voice and underplays the force of the intertextual (Barthes, 1974: 41). To call such a text 'readerly' is to foreground the manner in which its reader is positioned as a relatively passive receiver: the reader's task is to follow the linear development of the story until the truth, presumed to lie *behind* the narrated events, is finally unfolded before him or her. Readerly texts thus reinforce cultural myths and ideologies which Barthes symbolizes through the term *doxa*. The *doxa* suggests, and indeed embodies, the idea that stable meaning is possible, that a signified can be found for the text's signifiers, that language can uncomplicatedly represent the world, that a truth can finally be delivered by an author to a reader.

Readers of the classic, readerly text are, at best, detectives shifting through the clues sequentially provided by a narrative until the 'answer' is unveiled. It is not coincidental that Barthes chooses to analyse texts which have for their main narrative plot some kind of search for the truth. In Poe's 'The Facts in the Case of M. Valdemar', for example, a scientist concerned with the nineteenth-century pseudo-science of mesmerism writes of how a man on the brink of death becomes the subject of a mesmeric experiment. The case, and its shocking details, have been leaked to the public, we are informed at the tale's beginning, and the narrator now writes up the case to dispel the misconceptions, scandal and misguided public interest it has produced. The experiment had in fact succeeded in allowing M. Valdemar to make a statement never before made in human history: in a mesmeric state, after the time which his doctors had agreed would see his death, M. Valdemar had said: 'For God's sake! – quick! – quick! – put me to sleep – or, quick! – waken me! – quick! – I *say to you that I am dead!*' (Poe, 1986: 359). The doctor, whilst M. Valdemar reiterates 'dead! dead!', attempts to awaken his patient, only to see him collapse into a 'liquid mass of loathsome – of detestable putridity' (*ibid.*). Such a story leads us steadily towards a truth which is literally impossible and undermines the very notions of truth, certainty, science, meaning; the readerly text explodes into a plurality which undermines its status as a readerly text, which makes it, at least in its dénouement, writerly, plural, structured and yet infinite.

Balzac's *Sarrasine* contains a similarly disturbing narrative, and again, as Barthes demonstrates, contains a potential for the 'writerly' within its apparent 'readerly' form. The story begins with the narrator at a party given by the wealthy Lanty family. The narrator is enamoured of a young woman. When she sees and is shocked by the appearance of a man of extreme old age, the narrator forms a contract with the young woman: he will divulge to her the identity of the old man in exchange for one night of passion. The story of Sarrasine is thus framed by certain enigmas: not only is it concerned to explain the identity of the old man, but in the answer to that enigma the origin of the wealth of the Lanty family will also be divulged. The answer to both of these enigmas is in the story of a sculptor, Sarrasine, who, in visiting Rome falls in love with what he takes to be a beautiful young female singer at the theatre. Sarrasine does not know that women are banned from the Roman stage and that the singer, Zambinella is in fact a castrato. Sarrasine's infatuation with Zambinella drives him to attempt to capture his beloved in sculpture and to capture her heart. He makes a statue and is finally driven, refusing to believe the growing evidence of the real nature of his love, into a plot to kidnap Zambinella. Sarrasine is eventually murdered during the unsuccessful kidnapping, and Zambinella goes on to become a famous and wealthy castrato, thus founding the Lanty family's wealth.

The old man, so disgusting to the sight of the young woman, is in fact Zambinella. The statue of female beauty created by Sarrasine, and copied by painters subsequently, and the disgusting old man at the party turn out to be the same person. More shockingly still, the origin of the various enigmas is a case of castration – a nothingness, as Barthes, using psychoanalytical theories concerning the fear of castration, puts it. The young woman is so shocked by the truth (the nothingness) that is revealed by the narrative that she breaks the contract with the narrator and so, herself symbolically castrated by the story, also symbolically castrates, or makes nothing of, the desire that has driven the narrator to tell the story in the first place.

The text is a fantastically rich resource for Barthes to plunder. The story of an artist, Sarrasine, attempting to find the truth behind the appearance of Zambinella mirrors the ethos of the realist novel and still dominant ideas concerning language. The story seems to confirm that language can display a reality if we can penetrate behind its surface appearance (Barthes, 1974: 122). Balzac's narrative repeats the structure that lies at the foundation of traditional ideas concerning the work and the relationship it establishes between an author, who delivers meaning, and a reader, who interprets that meaning by progressing through to the work's presumed depth. However, the text also demonstrates that at the centre of the rising French bourgeois society of the nineteenth century – its wealth, its language, its art – is a shocking nothingness, which threatens to throw all that culture's values into question. Again, as Barthes demonstrates, the readerly text threatens to explode into something writerly, plural, paradoxical.

Barthes's analysis of such texts as those by Poe and Balzac, then, challenges the historical argument that intertextuality emerges in literary works only with the rise of Modernism. The modern avant-garde text, after Mallarmé, might be self-consciously intertextual, yet we can discover the disruptive power of the intertextual within earlier, apparently realist works. It is important to note that for Barthes a pure text, in the sense of a completely writerly text, is a utopian notion (see 1977b: 76– 7). Even a radically avant-garde text, Barthes suggests in *The Pleasure of the Text*, needs 'its shadow: this shadow is a *bit* of ideology, a *bit* of representation, a *bit* of subject' (1975: 32). At the beginning of his textual analysis of Balzac's story in *S/Z* Barthes states that the totally writerly text is an 'ideal' (1974: 5–6). The bourgeois realism of Balzac is a perfect site for Barthes to demonstrate how intertextuality achieves a goal for which Barthes always wrote: the exposure of the natural as cultural and ideological.

In the contract between the narrator and the young woman, *Sarrasine* thematizes the fact that narration, telling stories, is always a contract; the narrative itself, that which is readerly, is always an object of exchange-value. Intertextuality, the *already read*, however, conflicts with the commercialism of the readerly, and Barthes's textual analysis strives to open up this aspect of the text by cutting up its linear, sequential, readerly flow into small segments. Barthes divides the text into 561 *lexias*, small segments which can be a word, a phrase, a piece of action, one sentence, or a small group of sentences. Each *lexia* contains a limited number of meanings, sometimes only one, never more than four. The name, *Sarrasine*, also functioning as the title, is a *lexia*, as are other names including that of Zambinella or La Zambinella (feminine) as Sarrasine calls 'her'. Other *lexias* include the first and every subsequent posing of the enigma of the Lanty family's wealth, or of the old man's identity, or each reference to the framing narrative contract. In the analysis of the Poe story, each mention of mesmerism constitutes one of the text's *lexias*, but so does the fact that the dying man is nominated as 'M. Valdemar' rather than simply 'Valdemar'. These *lexias* are arbitrary, they could be more or less in number, they represent the reader's establishment of an operating field but also the productive manner in which the textual analyst treats the text (Barthes, 1981b: 136).

In the structural analysis of narrative a text is cut up into segments in order to demonstrate how those segments relate to the rules of combination and association which are presumed to form the *langue* of narrative. In Henrik Ibsen's *Hedda Gabler*, for example, the audience is made aware that there exists a gun within the Gabler household. From a structuralist point of view such an element, once noticed, must either be a functional signifier of a set of signifieds (danger, threat) or ultimately become part of the overall action; in the play Hedda Gabler does, in fact, finally use the gun to devastating effect. In structural analysis every signifier, once isolated and cut away from the linear flow of the narrative, is ultimately regrouped at a higher level of analysis, in which the text's component parts are related to the rules of narrative *langue*. Meaning is not a question in structural analysis of this variety, where every signifier is finally provided with a signifying place in the total system. Barthes cuts the text into *lexias* but, instead of explaining them, regrouping them at a higher level and thus closing off their meaning, he strives to detonate their meanings without any sense that these meanings can be contained at some higher level of analysis. The text, after all, is a plural phenomenon; it has structure, yet also an infinity of meaning. As Barthes writes, each *lexia* functions like a 'minor earthquake' (1974: 13), a minor explosion of meaning which provides the reader with a window not onto some ultimate structure or meaning but onto the realm of the intertextual. Barthes's cutting up of the text, in other words, strives to register the manner in which it is woven from the threads of the social text. Barthes strives to respect the text's non-linear, non-totalizable intertextuality.

For Barthes, both the traditional notion of the work and structural analysis of narrative present the illusion of a text which is finally 'unreversible'. The unreversible here is associated with all the myths encapsulated within Barthes's term *doxa*: for example, to raise the text into an explanatory higher model or metalanguage (*langue*) is to repeat the ideology in which texts are objects which can be consumed. However, for Barthes, the text is reversible. Every *lexia* is a signifying point which leads us out into the infinity of the social text, demonstrating the manner in which intertextuality reverses narrative progression, explodes and disperses within the text and shatters the illusion that narrative can provide an ultimate meaning. Textual analysis becomes, on this model, a 'step-by-step', 'slow-motion' procedure through which the reader strives to capture the text's detonation of meaning or, to employ Kristeva's term, of *signifiance*.

In his discussion of Kristeva in 'Theory of the Text' Barthes associates the term *signifiance* with the 'connotative' meaning of the text (1981a: 37–8). If we read a text and presume it has a stable meaning to offer us, then we read at the level of 'denotation'. Denotation concerns the notion that each signifier has a primary signified. Connotation, on the other hand, involves 'secondary meaning', meanings which are the intertextual threads of the classic, readerly text's *lexias*. As Barthes writes: 'Connotation is the way into the polysemy of the classic text, to that limited plural on which the classic text is based' (1974: 8). Connotation is that aspect of the readerly text which allows meaning to break free from a linear, consecutive order and to 'spread like gold dust on the apparent surface of the text' (*ibid.*: 9). Thus connotation is a 'deliberate static' and establishes various 'codes' by which Barthes attempts to register the intertextuality of the text's connotative meanings. Each connotation, 'is the starting point of a code (which will never be reconstituted), the articulation of a voice which is woven into the text' (*ibid.*).

These codes are not methodologically rigorous; they do not collect the text's *lexias* and meanings up into a higher system (*langue*), rather they are the reader's own way of registering the intertextual avenues of meaning which break into the text's apparent sequential order. The hermeneutic code (HER) concerns all those elements of the text, such as enigmas and questions, which force the reader to interpret the events being narrated. The code of the seme (SEM) concerns all the connotations which help to build up the sense of the special quality of a character or an action. Characters in a narrative are basically a collection of semes which Barthes often defines through single words: often next to mentions of 'the Lanty family' we find the singular '(SEM. Wealth)' (Barthes, 1974: 18). Various characters build up a set of recurrent semes as the analysis progresses, such as 'childishness' and 'mechanicalness'. Characters are then names to which groups of semes are attracted. As Barthes writes: 'As soon as a Name exists (even a pronoun) to flow toward and fasten onto, the semes become predicates, inductors of truth, and the Name becomes a subject' (*ibid.*: 191). Names, such as Zambinella, act as magnets, attracting to them various semes (beauty, mystery, danger); it is this build-up of semes which creates the impression of 'depth', and thus generates the illusion that these names refer to actual 'characters'.

The symbolic code (SYM) involves all the recognizable symbolic patterns, including traditional oppositions such as male–female or light and dark. The proairetic code (ACT) involves the narrative's various actions, which combine into sequences and which Barthes provides titles for, such as '*stroll, murder, rendezvous*' (*ibid.*: 19). Some of these actions derive 'from a practical reservoir of trivial everyday acts (*to knock at the door, to arrange a rendezvous*) and others from a written corpus of novelistic models (*the Abduction, the Declaration of Love, the Murder*)' (*ibid.*: 204). Lastly, the cultural code (REF) involves the 'numerous codes of knowledge or wisdom to which the text continually refers'. Despite recognizing that as part of the intertextual all the codes can be called cultural, Barthes restricts the cultural code to those elements which seem to refer directly to cultural authorities and communal thinking.

In one sense the tragedy of Sarrasine stems from how badly he plays the cultural code. Sarrasine convinces himself of Zambinella's femininity on the basis of a set of cultural assumptions: a 'narcissistic proof': 'I love her, therefore she is a woman'; a 'psychological proof': 'women are weak, La Zambinella is weak, etc.'; and what Barthes styles 'a kind of sorites (or abridged syllogism): beauty is feminine; only an artist can know beauty; I am an artist; therefore I know beauty and therefore I know woman, etc.'. (*ibid.*: 167). The only flaw in this collection of culturally encoded assumptions on the part of Sarrasine is that he is ignorant of the Papal ban on women appearing on the stage. That particular cultural code, shared by all the theatre-goers save Sarrasine himself, will, through his ignorance of it, cause Sarrasine's death. Sarrasine dies, that is, from 'a gap in knowledge' of the cultural codes in operation (*ibid.*: 184–5).

The five codes, then, are Barthes's non-systematic way of marking intertextuality within Balzac's text. As he puts it:

> they are so many fragments of something that has always been *already* read, done, experienced; the code is the wake of that *already*. Referring to what has been written, i.e., to the Book (of culture, of life, of life as culture), it makes the text into a prospectus of this Book. Or again: each code is one of the forces that can take over the text (of

which the text is the network), one of the voices out of which the text is woven. Alongside each utterance, one might say that off-stage voices (whose origin is 'lost' in the vast perspective of the *already-written*) de-originate the utterance: the convergence of voices (of the codes) becomes *writing*, a stereographic space where the five codes, the five voices, intersect.

(Barthes, 1974: 20–1)

It is important to remind ourselves of the convenient, even arbitrary, nature of Barthes's codes and of his use of them. The textual analysis of *S/Z*, as Barthes makes clear, is not an exhaustive interpretation, but is one reader's analysis, which is necessarily, given the nature of intertextuality, incomplete.

Barthes's codes allow for a further refinement of the distinction between readerly and writerly texts. The readerly text contains only a limited plural, since within it the proairetic and hermeneutic codes remain very strong. These codes 'constitute the strongest armature of the readerly ... by their typically sequential nature' (*ibid.*: 204). There is, to put it simply, in the classic, readerly text a strong illusion of narrative progression which the textual analyst can only seek to disturb, never completely overturn. Narrative, like the sentence, Barthes argues, encourages the reader to move from beginning to end. Both narrative and individual sentences are essentially readerly, in that they encourage an unreversible flow of reading. Readerly texts are, in this sense, sentential: based on the linear, sequential nature of the sentence. One defining feature of the modern writerly text, therefore, would be its attempt to downplay, or even eradicate, the two linear codes in favour of the other more nebulous, circulating codes. A good deal of modern avant-garde writing, in fact, goes so far as to repudiate any recognizably sentential order.

Mallarmé's *Un Coup De Dés* is often cited by poststructuralist theorists of the text, because in this work of the last years of the nineteenth century Mallarmé writes a poetry within which 'narrative is avoided' (Mallarmé, 1994: 122). The poem sets up a radical polysemy through its utilization of the spacing of words and through the employment of different typefaces. Both techniques puncture any simple narrative or linear progression from beginning to end. Various sentences run through the whole poem, such as the full title sentence, 'Un Coup De Dés Jamais N'abolira Le Hasard' ('A Throw of the Dice Will Never Abolish Chance'). Such sentences thus function as sentences whilst also incorporating themselves into the meaning of the particular words which surround them on the given page on which they appear. As demonstrated in the following page from the text (*ibid.*: 134), the poem offers the reader more than a single, linear line of words, thus setting up multiple possibilities for combination and thus for meaning:

AS IF
An insinuation   simple

in the silence   enrolled with irony
                                or
                                    the mystery
                                        hurled
                                            howled
in some nearby   whirlpool of hilarity and horror

    flutters   about the abyss
                            without strewing it
                                or fleeing

                        and out of it cradles the virgin sing

                                            AS IF

Do we begin by reading the text 'AS IF An insinuation simple in the silence enrolled with irony ... '? or do we begin by reading two columns of simultaneous text: 'AS IF An insinuation in the silence ... ' and 'AS IF simple enrolled with irony ... '? Such questions confront the reader throughout the poem and generate numerous signifying combinations. This is a text which is rich in what Barthes styles the symbolic and the cultural codes but constantly resists any of the more narrative codes.

The codes presented in Barthes's analysis of *Sarrasine* are, however, as we have seen, arbitrary and convenient. Despite the declaration that ends 'The Death of the Author', no reader can contain the social text and, just as importantly, every reader's relation to the social text mirrors that of Sarrasine, rich in places, lacking in others. The experience of reading Barthes's analysis is to witness a reader taking certain *lexias* far beyond what one would have previously imagined possible, but leaving others less discussed than another reader would have done. The comparison, for example, made between the Lanty family and 'Lord Byron's poems' in *lexia* 25 seems to contain far more potential connotative meaning than Barthes's simple 'REF. Literature (Byron)' (Barthes, 1974: 39). Was not Byron a man who was wealthy, famous, and yet the subject of scandal and mystery concerning his private life? The 'figure of Byron' as we know it contains an ambiguity on the sexual level, the ethical level and even the level of identity which might be interestingly related to the story of the Lanty family. Byron after all lived a life in which the artifice of his poetry and his actual self were constantly confused. Does not Sarrasine confuse artifice and substance? And does not Barthes himself demonstrate the conflict between the realistic and the cultural throughout his analysis? Similarly, the comparison of the Lanty family's mysteriousness to something out of the novels of Ann Radcliffe seems to set up a reference to the Gothic which some readers would feel deserves more attention than Barthes's 'REF. Literature (Ann Radcliffe)' (*ibid.*: 40). The textual analyst, however, traces the explosion of *signifiance* rather than of meaning as signification. This is a meaning within which both narrative 'I' and the 'I' which reads find themselves lost, overwhelmed, able merely to mark the points at which the intertextual explodes and disseminates. Forgetting meanings is, as Barthes reiterates, a part of reading.

Jonathan Culler, in a much read essay, has complained that poststructuralist theorists of intertextuality reduce intertextuality, when performing specific readings, to a restricted, manageable level and so undermine the claims made for that new term. To talk of the infinity of intertextuality but to then produce a curtailed version of it when analysing specific texts seems, Culler argues, somewhat contradictory (see Culler, 1981: 100–18). Yet

Barthes's textual analysis never sets out to explain the entirety of the text's connotative meanings; such a project is doomed, since both writer and reader exist and work within an intertextual field of cultural codes and meanings which can never be contained within an analysis. The tension that remains in Barthes's work is not, then, one between theory and practice but that tension we have associated with the clash between historical and theoretical versions of intertextuality: namely, the clash between *doxa* and *para-doxa*.

THE PARADOXICAL TEXT

In *S/Z* Barthes attempts to employ the readerly, classic text's intertextuality against that within it which would lead us towards a singular truth or representation of reality. At times, however, as the two linear or narrative codes begin to dominate, Barthes can speak of ennui or nausea brought on by the 'conformism, and disgust with repetition that establishes them' (Barthes, 1974: 139). Readerly texts, we might say, depend greatly on intertextual codes which are so stereotypical that following them can create a certain boredom in the reader. Even the cultural codes detected in *Sarrasine* can reach this level of predictability. Barthes imagines school-books within which could be arranged, for easy learning, many of the cultural codes operative in a readerly text such as *Sarrasine*. He goes on:

> Although entirely derived from books, these codes, by a swivel characteristic of bourgeois ideology, which turns culture into nature, appear to establish reality, 'Life'. 'Life' then, in the classic text, becomes a nauseating mixture of common opinions, a smothering of received ideas.
>
> (Barthes, 1974: 206)

We learn an important thing about Barthes's employment of the term intertextuality here which it is worth stating boldly: the intertextual can be the source of ennui or boredom. Intertextuality is not itself that which produces what Barthes and Kristeva call *jouissance*, the loss of unity and even identity

experienced by the reader when confronted by the plural, polysemous, non-unified text. Intertextuality is an important term for
describing the radically plural text, and is a crucial technique in
the work of those writers who eschew notions of the unified
work, yet it is also potentially what creates a sense of repetition,
cultural saturation, a dominance of cultural stereotypes and thus
of *doxa* over that which would resist and disturb the beliefs and
forms and codes of that culture, the *para-doxa*.

Barthes goes on to speak of a 'Replete Literature', very much
associated with the tradition of the bourgeois, realist novel,
which is 'stalked by the army of stereotypes it contains' (*ibid*:
206). In this kind of literature, it would seem, intertextuality
functions in terms of the unavoidability, the apparent naturalness,
of literary and cultural codes, the only defence against them appearing to be to employ them ironically. Against such a saturated
literature Barthes posits the radically plural text, which does not
allow one code to dominate over any other, and which therefore
liberates the disruptive force of the intertextual.

The opposition between the readerly and the writerly text is
transposed in Barthes's essay-length book *The Pleasure of the Text*.
In this book Barthes meditates on two kinds of texts: the 'text of
bliss' (*jouissance*) and the 'text of pleasure' (*plaisir*). On first reading
it might appear that Barthes's two kinds of texts correspond to the
two kinds of uses of intertextuality, one generating ennui because
saturated by dominant cultural codes, the other generating a pleasure analogous to sexual coming (*jouissance*) because radically plural and functioning as a conduit for the disruptive potential of
intertextuality. Barthes explains his two texts as follows:

> Text of pleasure: the text that contents, fills, grants euphoria; the text
> that comes from culture and does not break with it, is linked to a
> *comfortable* practice of reading. Text of bliss: the text that imposes a
> state of loss, the text that discomforts (perhaps to the point of a cer-
> tain boredom), unsettles the reader's historical, cultural, psychologi-
> cal assumptions, the consistency of his tastes, values, memories,
> brings to a crisis his relation with language.
>
> (Barthes, 1975: 14)

With this definition we are immediately made aware that Barthes associates the text of bliss rather than the text of pleasure with ennui, along with its opposite state of *jouissance*. Why is this? We return to the tension between historical and theoretical descriptions of the text and of intertextuality. From a historical perspective the text of pleasure appears to be related to the kind of readerly text Barthes analyses in *S/Z* and the essay on Poe. The text of bliss seems to correspond to modern, avant-garde writing. On that basis, ennui would surely only occur with regard to the former. Barthes, however, is not, through his distinctions, attempting to make an historically oriented point; or, at least, an historical account of the text is only one of the avenues, as he puts it in *S/Z*, which might be explored from the basis of his theory.

The purpose of *The Pleasure of the Text*, and indeed all Barthes's writings of the late 1960s and 1970s, is to articulate *para-doxa*. As he states in *Roland Barthes by Roland Barthes*: 'The *doxa* is current opinion, meaning repeated *as if nothing had happened*' (1977: 122). The *doxa* is a stereotypical meaning, a fragment from the intertextual environment of the social text, constituted by established discourses, by the already written and the already read. But *doxa* expresses the already written as if it were literal, representational, denotative and, thus, as if it were natural. For Barthes, as he makes clear in *The Pleasure of the Text*, it is not just conservative, monological discourse which relies on the *doxa*; left-wing, even Marxist discourses have their own unquestionable signifieds. *Doxa* is 'a kind of unconscious' and as such is 'the essence of ideology' (1975: 29). When politically right-wing people argue for the sanctity of the nuclear family, or for heterosexuality as the only legitimate sexuality, then we are clearly dealing with discursive arguments Barthes would nominate in terms of the *doxa*. The *doxa* here is relatable to Bakhtin's concept of the monologic. However, when left-wing groups argue that society can only be changed by a revolution of the workers, or that all art which does not reflect working-class conditions is elitist, then we are also dealing with Barthes's *doxa*. Barthes writes, in a fashion which is still at one level recognizably Bakhtinian, that the *doxa* is a cultural stereotype, and thus a fiction, functioning as a jargon, an unconscious or even lazy discourse:

> each jargon (each fiction) fights for hegemony; if power is on its side, it spreads everywhere in the general and daily occurrences of social life, it becomes *doxa*, nature: this is the supposedly apolitical jargon of politicians, of agents of the State, of the media, of conversation; but even out of power, even when power is against it, the rivalry is reborn, the jargons split and struggle among themselves. A ruthless *topic* rules the life of language; language always comes from some place, it is a warrior *topos*.
>
> (Barthes, 1975: 28)

Barthes's concepts of *doxa* and *para-doxa* may well be his unacknowledged transposition of the Bakhtinian notion of the clash between monologic and dialogic discourse. We might object, however, that Barthes's conception of these forces remains unattached to the specific social and institutional sites within which such utterances occur. As the US critics Clayton and Rothstein point out, many critics and theorists, unhappy with the abstract notions of language and discourse observable within poststructuralist theories such as Barthes's, have found a greater attention to the social situatedness of language in the work of Michel Foucault (Clayton and Rothstein, 1991: 27). In Foucault, a textualized vision of the human subject leads increasingly to an emphasis on social power relations. As Clayton and Rothstein write:

> Unlike Barthes and Derrida, with their boundless visions of textuality, Foucault attends to the forces that restrict the free circulation of the text. Although every text possesses countless points of intersection with other texts, these connections situate a work within existing networks of power, simultaneously creating and disciplining the text's ability to signify. Foucault insists that we analyse the role of power in the production of textuality and of textuality in the production of power. This entails looking closely at those social and political institutions by which subjects are subjected, enabled and regulated in forming textual meaning.
>
> (Clayton and Rothstein, 1991: 27)

It is one thing to discuss, we might say, a text's intertextual relation to cultural codes, but what kind of cultural codes are we referring to? Where do they come from? What kind of power relations are involved in their use? Bakhtinian dialogism and Foucault's account of discourse have seemed to some to allow for a rejection of poststructuralist textual theory and a return to a situated, historically specific account of texts and textuality.

We find here, once again, a tension between an historically oriented approach and an approach, such as Barthes's, which is concerned with the theoretical articulation of 'novelty', of a mode of writing which attempts to liberate the speaking and writing subject from the already said and the already written (Barthes, 1975: 40–1). Whilst for some a Foucauldian attention to the history of discourses and their place within institutional sites of power such as the hospital, the university and the family might appear to offer up the most politically radical theoretical model, Barthes's objective remains what he and his *Tel Quel* colleagues style as a radical refusal to remain within any dominant discourse, be it politically conservative or politically left-wing. As Barthes writes, the text 'is (should be) that uninhibited person who shows his behind to the *Political Father*' (*ibid*: 53). Barthes's objective remains throughout his work to challenge any *doxa* with *para-doxa*, to unleash the power of the text and of the intertextual to unsettle all dominant discursive positions, to unleash the paradoxical power of writing within the apparently natural, the *doxa*.

In his self-analytical text Barthes recognizes that the *doxa–para-doxa* opposition in his writing might itself have become an unchallenged opposition, and thus a *doxa*. Using the third- instead of the first-person pronoun, he writes of his own approach:

> Frequently he starts from the stereotype, from the banal opinion *which is in him*. And it is because he does not want that stereotype (by some aesthetic or individualist reflex) that he looks for something else; habitually, being soon wearied, he halts at the mere contrary opinion, at paradox, at what mechanically denies the prejudice (for

example: 'there is no science except for the particular'). He sustains,
in short, counter-relations with the stereotype – familial relations.

(Barthes, 1977b: 162)

It is precisely because of the ability of *doxa* to return and to solidify around a theoretical or critical style that Barthes, like Kristeva, eschews methodological rigour, one all-encompassing and explanatory metalanguage. Barthes is not a literary critic but a modern scriptor. In the passage above, after all, he is performing two apparently incompatible functions simultaneously. Interpreting existing texts (his own in this case), and so apparently functioning as a critic, he is also producing a new text. A writerly text itself, *Roland Barthes by Roland Barthes*, is cut up into small fragments with headings of a word or a phrase which are *almost* completely arranged upon the arbitrary order of the alphabet. The text also includes photographs, small marginalia, and yet teasingly refers to a narrative of writing the text one summer which is never fully incorporated into the text. The poststructuralist Barthes is a modern scriptor writing texts which are self-consciously intertextual rather than works of critical interpretation. His books embody the theory of textuality and intertextuality they articulate, and they constantly seek to find new ways of countering *doxa* and of unleashing the power of the plural text. His texts are an immense source of intertextual theory, and yet, with the exception of *S/Z*, they refuse to develop a rigorous theory of how intertextuality might be applied to other texts. Apart from *S/Z*, Barthes's poststructuralist texts are examples of a radical form of intertextuality rather than intertextual theory as it might exist in critical practice. It is perhaps no surprise that we have to move away from the poststructuralism of the 1960s and 1970s to discover examples of theorists committed to such a critical application of the term.

3

STRUCTURALIST APPROACHES: GENETTE AND RIFFATERRE

Since its appearance in poststructuralist work of the late 1960s intertextuality has been adopted and explored by theorists of a more structuralist frame of mind. To speak of a decisive fork in the river which flows from Kristeva's initial engagement with Bakhtin, a fork producing distinctly poststructuralist and distinctly structuralist accounts of our term, would be a mistake. However, it is still possible to locate what I will style a structuralist – by which I mean a more circumscribed – rendition of intertextuality in a number of theorists working from the late 1960s onwards.

We have already encountered the basic tenets of structuralism in this study. To remind ourselves of the characteristics of structuralist and semiological thought we might truncate a statement by the contemporary French theorist and critic Gérard Genette: 'the ability to constitute a system is precisely the characteristic of any set of signs, and it is this constitution that marks the passage from pure symbolism to the strictly semiological state' (Genette, 1982: 30). Semiology and structuralism appear to be defined by the desire to study the life of cultural sign-systems. Genette's statement concerns not individual symbols or individual works but the ways in which signs and texts function within and are generated by describable systems, codes, cultural practices and rituals. In this sense, the essential thrust of the structuralist project seems to be towards the intertextual, in that it denies the existence of unitary objects and emphasizes their systematic and relational nature, be they literary texts or other art works.

In his influential essay 'Structuralism and Literary Criticism', Genette elaborates on Claude Lévi-Strauss's notion of the *bricoleur* in order to flesh out a structuralist account of the practice of the literary critic (*ibid.*: 3–25). The *bricoleur*, states Genette, whether he be one of Lévi-Strauss's primitive myth-makers or a Western literary critic, creates a structure out of a previous structure by rearranging elements which are already arranged within the objects of his or her study. The structure created by this rearrangement is not identical to the original structure, yet it functions as a description and explanation of the original structure by its very act of rearrangement. To put this simply, the *bricoleur*-critic breaks down literary works into 'themes, motifs, key-words, obsessive metaphors, quotations, index cards, and references' (*ibid.*: 5); in other words, s/he rearranges the original literary work into the terms of literary criticism. The critic can then display the work's relation to the system of 'themes, motifs, key-words' which make up the literary system out of which the work was constructed.

Literary works, for a theorist like Genette, are not original, unique, unitary wholes, but particular articulations (selections and combinations) of an enclosed system. The literary work might not display its relation to the system, but the function of criticism is to do precisely that by rearranging the work *back into its relation to the closed literary system*. As Genette states: 'literary "production" is a *parole*, in the Saussurean sense, a series of partially autonomous and unpredictable individual acts; but the "consumption" of this literature by society is a *langue*'. Readers, that is, tend to order literary texts 'into a coherent system' (*ibid.*: 18–19). Both critic and author, then, can be termed *bricoleurs*, but with one difference. The author takes elements of the enclosed literary system or structure and arranges them into the work, obscuring the work's relation to the system. The critic takes the work and returns it to the system, illuminating the relation between work and system obscured by the author.

As we have seen, poststructuralists deny that any critical procedure can ever rearrange a text's elements into their full signifying relations. Structuralists retain a belief in criticism's ability to locate, describe and thus stabilize a text's significance, even if that significance concerns an intertextual relation between a text and other texts. Thaïs Morgan makes the same point by dividing theorists into two camps: one camp, poststructuralist in nature, 'emphasizes the ambiguity of the basic sign relation (signifier – signified) and the infinite regression or *mise en abîme* of signification'; the other, structuralist, camp 'assumes that the signification of a text or corpus of texts can be contained and fully explicated by description of elementary units and their systematic or recurrent relations' (Morgan, 1985: 9). For the theorists we are about to examine, placing a text back into its presumed system produces a form of knowledge and of stable reading which is unavailable in poststructuralist theories of intertextuality and the text.

STRUCTURALIST POETICS: GENETTE

Jonathan Culler, in his *Structuralist Poetics*, reminds us that poetics is essentially a theory of reading and thus has a very long history, going back particularly to Aristotle's *Poetics*. Structuralism's particular contribution to this tradition is to refocus attention away from the specificities of individual works to the systems out of which they can be said to have been constructed. Culler cites Genette's statement that literature 'like any other activity of the mind, is based on conventions of which, with some exceptions, it is not aware' (quoted in Culler, 1975: 116). These systems, rather than individual works, are the object of study for structuralist poetics, their description constituting a mapping of the closed system of literature and thus providing the basis for any meaningful analysis of individual works. To slightly adapt Culler's example, although a critical interpretation of a work might style it as a tragic novel, we need to understand how tragedy and the novel relate to each other and to all the other possible generic and modal elements which make up the literary system before that statement can be fully meaningful. We might wish to call works such as Shakespeare's *Hamlet*, Emily Brontë's *Wuthering Heights* and Thomas Hardy's *Tess of the D'Urbervilles* tragedies, but what do we mean when we use the word 'tragedy' to refer to such different texts? We might think we understand what tragedy is, but, unless we have proper knowledge of its position within the system of literary genres, we have at best an impressionistic sense of the term, reliant on our knowledge of individual examples *named for us, by others*. Poetics is primary; interpretation is secondary.

Richard Macksey has described Gérard Genette as 'the most intrepid and persistent explorer in our time of the relations between criticism and poetics' (Genette, 1997b: xii). Such a reputation is dependent largely on Genette's ground-breaking studies of the nature of narrative discourse and especially narrative fiction. This work is a significant part of Genette's development of structuralist poetics, but our focus will be on three related works: *The Architext, Palimpsests*, and *Paratexts*. In this trilogy Genette pushes the practice of structuralist poetics into an arena which can be termed intertextual. In so doing, Genette not only makes major revisions in the practice of poetics, he also produces a coherent theory and map of what he terms 'transtextuality', which we might style 'intertextuality from the viewpoint of structural poetics'.

The first book in this trilogy, *The Architext* (Genette, 1992), is a revisiting of the history of poetics since Plato and Aristotle, astonishing for the manner in which Genette lays out, in less than one hundred pages, the major distortions and misconceptions which have bedevilled poetics since its inception a millennium ago. These misconceptions go back, Genette argues, to the definition of the three main genres – epic, lyric, dramatic – in Plato and especially in Aristotle's *Poetics*. To re-employ our example, what do we mean when we say a work of literature is tragic? Genette, running through the argument in Aristotle's *Poetics*, points to Aristotle's rather lax use of the word tragedy to mean both a facet of a genre (in this case high drama) and a theme involving tragic human situations. We need to note, then, something not always kept in view by post-Aristotelian poetics, that there is a distinction between the generic and the thematic. This can help us to answer our previous question concerning *Hamlet*, *Wuthering Heights* and *Tess*. From a generic point of view tragedies should concern characters from the highest rungs of society. That at least was part of Aristotle's definition of the genre. From that generic definition, out of our examples only *Hamlet* qualifies as a tragedy. If we switch to a thematic definition of tragedy, however, *Wuthering Heights* and *Tess* can be included. The question still remains, however, whether tragedy really is partly defined through the representation of socially 'high' characters like Hamlet, or whether it can include our two novelistic examples which deal with themes of unrealizable love, jealousy, the abuse of power and social estrangement.

Genette's second point is that there is a general 'confusion between modes and genres' (*ibid.*: 61). Genres, he reminds us, are essentially literary categories. Modes, on the other hand, are 'natural forms', or at least aspects of language itself, and can be divided into 'narrative' and 'discourse'. Narrative here concerns the recounting of facts or events without attention being placed on the person who is doing that recounting. Discourse, however, places its focus on the person who speaks and the situation from within which that person is speaking. The two modes, narrative and discourse, thus involve what Genette styles as two distinct 'modes of enunciation' (see 'Frontiers of Narrative' in Genette 1982). Genette's main point here is that the traditional modal triad of narrative, dramatic and epic can be viewed either in terms of mode or in terms of generic categorization. Once again, however, there is often a confusion between generic and modal definitions. There may be, that is, a good deal of narrative, in terms of a mode of enunciation, in a dramatic text, but, unless we distinguish between modes and genres, poetics will forever find itself unable to stabilize its presentation of the system of literary conventions, including a viable definition of the various generic and sub-generic classes.

The desire to establish a viable and stable poetics of theme, genre and mode depends, as Genette argues, on the notion of *architexts*, basic, unchanging (or at least slowly evolving) building blocks which underpin the entire literary system. However, the issue of the slow evolution of such categories means that eventually even Genette has to admit to an inability to finally, and for all time, determine such 'architextual' building blocks (1992: 78). At this juncture other critics might be tempted to recast their work as a radical poststructuralist call for plurality, or a deconstructive unravelling of a major Western tradition of thought, but Genette attempts to save the notion of poetics by moving to a higher field of examination. His resolution of these problems is based on his decision to redescribe the entire field of poetics from a new perspective: that of *transtextuality*.

Textual transcendence, or transtextuality, is, according to Genette, precisely what poetics has been attempting to describe via the confused and misleading tools so far discussed. It includes issues of imitation, transformation, the classification of types of discourse, along with the thematic, modal, generic and formal categories and categorizations of traditional poetics. This change in perspective allows Genette to conclude his examination of the history and current state of poetics by moving to what in his next work in this series of studies, *Palimpsests* (Genette, 1997a), he will call an *open structuralism*. That is, a poetics which gives up on the idea of establishing a stable, ahistorical, irrefutable map or division of literary elements, but which instead studies the relationships (sometimes fluid, never unchanging) which link the text with the architextural network out of which it produces its meaning (Genette, 1992: 83–4). As Genette states, emphasizing the *open* nature of this vision of poetics: 'The architext is, then, everywhere – above, beneath, around the text, which spins its web only by hooking it here and there onto that network of architexture' (*ibid.*: 83). Transtextuality, and what he calls architextuality, allow for an 'endlessly forming and reforming poetics, whose object, let us firmly state, *is not the text, but the architext*' (*ibid.*: 84). This, it must be noted, is not a radical instability or pluralism à la Barthes or Kristeva, but a *pragmatic* structuralism which Genette goes on to exemplify in the two studies which succeed *The Architext*.

Transtextuality

Genette begins his massive study *Palimpsests* by reaffirming his new approach to poetics: 'The subject of poetics,' he writes, 'is not the text considered in its singularity .... but rather the *architext* or, if one prefers, the architextuality of the text ... the entire set of general or transcendent categories – types of discourse, modes of enunciation, literary genres – from which emerges each singular text' (Genette, 1997a: 1). Never one to rest on a settled critical vocabulary, Genette immediately refines such a point by subsuming architextuality within what he now calls *transtextuality* 'or the textual transcendence of the text, which I have already defined roughly as "all that sets the text in a relationship, whether obvious or concealed, with other texts"' (*ibid.*). Transtextuality is, basically, Genette's version of intertextuality and architextuality one of its types. However, since Genette wishes to employ this concept to chart ways in which texts can be systematically interpreted and understood, and since he wishes to distance his approach from poststructural approaches, he coins the term transtextuality to cover all instances of the phenomenon in question and then subdivides it into five more specific categories.

Genette terms his first kind of transtextuality, perhaps a little confusingly, *intertextuality*. Genette's *intertextuality* is, however, not the concept employed within poststructuralism, since he reduces it to 'a relationship of copresence between two texts or among several texts' and as 'the actual presence of one text within another' (*ibid.*: 1–2). Reduced now to issues of quotation, plagiarism and allusion, intertextuality thus defined is no longer concerned with the semiotic processes of cultural and textual signification. Genette's redescription gives us a very pragmatic and determinable intertextual relationship between specific elements of individual texts. Acknowledging the change in focus and theoretical vocabulary, Genette defends this transformation of the term by pointing to the fact that previous theorists of the term have tended to concentrate on 'semantic-semiotic microstructures, observed at the level of a sentence, a fragment, or a short, generally poetic, text' (*ibid.*: 2).

Taking up an analogy with the pictorial arts, Genette writes: 'The intertextual "trace" ... is therefore more akin (like the allusion) to the limited figure (to the pictorial detail) than to the work considered as a structural whole' (*ibid.*: 2–3). It is the 'structural whole', the 'total field of relevant relationships' which Genette directs his work towards. At stake here is a distinction between the poststructuralist recognition of the text's relation to the entirety of cultural signification and a more restricted, structuralist-inspired focus on the supposedly closed, or at least semi-autonomous, field of literature. Such a distinction involves a complex clash of critical and theoretical motivations, which include a clash between a desire like Barthes's to observe how the text 'explodes and disperses' (Barthes, 1981a: 135) and a desire like Genette's to place any specific example of textuality within a viable system. What is involved, we might say, is an opposition between *dissemination* and *rearrangement* which is certainly not resolvable, but which requires to be noted if we are to be able to read Genette's open structuralist approach within the broader perimeters of modern literary and cultural theory.

Genette describes his varieties of transtextuality out of strict numerical order. In order to follow his arguments I will do the same. The third type concerns what Genette calls *metatextuality*; that is, when a text takes up a relation of 'commentary' to another text: 'It unites a given text to another, of which it speaks without necessarily citing it (without summoning it), in fact sometimes even without naming it' (Genette, 1997a: 4). The very practice of literary criticism and poetics is clearly involved in this concept, which remains rather underdeveloped by Genette.

We have already examined architextuality, the fifth type of transtextuality in Genette's map. This aspect of the text, he suggests, has to do with 'the reader's expectations, and thus their reception of a work' (*ibid.*: 5). Novels may signpost their architextual relation to certain genres, sub-genres or conventions by including a subtitle, as in Anne Radcliffe's Gothic novel *The Mysteries of Udolpho: A Romance*; other works perform similar functions, as in David Bowie's rather excessively denominated 1995 album, *1. Outside. The Diary of Nathan Adler, or The Art-Ritual*

Murder of Baby Grace Blue: A Non-Linear Gothic Hyper-Cycle. Other texts may obscure their architextual relations to such genres, as is the practice in most realist novels. We expect love poems to be in the first person and directed to a specific addressee, whilst in epic poems we expect other kinds of themes and narrative styles than those we might find in a sonnet. The architextual nature of texts, as we have seen, includes generic, modal, thematic and figurative expectations about texts, although, as Genette warns his readers, the five types of transtextuality, of which architextuality is one, are not 'separate and absolute categories without any reciprocal contact or overlapping' (*ibid.*: 7).

Genette's second type of transtextuality is styled *paratextuality*. This is clearly a concept of some importance to Genette and we will break our discussion of *Palimpsests* to explore his study devoted to paratextuality: *Paratexts: Thresholds of Interpretation* (Genette, 1997b).

Paratextuality

The paratext, as Genette explains, marks those elements which lie on the threshold of the text and which help to direct and control the reception of a text by its readers. This threshold consists of a *peritext*, consisting of elements such as titles, chapter titles, prefaces and notes. It also includes an *epitext* consisting of elements – such as interviews, publicity announcements, reviews by and addresses to critics, private letters and other authorial and editorial discussions – 'outside' of the text in question. The paratext is the sum of the peritext and the epitext. Genette, at the beginning of his study, refers to the deconstructive critic J. Hillis Miller's meditation on the prefix 'para' and the manner in which examining the threshold, or paratext, of a text positions us at once inside and yet outside its material boundaries (Hillis Miller, 1979). The paratext does not simply mark but occupies the text's threshold – the space which is both inside and outside (or 'para') – and thus, in a logic explained before Genette by Jacques Derrida, it paradoxically frames and at the same time constitutes the text for its readers (Derrida, 1987b). As Genette puts it elsewhere: 'the paratext consists, as [the] ambiguous prefix suggests, of all those things which we are never certain belong to the text of a work but which contribute to present – or "presentify" – the text by making it into a book. It not only marks a zone of transition between text and non-text ("*hors-texte*"), but also a transaction' (Genette, 1988: 63). What interests Genette is not the kind of philosophical problem derived from this aspect of textuality by deconstructionists like Hillis Miller and Derrida, but rather the transactional nature of the paratext.

The text you are currently reading is heavily marked by paratextual elements in Genette's sense. The design of the cover is not without meaning, since it signals this text's place within a series of texts, The New Critical Idiom series, all of which share a black cover design and a lower border which, in each text, contains in colour a portion of a different photographic or computer-generated image. Various other elements which stand on this text's threshold, such as the notice concerning the objectives of The New Critical Idiom series and the description of the study on the back cover serve as paratextual elements which are designed to assist the reader in establishing what kind of text they are being presented with and how to read it.

The paratext, for Genette, performs various functions which guide the text's readers and can be understood pragmatically in terms of various simple questions, all concerned with the manner of the text's existence: when published? by whom? for what purpose? Such paratextual elements also help to establish the text's intentions: how it should be read, how it should not be read.

Such an approach leads Genette into a densely packed study of textual minutiae. The size of books, for instance, can signal various paratextual significations, and so can the typeface chosen – as Genette's example of Thackeray's *Henry Esmond* demonstrates. The original Queen-Anne typeface was chosen by Thackeray to support his novel's thematic and stylistic pastiche; in modern editions, in regularized typefaces, we lose this important aspect of the text. Likewise, modern editions of Mary Shelley's *Frankenstein* might be said to eradicate an important paratextual function, including the text's original anonymity. The image which was included before the text of Mary Shelley's 1831 edition of *Frankenstein* presents us with the creature starring in horror at a skeleton which lies scattered below his bent legs. Frankenstein holds open the door whilst he too stares in horror at the skeleton. The moon, which is visible through the open window, seems to shine down at precisely the same spot. The design is heavily symbolic and suggests various readings, including one in which the centre of horrified speculation is either the skeleton beneath the creature's bent legs or the naked creature's genitalia, which are hidden from the viewer's direct gaze but open to the gaze of the creature and his creator alike. Such a design clearly acts as a powerful paratextual element, and modern readers of editions of *Frankenstein* which do not include this frontispiece begin their reading of the novel in a different fashion to readers of the 1831 edition.

As Genette demonstrates, there are a number of ways in which the naming of the author or the titles of works can function to control reception of the text. Genette distinguishes between *thematic* titles which refer to the subject of the text and *rhematic* titles which refer to the manner in which the text performs its intentions. Genette gives the title and subtitle of Baudelaire's *Le Spleen de Paris: Petits Poèmes en prose* as an example. *Le Spleen de Paris*, which is translated by Francis Scarfe as 'Paris Blues', relates to the thematic element of the poem; *Petits Poèmes en prose* relates to the rhematic element in that it establishes the kind of poetry which will convey that theme.

A major peritextual field involves dedications, inscriptions, epigraphs and prefaces; a field which, as Genette demonstrates, can have major effects upon the interpretation of a text. It is clearly not a matter of indifference whether a text is dedicated to 'The Queen' or 'To the Masses'. Just as obviously, particular quotations used as inscriptions or epigraphs can set up important resonances before the reader begins the text in question. A famous example of this paratextual practice from the field of literature comes in the epigraph to T. S. Eliot's 'The Hollow Men': 'Mistah Kurtz – he dead' (Eliot, 1974: 87). The quotation is from Joseph Conrad's *Heart of Darkness* and it establishes a host of intertextual resonances which the reader then both brings to the poem and discovers within the poem itself. These include issues of failed quest, juxtapositions between the 'dead land' of Eliot's poem and Imperial England, along with the colonized and the uncolonized Africa of Conrad's novel and, perhaps most importantly, Kurtz's often-quoted words 'the horror – the horror'. So crucial, in fact, does the epigraph become to Eliot's poem that to read the text without it would be to drastically diminish its significance.

A major distinction running throughout Genette's *Paratexts* is that between paratexts which are *autographic*, by the author, and *allographic*, by someone other than the author, such as an editor or publisher. At times, as Genette demonstrates, the autographic and allographic can slip into modes of ambiguity crucial for an interpretation of the text. We might think here of P. B. Shelley's anonymous allographic Preface for the first anonymous edition of Mary Shelley's *Frankenstein*, a paratextual element that has caused radically misconceived claims about that novel, including erroneous claims for P. B. Shelley's authorship. The essential function of the autographic or allographic preface is, Genette asserts, to encourage the reader to read the text, and to instruct the reader in how to read the text properly. A similar function can be ascribed, he argues, to such epitextual features as the decision to leave out of the published version the various Homeric chapter titles of *Ulysses*, or Joyce's 'leaking' to critics various plans demonstrating the relations between *Ulysses* and its Homeric and other literary and cultural inter-texts. We can add to such phenomena manuscript revisions returned to a text by modern scholarly editors, down to newspaper and magazine interviews, authorial public performances or publishers' decisions over book design. Modern scholarly editions of texts, for example, crammed as they are with such peritextual features as prefaces and notes, and with what were originally epitextual features (such as private letters, journal entries, original and later reviews), clearly signify a text's status as part of a literary canon and thus worthy of study. We read such editions in a very different manner to the text's original readers and texts are radically transformed by the addition of these paratextual elements.

Such an account of paratextuality clearly marks it out, in Genette's hands, from the poststructuralist dismissal of authorial intention we have observed as a major facet of intertextual theory. Manfred Pfister has argued that such a reassertion of the importance of authorial intention is a ruling characteristic of structuralist versions of intertextuality, though seen from a poststructuralist perspective such an approach seems merely to strip the term of its original vitality and ideologically disruptive force (Pfister, 1991: 210–11). Genette in fact asserts that the single most important aspect of paratextuality is 'to ensure for the text a destiny consistent with the author's purpose' (Genette, 1997b: 407). He goes on: 'the correctness of the authorial (and secondarily, of the publisher's) point of view is the implicit creed and spontaneous ideology of the paratext' (*ibid.*: 408). Such an emphasis on authorial intention is not only contrary to poststructuralist theory and practice but also runs counter to the major thrust of structuralism, in which system (*langue*) is privileged at the expense of work (*parole*) and thus signification and function privileged at the expense of intention. It would appear, however, that to keep transtextual relations within a determinate and determinable field Genette must neutralize the radically destabilizing and deauthorizing nature of intertextuality. The author of the paratext may not originate or really affect the paratextual system painstakingly described by Genette, yet Genette himself cannot do without what Foucault would call the 'author-function' if he is to retain the pragmatic, open structuralist approach he takes up with regard to his subject. The same reliance on notions of authorial intention can be observed if we return to the centre of his study of transtextual relations, *Palimpsests*.

Hypertextuality

Having passed through four of the five kinds of transtextuality posited by Genette, we are left with the kind which forms the focus of attention of *Palimpsests* itself, namely *hypertextuality*. This phenomenon, according to Genette, involves: 'any relationship uniting a text B (which I shall call the *hypertext*) to an earlier text

A (I shall, of course, call it the *hypotext*), upon which it is grafted in a manner that is not that of commentary' (Genette, 1997a: 5). What Genette terms the *hypotext* is termed by most other critics the *inter-text*, that is a text which can be definitely located as a major source of signification for a text. In this sense, Homer's *Odyssey* is a major inter-text, or in Genette's terms hypotext, for Joyce's *Ulysses*. In his use of hypertextuality Genette particularly refers to forms of literature which are intentionally inter-textual. He writes: 'let us posit the general notion of a text in the second degree .... i.e., a text derived from another pre-existent text' (*ibid.*: 5). The Oxford English Dictionary defines the word *palismpsest* as 'a parchment, etc., which has been written upon twice, the original writing having been rubbed out'. Palimpsests suggest layers of writing and Genette's use of the term is to indicate literature's existence in 'the second degree', its non-original rewriting of what has already been written.

Genette's concern is with intended and self-conscious relations between texts. Hypertextuality marks a field of literary works the generic essence of which lies in their relation to previous works. As Genette puts this point:

> Above all, hypertextuality, as a category of works, is in itself a generic or, more precisely, *transgeneric* architext: I mean a category of texts which wholly encompasses certain canonical (though minor) genres such as pastiche, parody, travesty, and which also touches upon other genres – probably all genres.
>
> (Genette, 1997a: 8)

Concerned here, then, not with a general facet of language, or culturally signifying practices, but with a generic aspect of the closed system of literature, Genette's hypertextuality might seem rather similar to his architextuality. The main difference between hypertextuality and architextuality is that whilst pastiche, parody, travesty and caricature are essentially and intentionally hypertextual, tragedy, comedy, the novel and the lyric are based on the notion of the imitation of generic models rather than specific hypotexts. The meaning of hypertextual works, Genette argues, depends upon the reader's knowledge of the hypotext which the hypertext either satirically transforms or imitates for the purpose of pastiche.

The bulk of Genette's study concerns the manner in which hypertextual transpositions are made of specific hypotexts. Texts can be transformed by processes of self-expurgation, excision, reduction, amplification and so on. An example of self-expurgation might be seen in the differences between the first serialized version and the final published edition of Thomas Hardy's *Tess of the D'Urbervilles*. Hardy's novel was for financial reasons first published in serialized form between 4 July and 26 December 1891 in the literary magazine *The Graphic*. In order to conform to the expectations of the late-Victorian audience of *The Graphic* Hardy had to alter his narrative so that Tess, instead of being raped by Alec D'Urberville, goes through a fake marriage with him. Many other changes to the novel were forced on him. The novel, as it was originally imagined by Hardy, was finally published in 1912. In the modern Penguin edition of *Tess*, the original *Graphic* version, present through the scholarly notes at the back, exists as a hypotext to the canonical version of 1912.

Excision and reduction might make us think of what in Britain are known as bowdlerized versions of texts, versions of Shakespeare or popular novels which Victorian publishers often published minus the 'sexy' or religiously controversial bits. Although Genette does not mention it, the phenomenon of film adaptations of literary classics clearly constitutes another version of such a hypertextual activity. The classic film adaptation of Emily Brontë's *Wuthering Heights*, starring Laurence Olivier and Merle Oberon, concentrates on only the first nineteen chapters of the novel. Film versions of the bulky novels of the Victorian period such as those by Dickens or George Eliot, can clearly only represent small sections of the actual text they hypertexually transpose. Most film adaptations do not, of course, include the all-pervading voice of third-person narrators which characterize novels by authors such as Jane Austen or Henry James.

Amplifications are, of course, as prevalent and as significant as hypertextual processes which reduce the hypotext. As Genette demonstrates, hypotexts can go through processes of extension, contamination and expansion, as in Thomas Mann's *Joseph and His Brothers*, which amplifies a Biblical hypotext of approximately 26 pages to a novel of approximately 1,600 pages. A more recent example of amplification comes in Dreamworks' animated film *Prince of Egypt* about Moses and the Biblical story of the escape from Egypt of the Jewish people. In Exodus 2: 5–11 we find the account of how the infant Moses is discovered by the Pharaoh's daughter, is given to a maid and comes to manhood. The film version spends a great part of its time developing a narrative in which Moses is brought up by the Pharaoh and his wife, is fully integrated into Egyptian social life, and finally rebels against his father, brother and the whole of Egyptian culture. *Prince of Egypt* can be said to amplify a possibility which is unstated in Exodus, that Moses may have been influenced by Egyptian culture. It elaborates out of this potential within the hypotext a whole narrative of royal adoption and so finally amplifies the gaps within the Biblical narrative into a film in which the exodus of the Jewish people is conceived in terms of a story of one individual's rebellion against familial values.

One of the transformations produced by such amplification involves another dimension of Genette's study, namely 'transmotivization'. The transformation of motivation in hypertexts can be a fruitful area of study, as Genette demonstrates. Hypertexts can give a character motivations lacking in the hypotext, as in the example of *Prince of Egypt*. At other times there can be a suppression or eliding of motivation. In Homer's *Odyssey* Ulysses is questing to return home after the war between the Greeks and the Trojans dramatized in Homer's *Iliad*. In Joyce's *Ulysses* we spend a day in the life of his novel's protagonist, Leopold Bloom, and, although the narrative is structured by and shot through with references to Homer's *Odyssey*, no international conflict is explicitly mentioned, at least in relation to Bloom himself. Leopold Bloom may well be a traveller of the mind, and a figure not completely at home in his home town of Dublin, yet it remains true to say that his motivations involve a set of expectations and desires radically different from that of Homer's Ulysses.

Genette's study of hypertextuality, as he admits near the end of his study, has a major source in his love of Jorge Luis Borges's 'Pierre Menard, Author of *Don Quixote,*' a short story in which Menard writes 'with his own resources a new version of *Don Quixote*, which was rigorously and literally identical with Cervantes's text but which two intervening centuries of history had invested with new complexity and depth and with an entirely different meaning' (Genette, 1997a: 317; 393–4). Such acknowledgement of the effect upon his study of the 'vagaries' of his own 'personal readings' (*ibid.*: 394), the fact that no individual study of the literary system can hope to be 'exhaustive', is typical of Genette's open structuralism. As stated at the end of his study, Genette seeks merely to explore the ways in which texts are read in relation to other texts. He contrasts such an open approach to what we might style a closed structuralism, which is 'concerned with the closure of the text and with deciphering its inner structures' (*ibid.*: 399). Thinking of the text by Borges, we might object that it is one thing to examine the hypertextual relations and functions of a text which explicitly foregrounds its reliance on and transformation of a hypotext; it is quite another to deal with a text which hides its hypotext or depends upon a hypotext no longer available to or known by modern readers.

This problem of the missing or forgotten hypotext crops up a number of times in Genette's study. During his discussion of hypertextual continuation, Genette considers what occurs when a continuation's hypotext is no longer available to a culture; he argues that in the case of texts such as Rabelais's *Pantagruel* the text's status changes from hypotext to autonomous text. Most teachers of literature confront the same problem when attempting to teach certain canonical texts. We cannot necessarily presume that the mythical hypotext standing behind P. B. Shelley's *Prometheus Unbound* will be recognized by modern readers. Sometimes even the scholarly community forgets important hypotexts, long buried in forgotten traditions. In such cases the hypertext becomes merely a text, a non-relational, non-transformational work. Genette also argues that all texts are potentially hypertextual, but that sometimes the existence of a hypotext is too uncertain to be the basis for a hypertextual reading. He gives the example of Flaubert's novel *Leuwen*, which may have a hypotext in a manuscript draft of a novel entitled *Le Lieutenant* sent to the author by Mme Gaulthier in 1833. Genette's response to this kind of indeterminate case is perhaps revealing: 'This is the most irritating palimpsest of all, which reduces me to hunches and to questionings' (*ibid.*: 383). We might want to suggest, however, that it is precisely in that critical act of interpretation of the text which he eschews that such hunches and questionings are positively embraced. Genette's resolution of his own unease with regard to uncertain cases is to remind himself and his readers that ultimately every hypertext 'can be read for itself and in its relation to its hypotext' (*ibid.*: 397). For Genette, indeterminacies within an individual text are unimportant, since his task is to establish a general system of possibilities and functions. As he puts it:

> Every hypertext, even a pastiche, can be read for itself without becoming perceptibly 'agrammatical'; it is invested with a meaning that is autonomous and thus in some manner sufficient. But sufficient does not mean exhaustive. In every hypertext there is an *ambiguity* that Riffaterre denies to intertextual reading.
>
> (Genette, 1997a: 397)

It might be argued here that Genette's project, grounded on the assertion that a structuralist poetics must uncover the transtextual nature of texts, cannot perhaps quite so easily retreat to the apparently commonsensical argument that texts have a dual existence: as autonomous texts and as inter-texts. Various problems lurk behind Genette's approach here: the establishment with regard to paratextuality of the 'inside' and the 'outside' of the text; the question of the relationship between literature, the other arts and the cultural text generally; the question of authorial intention, its establishment by the reader, and the reader's own role in the production of meaning.

The French theorist Laurent Jenny, in his 'The Strategy of Forms', distinguishes between works which are explicitly intertextual – such as imitations, parodies, citations, montages and plagiarisms – and those works in which the intertextual relation is not foregrounded. Texts, Jenny argues, clarifying Genette's distinctions, can, at one and the same time, have their intertextual determinants directed towards a specific work (hypotext) or towards a model of a kind of textuality such as parody or montage, à la Genette's architextuality. When a work enters into a relation of intertextuality with a genre, what was, in that architextual genre, a code (a generic structure) can become part of the text's or the hypertext's message (Jenny, 1982: 42). We move, in such cases, from general codes within a genre to a meaningful element of a particular text. A modern novelist, for example, might portray the collapse of a protagonist's fortunes but without suggesting that this misfortune is unmerited, or a cause for pity. In this case, a code (the 'fall' of the tragic hero) from the genre of tragedy has been intertextually utilized, but it has also been given a specific meaning within the text in question, a meaning not evident in the general principles of the genre of tragedy. Jenny's point is close to Genette's, in that, whilst it plays down the interpretive role of the reader, it also recognizes that the processes of transtextuality involved in hypertextual translation are never neutral and always involve a resignification or a semiotic utilization of a previous formal structure for means other than those produced within the original structure. We are close here to Kristeva's point that intertextuality involves the transposition of elements from existent systems into new signifying relations.

The heart of Jenny's argument comes in the section of his essay entitled 'Status of Intertextual Discourse', where he writes in a manner which cannot but remind us of the poststructural approach of Kristeva and, particularly, Barthes:

> What is characteristic of intertextuality, is that it introduces a new way of reading which destroys the linearity of the text. Each intertextual reference is the occasion for an alternative: either one continues reading, taking it only as a segment like any other, or else one turns to the source text, carrying out a sort of intellectual anamnesis where the intertextual reference appears like a paradigmatic element that has

been displaced, deriving from a forgotten structure. But in fact the alternative is only present for the analyst. These two processes really operate simultaneously in intertextual reading – and in discourse – studding the text with bifurcations that gradually expand in semantic space.

(Jenny, 1982: 44–5)

In other words, to say, as Genette finally does in *Palimpsests*, that the reader has a choice between reading the text *for itself* or in terms of its intertextual relations is a kind of bad faith. Such an approach divides up what is indivisible within the work, its textual structure and its intertextual relations. This is a division which can only be achieved by the reader performing a kind of negative forgetting of the intertextual dimension.

Jenny is particularly challenged by the manner in which the intertextual dimension disrupts any work's formal structure. 'Intertextuality,' he writes, 'speaks a language whose vocabulary is the sum of all existing texts. There takes place a sort of release on the level of *parole*, a promotion to discourse of a power infinitely superior to that of everyday monologic discourse' (Jenny, 1982: 45). If the reader's initial desire is to find the 'meaning' of a work, then intertextuality comes to be seen as that phenomenon of textuality which disturbs such a project by potentially shattering the work's structure: 'The problem of intertextuality is to bind together several texts in one without their destroying each other and without the [text] ... being torn apart as a structural whole' (*ibid.*: 45).

Jenny's essay is largely concerned with charting how different textual practices, from Modernism to Surrealism to the cut-up techniques of William Burroughs, seek to utilize and/or control the disruptive tendencies of intertextuality. Such a study might be viewed as complementary to Genette's work, gesturing towards a poetics of the kind of ambiguities and disturbances referred to by Genette at the conclusion of his *Palimpsests*. On the other hand, Jenny's insistence that intertextuality's essence lies in the 'perturbation' of formal and thematic structures, might strengthen the argument against Genette that what is required is not a poetics which can separate textual from intertextual dimensions but a theory of interpretation which can explore the interpretive processes by which the clash of these two dimensions is registered and reconciled. To say this is to suggest a shift of focus from Genette to the theorist who most seriously haunts his work, Michael Riffaterre.

STRUCTURALIST HERMENEUTICS: RIFFATERRE

Michael Riffaterre's work can be said to straddle structuralism, poststructuralism, semiotics, psychoanalytic theories of literature and various other theories of reading. Yet it can be said that his work is grounded on the belief in a stable and accurate account of textual meaning and intertextual relations which we are, in this Chapter, calling structuralist.

The core of Riffaterre's semiotic approach is his belief that literary texts are not referential (mimetic). On the contrary, he argues that they have their meaning because of the semiotic structures which link up their individual words, phrases, sentences, key images, themes and rhetorical devices. At the beginning of his seminal study *Semiotics of Poetry* he writes of the reader's need to 'surmount the mimesis hurdle' (Riffaterre, 1978: 6). The centrality of intertextuality in Riffaterre's work is signalled by this anti-referential approach, since, as we have seen, intertextual theory argues that texts and signs refer not to the world or even primarily to concepts, but to other texts, other signs. Riffaterre frequently alludes to what he calls the 'referential fallacy' and asserts that 'the text refers not to objects outside of itself, but to an inter-text. The words of the text signify not by referring to things, but by presupposing other texts' (1980b: 228). However, surmounting the 'mimesis hurdle' also means, for Riffaterre, paying tribute to 'the self-sufficient text'. For Riffaterre, true analysis seeks to describe the uniqueness of the literary text. Whilst poetics 'generalizes and dissolves a work's uniqueness into poetic language', the textual analysis Riffaterre favours attempts to explain its uniqueness (1983: 2). Riffaterre states that the 'largest analysable corpus that we conceive in literature should be the text and not a collection of texts' (*ibid.*: 5). The text itself, because of its uniqueness, can, as Riffaterre puts it, 'control its own decoding' (*ibid.*: 6).

What is at face value a rather paradoxical insistence on intertextuality *and* on the text's self-sufficient uniqueness is only explicable when we enter into the minutiae of Riffaterre's theory of reading and of textuality. However, it should immediately alert us both to the circumscribed domain of enquiry Riffaterre allows for the hermeneutic project and to his belief that such a project can produce right or proper reading.

The reading strategy Riffaterre charts is one in which the reader at first seeking for a textual mimesis is forced, by the indeterminacies of the text, into a deeper examination of the text's non-referential structures. Reading, then, takes place on two successive levels: first, a mimetic level which tries to relate textual signs to external referents and tends to proceed in a linear fashion; second, a retroactive reading which proceeds, in a non-linear fashion, to unearth the underlying semiotic units and structures which produce the text's non-referential significance. What forces the reader into the leap from a mimetic to semiotic interpretation of the text is recognizing what Riffaterre calls the text's 'ungrammaticalities'. These are aspects of the text which are contradictory on a referential reading but resolved when we reread the text in terms of its underlying sign structures.

In the following poem by Sylvia Plath, for example, the reader working with a referential model might presume that the poem's title refers to the addresser's own name; there seems no other referential reason why the poem should have this title:

Mary's Song

The Sunday lamb cracks in its fat.
The fat
Sacrifices its opacity ...

A window, holy gold.
The fire makes it precious,
The same fire

Melting the tallow heretics,
Ousting the Jews.
Their thick palls float

Over the cicatrix of Poland, burnt-out
Germany.
They do not die.

Grey birds obsess my heart,
Mouth-ash, ash of eye.
They settle. On the high

Precipice
That emptied one man into space
The ovens glowed like heavens, incandescent.

It is a heart,
This holocaust I walk in,
O golden child the world will kill and eat.

(Plath, 1981: 257)

Having performed an initial reading, the alert reader will begin to recognize a series of connections on what Riffaterre calls
the semiotic level: the level we reach after the referential level has
failed to explain the text to us. The poem is full of references to
people persecuted for their religious beliefs: the 'tallow heretics',
Catholics or Protestants persecuted and killed after the
Reformation; the Jews who suffered genocide under the Nazi
regime; the 'one man' who reminds us of Christ, persecuted and
crucified in the Gospel story. Having made these connections, the
reader might then recognize the manner in which the domestic
scene with which the poem begins and ends, a mother with child
preparing the 'Sunday roast', is connected to these historical referents. The mother, in fact, compares herself to the Biblical Mary:
her child becomes symbolically a Christ-figure, whom the world
will 'kill and eat'. The semiotic connections between the domestic scene and the historical referents are extended by the last line,
which on this level seems to refer to the ritual of the Eucharist in

which Christ's body is re-membered in the taking of holy wine and bread. To interpret the poem in this manner, then, we need to move from a mimetic level to a semiotic level in which apparently ambiguous images and phrases are connected on a deeper, non-referential level.

Riffaterre resists the traditional literary critical notion of 'ambiguity' and the various poststructuralist and deconstructionist versions of that concept. Whilst concepts like ambiguity or ambivalence serve to highlight the undecidability of textual meaning, Riffaterre prefers to substitute alternative figures and explanatory concepts which work to reinforce the notion of a move from initial ambiguity or ungrammaticality on a mimetic level to final decidability on a semiotic level. Against the term ambiguity, Riffaterre offers the rhetorical term 'syllepsis', a word which means something in one context and has an opposed or clashing meaning in another context. Another term frequently invoked by Riffaterre, the 'interpretant', is taken from the linguist C. S. Pierce and also emphasizes the possibility of resolving undecidable textual units by moving to another, more structurally coherent, dimension. An interpretant, Riffaterre informs his readers, is a sign which explains the relation between one sign and another sign. 'Persecution' might be said to function as an interpretant in *Mary's Song*.

In Riffaterre's theory of reading, then, we surmount the mimetic hurdle by moving to the structurally more coherent level of semiosis. In Plath's poem, for example, the connection between a domestic scene and the images of persecution and murder might be seen as 'ungrammatical' on a referential level (Riffaterre does not restrict ungrammaticality to breaks in the rules concerning the construction of sentences). To make sense of Plath's text we need to dispense with the idea that it has anything literal to say about the world and to move to a recognition that its meaning, or what Riffaterre terms its 'significance', is based on an inversion of culturally normative associations: the roasting of a joint of lamb being unconnected to historical events, for example. The poem inverts these culturally normative associations by taking the roasting of the 'Sunday lamb' as a cue for a series of references to historical scenes of violence. Once we recognize this inversion of context and the common discourse for that context, we have recognized the semiotic principle or system upon which the whole poem depends, and out of which it produces not only its significance but its idiosyncratic unity.

For Riffaterre, texts produce their significance out of transformations of socially normative discourse, which he calls the 'sociolect'. A text's significance, we might say, depends on an 'idiolect' which transforms a recognizable element of the sociolect by means of inversion, conversion, expansion or juxtaposition. The way the reader recognizes this transformation, and so recognizes the text's semiotic unity, is to discover what Riffaterre calls the poem's 'matrix', a word, phrase or sentence unit which does not necessarily exist in the text itself but which represents the kernel upon which the text's semiotic system is based. As Riffaterre puts it: 'The matrix is hypothetical, being only the grammatical and lexical actualization of a structure' (1978: 19). The text's structural unity is created by the transformation of this matrix. In Plath's poem the matrix perhaps concerns the common cultural assumption that mothers wish to preserve their children's innocence or that the preservation of childhood purity is an important thing when individuals come to adulthood. Since Plath's poem focuses on what the 'world' does to those seeking to retain religious belief and thus a kind of spiritual innocence, the poem might be said to work by negating a matrix expressible in something like the following phrase: 'blessed are the innocent'.

Only when we have recognized the matrix and passed to the semiotic significance of the text, do the text's various apparent 'ungrammaticalities' become understandable as referring to an 'invariant' structure. The invariant structure is the manner in which all elements of the text can be said to work by transforming the matrix. This fundamental level of the text may be signposted by aspects which, though they are not the matrix, point to or embody it in some way. This is what Riffaterre styles as the 'model', and for Plath's poem we might imagine for the model phrases such as: 'the innocent or pure or faithful are made victims by the world'. Such phrases might alert the reader to the 'descriptive system' normally associated with the words 'innocence' or 'pure' or 'faithful': a descriptive system which would include a series of notions which refer to precisely opposite situations and contexts to those invoked in the poem. Texts, on this model, are expansions and developments of small signifying units. As Riffaterre writes:

> The poem results from the transformation of the *matrix*, a minimal and literal sentence, into a longer, complex, and non-literal periphrasis. The matrix is hypothetical, being only the grammatical and lexical actualization of a structure. The matrix may be epitomized in one word, in which case the word will not appear in the text. It is always actualized in successive variants; the form of these variants is governed by the first or primary actualization, the *model*. Matrix, model, and text are variants of the same structure.
>
> (Riffaterre, 1978: 19)

Riffaterre is a superb close reader of texts, his characteristic manner of presenting theoretical points being through intricate interpretations of canonical texts. Such an approach tends to generate more and more refinements to its key concepts. The attempt to follow his vision of textuality and intertextuality is, indeed, an experience in which key words such as 'matrix' and 'model' tend to blend and merge into each other. Riffaterre's concern is with what it is to read, with what it is to *produce* a text. He is not concerned, that is, with what might constitute the unchanging dimensions of the literary system itself. This concern with the phenomenology of reading can be discerned in the rather blurred relationship drawn in his work between the notion of the 'intertext' and of the 'hypogram'. An understanding of these terms brings us closer to Riffaterre's vision of intertextuality.

Riffaterre distinguishes between what he calls the inter-text and intertextuality itself: the 'latter,' he writes, 'is the web of functions that constitutes and regulates the relationship between text and intertext' (1990a: 57). As he states, the inter-text is not to be viewed in terms of 'sources' and thus in terms of one text's purposeful 'influence [by] or imitation [of]' another text or group of texts. An inter-text, rather:

> is a corpus of texts, textual fragments, or text-like segments of the sociolect that shares a lexicon and, to a lesser extent, a syntax with the text we are reading (directly or indirectly) in the form of synonyms, or even conversely, in the form of antonyms. In addition, each member of this corpus is a structural homologue of the text.
>
> (Riffaterre, 1984: 142)

The origin of a text's significance is not found, Riffaterre is implying, by discovering a text or group of texts which supposedly lie behind it; specific prior texts need only be invoked if such exist which sufficiently characterize the aspect of the sociolect which is being transformed by the text in question. Even when there is indisputably a text-to-text relationship involved in a specific text's generation of significance, the point of interpretive emphasis is not necessarily that relationship but the structural homologue (*homologous*: having the same relation, proportion, relative position; corresponding) which that relation foregrounds. Because the inter-text is an aspect of the sociolect rather than a specific text or group of texts, Riffaterre can go on to assert that, for semiotic interpretation to occur, all that is required is what he calls the presupposition of the inter-text. We do not, that is, need to discover specific inter-texts behind the texts we read; all we need to do to produce a sufficient interpretation is to assume that such an inter-text – either a specific text or a piece of socially significant language – is being transformed by the text in question. Riffaterre's answer to the problem of the missing inter-text, which we observed in our analysis of Genette, is simply to argue that it can be presupposed by the reader. Writing of the act of widening out of the comparison of textual units *beyond the text itself*, Riffaterre states:

> Intertextual reading is the perception of similar comparabilities from text to text; or it is the assumption that such comparing must be done if there is no intertext at hand wherein to find comparabilities.

> In the latter case, the text holds clues (such as formal and semantic
> gaps) to a complementary intertext lying in wait somewhere,
>
> (Riffaterre, 1980a: 626)

We have seen in our analysis of Plath's poem that a semiotic
interpretation of that poem need not locate a specific inter-text or
group of inter-texts in order to describe the sociolectic codes
upon which it builds its significance. The reason why the inter-
text need not be located, but only presupposed, leads us on to the
hypogram, which is, as Riffaterre puts it, 'the text imagined by
him [the reader] in its pretransformational state':

> This hypogram (a single sentence or string of sentences) may be
> made out of clichés, or it may be a quotation from another text, or a
> descriptive system. Since the hypogram always has a positive or a
> negative 'orientation' (the cliché is meliorative or pejorative, the quo-
> tation has its position on an esthetic and/or ethical scale, the descrip-
> tive system reflects the connotations of its kernel word), the
> constituents of the conversion always transmute the hypogram's
> markers ... This means that the significance will be a positive valoriza-
> tion of the textual semiotic unit if the hypogram is negative, and a
> negative valorization if the hypogram is positive.
>
> (Riffaterre, 1978: 63–4)

Although the terms inter-text and hypogram may seem to
merge into one another, the hypogram represents specifically literary or 'poeticized' signs. A hypogram depends on the notion
that certain words or word groups already possess a 'poetic' function in the sociolect. Our reading of Plath's *Mary's Song* depends
upon long-standing cultural associations connected to the word
'innocence'. A text's hypograms will be those of its signs which
relate to already existent semiotically signifying words or word-
groups within the sociolect. 'Hypogrammatic derivation,'
Riffaterre writes, exists whenever 'the verbal sequence patterns itself upon word groups which pre-exist in the language and have
usually been long tried and tested in literature' (1977: 111).

In *Semiotics of Poetry* Riffaterre gives the following example from Apollinaire (1978: 97):

> Et vous cils roseaux qui vous mirez dans l'eau profonde et claire
>   de ses regards
> Roseaux discrets plus éloquents que les penseurs humains ô
>   cils penseurs penchés au-dessus des abîmes

[And you eyelashes reeds looking at yourselves in the deep clear water of her gaze/ Reeds discreet more eloquent than human thinkers oh eyelashes thinkers leaning over chasms]

Although on a referential level this verse, with its prominent eyelashes acting as addressee, and its association of those eyelashes with reeds, doesn't appear to make much sense, when we remember that the metaphor 'eyelash–reeds' is 'a traditional image for feminine eyelashes, themselves metonymic of woman as love-object' (1978: 98) we begin to unravel the poem's significance. The woman need not be addressed herself, since conventionally her eyelashes can stand in for her whole body, and thus her beauty *in toto*. The verse's matrix is something like 'You are beautiful': 'The model then expands in a descriptive sequence where the eyelashes in turn exemplify that beauty' (*ibid.*). The metaphor takes us to one of the verse's hypograms, the 'descriptive system of the word *eye*', since conventionally, in love poetry, 'eyelashes are to the eye what reeds are to a lake' (*ibid.*). Activating the eye-hypogram means that the addressee's eyes need not be referred to directly at all, since they are necessarily invoked by the cliché involved in the metaphor of eyelash–reeds.

Riffaterre goes on to demonstrate how various inter-texts can explain elements of the second line, specifically the initially puzzling 'discreet' and 'human thinkers': the first relating to the story of King Midas and the place of reeds within it; the second 'an oft-quoted sentence of Pascal's' which itself, because of its subsequent conventionality, functions as a hypogram: "l'homme n'est qu'un roseau, mais c'est un roseau pensant" [man is a reed, but a reed that thinks]' (1978: 99).

In Riffaterre's work, therefore, the hypogram represents what Barthes calls 'the already read'. As Jonathan Culler puts it:

> the hypogram is not located in the text itself but is the product of past semiotic and literary practice, and it is in perceiving a sign's reference to this pre-existing phrase or complex that the reader identifies the sign as 'poetic'. The apparently mimetic sign is seen as a transformation of past poetic discourse. But 'for the poeticity to be activated in the text, the sign referring to a hypogram must also be a variant of that text's matrix' [1978: 23]. In other words, poetic signs in a text are powerfully overdetermined: they both refer to a pre-existing hypogram and are variants or transformations of a matrix.
>
> (Culler, 1981: 83)

It is, above all, this overdetermination of the poetic sign which marks the difference between Riffaterre's approach and that of the poststructuralist utilizations of semiotic theory we have previously examined. The overdetermined nature of the literary sign might indeed lead us to locate or presuppose inter-texts and hypograms which clarify the structural significance at the heart of a text; yet such intertextual functions can be presupposed by the reader, and what counts is the unravelling of the code, just as an analyst would unravel the overdetermined dream symbols of a patient. In this approach Riffaterre manages to avoid unravelling the text into the infinitely regressive domains of a poststructuralist vision of the general or social text.

Riffaterre's interpretive practice is dependent on discovering the ways in which texts produce semiotic unity by transforming socially shared codes, clichés, oppositions and descriptive systems; yet such an approach refuses to accept that such a reliance on the sociolect involves the text in anything other than its own self-generating system, its idiolectic and thus unique significance. Whilst Barthes, Kristeva and other poststructuralist textual or semiotic analysts move outwards from the text to what we have called the general or social text and so explode the traditional idea of textual unity, Riffaterre reads in a backwards movement, from text to textual invariant, from mimetic ungrammaticalities to semiotic (textual) unity. As he puts it: 'A poem is read poetically backwards' (1978: 19). In this sense, the poem's significance depends upon the reader's bringing to the text of a knowledge of the sociolect which will unlock its initially hidden meanings. Texts presuppose inter-texts, which the reader must then actualize within a semiotic reading of the text. The theory depends heavily on the belief not only that texts give us clear clues to their decoding (a belief, that is, that texts *can* be properly decoded in their own terms), but also that readers have the capacity, the knowledge of the sociolect and of literary traditions, which will allow them to perform such a successful decoding.

Literary competence

Riffaterre is a celebrated theorist and practitioner of literary criticism. However, his reliance on a notion of linguistic or literary competence has produced a series of criticisms and objections. The question of what happens when specific inter-texts are culturally lost returns with even more frequency in Riffaterre's work than in Genette's. Riffaterre argues that such a problem is surmounted by his theory of linguistic/literary competence and thus the reader's ability to presuppose the inter-text. At the conclusion of his essay 'Interpretation and Undecidability', for example, he asks: 'Does not undecidability become final, a genuine impasse, when the intertext disappears from readers' memories and traditions? Can interpretation impede the gradual obsolescence of the intertext without the aid of philology, an archaeology of reading?' His answer to these questions is characteristic:

> Interpretation remains relatively impervious to the intertext's obsolescence because the text, as the ungrammatical reverse of a sociolectic obverse, goes on pointing to this obverse even after the latter has been effaced by time; all that is needed for communication is the postulation of the absent meaning. All that is needed for the text to function is the presupposition of the intertext. Certainly, presupposition itself cannot exist unless the reader is familiar with the structures or-

ganizing a representation of reality: but these are the very stuff of our linguistic competence.

(Riffaterre, 1980b: 239)

To argue that different readers have different levels of literary competence, and come from different literary and cultural traditions, might seem a simple enough rebuff to this statement (see Clayton and Rothstein, 1991: 26). However, when he is evoking literary competence Riffaterre is not referring to knowledge of texts and canons, but is rather referring to an adequate possession of the sociolect. Thus, the competence he is referring to involves the reader's awareness of language as it is presently used in communication and as it has been used in previous eras. To this we might object that the reference to a single, communal sociolect is a naïve generalization. We might also object that the contemporary currency of past literary and cultural symbols, descriptive systems, themes, generic and other codes, is insufficiently analysed in Riffaterre's work. Riffaterre, we might want to say, relies on an insufficient historical understanding of text production.

More specific objections can be established with regard to the Riffaterrean system if we focus on one specific example of his interpretive method. In his essay 'Intertextual Representation: On Mimesis as Interpretive Discourse', Riffaterre, along with claims about the modes of conversion associated with the hypogram, develops his thoughts concerning the 'obligatory' nature of intertextuality in textual decoding. In mimetic or representational poetry, for instance, texts produce semiotic unity, Riffaterre argues, either by 'resorting to an intertext incompatible with [the] reality [being depicted]' or 'by negating an intertext compatible with that reality' (1984: 143). His example of the first variety is William Carlos Williams's Modernist poem 'The Red Wheelbarrow' (quoted in Riffaterre, 1984: 144):

so much depends
upon

a red wheel
barrow

glazed with rain
water

beside the white
chickens

The poem, argues Riffaterre, produces its significance by comparing a common object to the highly crafted objects of the art world. The word which alerts us to this transformative deployment of the language of high art in the description of such a commonplace object as a wheelbarrow is the word 'glazed'. Riffaterre writes: '"Glazed" conjures up a vast intertext of artefacts made with aesthetic intent. The representations it evokes are everything that a wheelbarrow emphatically is not ... Our perception of the wheelbarrow is determined by the intertext rather than by the fact that the poem's construction gives us the elemental thing – unattached, unmotivated reality' (1984: 145).

His example of the second kind of poem, where the text negates an intei-text compatible with the reality being represented, is Wordsworth's sonnet 'Composed Upon Westminster Bridge, September 3, 1802':

Earth has not anything to show more fair:
Dull would he be of soul who could pass by
A sight so touching in its majesty:
This city now doth, like a garment, wear
The beauty of the morning; silent, bare,
Ships, towers, domes, theatres, and temples lie
Open unto the fields, and to the sky;
All bright and glittering in the smokeless steep
In his first splendour, valley, rock, or hill;
Ne'er saw I, never felt, a calm so deep!
The river glideth at his own sweet will:
Dear God! the very houses seem asleep;
And all that mighty heart is lying still.

(Riffaterre, 1984: 149)

Riffaterre's reading of this poem depends upon a recognition of the polarities and equivalencies established within it between natural and urban imagery. More precisely, the poem is said to negate the sort of city-code we might expect to dominate a poem on the subject of London:

> Wordsworth chooses the most powerfully representative of all the metonyms of London in common parlance. In all allusions to the modern Babylon [i.e. London], 'smoke' summarizes every stereotype about urban pollution that arose from the conflicting ideologies of the sublime in nature and of the realism born of the industrial revolution. 'Smokeless' literally quotes from the intertext, in accordance with the law that we cannot negate anything in language without naming it.
>
> (*ibid.*: 153)

The inter-text here, then, is the conventional sociolectic code concerning the city as a place antithetical to a positively encoded nature. The poem's significance depends on a negation of that city-code, which not only has the effect of invoking the nature-code but of producing a kind of positive representation out of a double negative. Negating the expected relation between the city of London and a smoke-filled environment, Riffaterre argues, the poem merely reinforces our cultural opposition between city and nature in the very act of negating that opposition. We remain, that is, with our sociolectic sense of the city as smoke-filled and of nature as smokeless, only here we view the city of London *in terms of* the nature-code rather than the city-code. A confirmation of such points can be found, Riffaterre argues, by noting the representation of the Thames as free-flowing rather than its expected representation in terms of something approximating William Blake's 'charter'd Thames' in his poem 'London'. Riffaterre concludes: 'The spectacle therefore is born not of a spectator's delusion but of a cancellation of sociolectic conventions: this is enough to make it [the poem's representation of London] a coded sign, the self-sufficient icon of a truth deeper than conventional representation' (*ibid.*: 154).

Riffaterre's argument that the decoding of such texts is 'obligatory', that if we are attentive to their deeper structural transformations of sociolectic units we cannot but locate their semiotic unity, is, as various commentators have remarked, belied by the fact that he invariably posits his readings as correctives to prior interpretive traditions. As Culler puts it: 'it is difficult to treat the efforts of previous readers simultaneously as the phenomena one wishes to explain and as the errors one is attempting to surpass' (Culler, 1981: 94).

One possible objection is that, because Riffaterre's theoretical model interprets all texts as elaborations of small semiotic kernels, matrixes, intertextual or hypogrammatic units, it evades the generic and formal differences between texts. To read a novel in terms of an invariant subtext is perhaps to misread it as a kind of elaborate lyric poem. To read a descriptive poem such as Wordsworth's sonnet on Westminster Bridge in terms of its negation of general sociolectic codes is, perhaps, to miss its ideological imperatives.

A related critique is voiced by Culler, and the critics Paul de Man and Geoffrey Hartman. This concerns Riffaterre's oversimplification of figurative language. De Man, for example, writes of Riffaterre's inability to 'cope with the sheer strength of figuration, that is to say, master their power to confer, to usurp, and to take away significance from grammatical universals' (de Man, 1986: 45). A striking example of this point might be said to come in the sonnet's last line. It does not seem very likely that Wordsworth was intending a pun in the penultimate word. Is not the possibility of such a pun, however, a perfect expression of the act of refiguration Wordsworth has performed upon the city of London? Wordsworth's poem could be said to 'lie' in presenting a London reconfigured into an organic unity which the great proportion of the rest of his poetry on that subject fails to discover within it. The ability of local figures to produce overdetermined significance irresolvable on a grammatical model cannot be contained within Riffaterre's vision of self-sufficient textuality. Such figures explode that unity and force the text's readers into the recognition of indeterminate elements; the text does and does not have this meaning, i.e. of lying and deceit. Such elements also force the reader out into figurative and semiotic chains which explode any notion of textual self-sufficiency.

A reader well-versed in Wordsworth's poetry will surely finish Riffaterre's reading with a host of questions. What is the relation between the 'smokeless' scene in the sonnet and the conspicuous smoke which arises from amongst the trees in the Wye valley of 'Tintern Abbey'? And how does that relate to Riffaterre's model of the negation of a city-code which includes the idea of the city as an exclusively smoke-related environment? Is the opposition between an industrialized city and a pre- or non-industrialized nature as conventional in the first decade of the nineteenth century as Riffaterre suggests? Or is it actually being formed and figured within poetry such as Wordsworth's? In Books 7 and 8 of *The Prelude* (1805 and 1850) Wordsworth presents fundamentally negative accounts of his time as a young man in London. How does Wordsworth's tendency, described in those Books of *The Prelude*, to seek out places of seclusion, or to locate fixed objects among the city's bewilderingly heterogeneous parts, relate to the unitary but distanced scene presented in the sonnet? What is the sonnet's relation to the common poetic representations of London in the eighteenth century?

The list of possible questions widens as the potential intertextual boundaries of Wordsworth's sonnet are widened by its reader. Various commentators have pointed to the tension, even confusion, in Riffaterre's work between *aleatory* and *determinate* intertextuality. The latter would involve instances where an inter-text clearly stands behind a text; the former involve instances in which many potential inter-texts can be found for a specific text. Yet it seems difficult to imagine how Riffaterre can deal with aleatory intertextuality. Such a notion seems to return us to a poststructuralist emphasis on the reader's productive role in reading; an emphasis which Riffaterre's approach strenuously denies.

John Frow has argued that the tension between determinate and aleatory intertextuality is paralleled in Riffaterre's work by the conflation of matrix and hypogram. For Frow, the matrix depends upon a notion of *intra*textuality, which he describes as 'the elaboration of a text from a semantic core'. The hypogram, however, depends upon intertextuality, which Frow defines as 'the elaboration of a text in relation to other texts' (Frow, 1986: 152). He writes: 'Because he needs the concept of matrix as a guarantee of textual unity Riffaterre tends ... to confuse the intratextual matrix with the intertextual *hypogram*.' Frow goes on to define the hypogram as: 'a semantic structure – thematic field, cliché, norm, or actual text – which is referred to and transformed by a particular poem' (*ibid.*). We might go one step further and question the very necessity for the concept of intentional reference when speaking of the hypogrammatic intertextual field.

De Man's reading of Riffaterre can be said to complement Frow's, particularly in its attention to the manner in which the notion of the hypogram in his work implicitly evokes the work on anagrams which Saussure conducted but then abandoned. As de Man puts it, Saussure's work on the anagram argues that 'Latin poetry was structured by the coded dispersal (or dissemination) of an underlying word or proper name throughout the lines of verse' (de Man, 1986: 36). Such a theory is so close to that of Riffaterre that it seems remarkable that Riffaterre has not given more space to its discussion within his critical and theoretical works (see, however, Riffaterre, 1983: 75–89). It may be that Riffaterre's arguments about hypogrammatic structures, and more generally about the essential semiotic unity of texts, represent the fullest articulation of one source of the whole post-Saussurean project of semiology. But one must also recognize the possibility, as articulated by Kristeva and others, that Saussure's theory, clearly one rather unnoticed source of the concept of intertextuality, can be turned another way. Saussure's work on anagrams, as Kristeva demonstrates, can be made to emphasize not textual unity so much as the dialogic quality of the literary sign and thus the literary text. That Saussure may have abandoned his project, of finding anagrammatic key-words fragmented into 'syllable-pairs' and 'potentially into letters' (de Man, 1986: 38) within Latin poems, because of an inability to determine whether such intertextual relations were 'random or determined' (*ibid.*: 43), seems to reinforce, rather than resolve, the tension between aleatory and determinate intertextual relations in Riffaterre's system.

Ultimately, the above points might all be said to extend Hartman's criticism of Riffaterre's elision of the role of author and reader (Hartman, 1987: 129–51). Riffaterre, we might say, not only confuses issues of determinate and random intertextuality, he also evades the full nature of the reader's presuppositions, those things the reader presumes *before* coming to a text. As de Man and Culler have suggested, arguing that the text compels the reader to read in a certain way evades the tension between a formalist emphasis on the self-sufficiency of the text and an interpretive theory and practice which, by recognizing the vital role the reader plays in producing textual significance, does the opposite. In this sense Riffaterre's theory, for all its significance within the area of textual and intertextual studies, remains blind to the disrupting effect of what has been called 'the hermeneutic circle'. This phrase is employed to refer to the fact that it is impossible to ascertain whether reading produces the theory of textuality or whether reading supports and is driven by that theory. Do we begin with texts and produce theories about them after we have read them? Or do we begin with theories about texts and then read specific texts in the light of those theories? Such a question, in twentieth-century theories of literature, has proved notoriously difficult to answer. Riffaterre's notion of presupposition and its ability to assist the reader in locating a text's meaning, seems a rather inadequate response to such a question. Readers come from numerous backgrounds and have numerous reading experiences. They clearly do not share a single 'sociolect'. We cannot, therefore, refer to the presupposition of readers as if it were a singular, or predictable phenomenon. A greater recognition of the situatedness of the reader and the historical, social, ideological and even individual specificities of text production, might appear an alluring prospect after the apparently stable, de-situated theories discussed in this Chapter.

4

SITUATED READERS: BLOOM, FEMINISM, POSTCOLONIALISM

INFLUENCE REVISITED: BLOOM

The kinds of theories we have so far studied have had a major impact on literary critics and theorists working in North America. Of all these critics Harold Bloom remains the most conspicuously dedicated to a version of intertextual theory and practice. To understand Bloom's version of intertextual theory we must first turn to his work on Romantic poetry.

Bloom has always had a concern for nineteenth-century and particularly for Romantic poetry. From the mid-1960s onwards, this concern developed a rather singular bent which can best be expressed in a question: If Romantic poets such as Blake, Wordsworth, Keats or P. B. Shelley believed so passionately in the idea of the imagination, an idea which ascribes uniqueness of vision to those possessed by or with it, why do they all consistently return, by direct and indirect means, to Milton as a figure of poetic authority? Bloom's answer to the question is expressed neatly by one of his chapter titles: 'The Belatedness of Strong Poetry' (1975a: 63–80). Belatedness is defined by Bloom as the experience of coming after the event. The reason the Romantic poets could not rid their poetry of explicit or implicit references and allusions to Milton was, it would appear, that they were late for an event. Bloom has no doubt that Milton's poetry is that event, and that Milton's poetry makes all poets after him, including the canonical male Romantics, belated.

Employing a vocabulary taken from Freud's theory of the Oedipus Complex, in which sons wish to marry or sexually possess their mothers and so wish to supplant or even kill their fathers, Bloom writes of the 'poetic father' as a scandalous figure, scandalous because he cannot die or be murdered. Bloom also employs a Greek vocabulary of 'precursor' (father) and 'ephebe' (son) to figure this relation between Milton and all poets who come after him in the tradition of British poetry. He writes:

> A poet, I argue ... is not so much a man speaking to men as a man rebelling against being spoken to by a dead man (the precursor) outrageously more alive than himself. A poet dare not regard himself as being *late*, yet cannot accept a substitute for the first vision he reflectively judges to have been his precursor's also.
>
> (Bloom, 1975a: 19)

The ideas contained in that last sentence are crucial and lead us on to Bloom's conflictual vision of the intertextual process. Poetry in the post-Miltonic period, Bloom argues, stems from two motivations, or, to employ the Freudian terminology which Bloom adapts, *drives*. The first concerns the desire to imitate the precursor's poetry, from which the poet first learnt what poetry was. The second concerns the desire to be original, and defend against the knowledge that all the poet is doing is imitating rather than creating afresh. Bloom's vision of poetry is thus intertextual. It argues that poetry, and indeed literature in general, can only imitate previous texts. In his most widely read critical work, *The Anxiety of Influence*, Bloom articulates these points as corrections to previous critical approaches which either misguidedly presume the literary text to possess in itself unity, and thus determinable meaning, or which misguidedly seek the meaning of literary texts in non-literary contexts. His own resolution of these critical 'errors', based on the recognition of the intertextual nature of poetic texts, he styles 'Antithetical Criticism':

> All criticisms that call themselves primary vacillate between tautology – in which the poem is and means itself – and reduction – in which the poem means something that is not itself a poem. Antithetical criticism must begin by denying both tautology and reduction, a denial best delivered by the assertion that the meaning of a poem can only be a poem, but *another poem – a poem not itself.* And not a poem chosen with total arbitrariness, but any central poem by an indisputable precursor, even if the ephebe *never read that poem.* Source study is wholly irrelevant here; we are dealing with primal words, but antithetical meanings, and an ephebe's best misinterpretations may well be of poems he has never read.

(Bloom, 1973: 70)

Bloom refers to 'source study' in order to distance his use of the word 'influence' from traditional uses of that word. As the passage explains, poets write by misinterpreting and misreading the poems of specific precursor poets. Poets become poets by becoming 'hooked', we might say, on the poetry of an earlier poet. However, to be 'strong poets', to employ Bloom's combative terminology, new poets must do two things: they must rewrite the precursor's poems, and in that very act they must defend themselves against the knowledge that they are merely involved in the process of rewriting, or what Bloom calls misreading. For Bloom, poets employ the central figures of previous poetry but they transform, redirect, reinterpret those already written figures in new ways and hence generate the illusion that their poetry is not influenced by, and not therefore a misreading of, the precursor poem.

Mapping misreading

Bloom develops an expanding 'map of misreading' in his work of the 1970s. This map is meant to enumerate and specify the kinds of figurative misreadings which dominate modern poetry. The map of misreading is in six stages, each stage concerning what Bloom calls a 'revisionary ratio', a specific technique of misreading. Each stage is also presented through the use of an archaic terminology characteristic of Bloom's tendency to mix and merge modern critical theory with ancient traditions. He also employs other modern vocabularies, most notably that of Freudian psychoanalysis. We need not describe each of the six stages of the map of misreading here (see Allen, 1994: 26–9, 49–54), but we do need to recognize that Bloom's fully developed map of misreading allows him to articulate one of his cardinal theoretical points: that poetry, and indeed all literature, involves both figurative language and psychological defence mechanisms. For each kind of misreading, Bloom associates a defence mechanism taken from Freudian psychoanalysis, and particularly from Anna Freud's mapping of the defence mechanisms in *The Ego and the Mechanisms of Defense* (Freud, 1948). Defence mechanisms concern the manner in which people defend themselves against that which they need to keep repressed in the unconscious. Thus, 'projection' involves the transference of elements repressed in the unconscious on to another person or some other external phenomenon. Someone who is terrified of lightning may well be projecting onto an external phenomenon an aspect of their own unconscious which terrifies them. In another defence mechanism, 'reaction-formation', people fix on an idea which is opposite to the idea which must remain repressed in the unconscious. Someone who complains about the slow work-rate of others may well be reacting against an unconscious anxiety concerning their own work-rate.

The combination of a rhetorical and a psychoanalytical approach to intertextuality is Bloom's particular contribution to contemporary literary theory's movement beyond the study of literary texts as if they alone contained meaning. For him all texts are inter-texts. As he writes in *Kabbalah and Criticism*: 'A single text has only part of a meaning; it is itself a synecdoche for a larger whole including other texts. A text is a relational event, and not a substance to be analysed' (1975b: 106). What makes Bloom unique is what he does with this relational feature of literature. Intertextuality is for Bloom a product of the 'anxiety of influence'. This anxiety, the keystone of Bloom's account of literary writing *and* critical reading, not only concerns the inability to avoid what Barthes styles the 'already written and read', but also concerns writers' and readers' refusal to accept this state of affairs. The fact that any writing is necessarily a misreading must, in Bloom's account, be resisted. As he puts it in *The Anxiety of Influence*: 'If influence were health, who could write a poem? Health is stasis' (1973: 95). Bloom's account of intertextuality is concerned with motivation, with the reasons why people write in a culture in which everything seems to have already been written, and written in better ways – and in which, as a consequence, there is no way of ever producing writing that is representational of the world, of producing writing that does anything more than rewrite what has already been written. Bloom directly confronts the way in which the intertextual dimension of writing might affect the desire to write.

Bloom's characteristic method of reading involves an intertextual assessment of the patterns of misreading observable between a poetic text and a precursor poem or set of poems. Once these figurative patterns are established, the psychological motivations which generated the particular figurative misreadings observable within the text in question can be discussed. Often, however, Bloom's intense awareness of canonical literature opens this procedure out into a wider framework and includes the precursor's own misreading of previous figurative patterns within his or her own precursor's poem or poems.

There are many similarities between Bloom's approach and that of Riffaterre. Both theorists reduce intertextuality to a model of text and inter-text, and by so doing produce very compelling, reading strategies. However, whilst for Riffaterre such an approach produces interpretive certainty, for Bloom critical reading is itself always a form of misreading, and suffers from the same anxieties of influence as we find in what he insists on calling 'strong poetry'. As Bloom writes:

> Poetic meaning ... is ... radically indeterminate. Reading, despite all humanist traditions of education, is very nearly impossible, for every reader's relation to every poem is governed by a figuration of belatedness. Tropes or defenses (for here rhetoric and psychology are a virtual identity) are the 'natural' language of the imagination in relation to all prior manifestations of imagination. A poet attempting to make this language new necessarily begins by an *arbitrary act of reading* that does not differ in kind from the act that *his* readers subsequently must perform on him.
>
> (Bloom, 1975a: 69)

We can better understand why Bloom argues that critical reading is itself misreading, and is motivated by the same act of defence that motivates literary writing, by returning to the passage quoted earlier regarding 'Antithetical Criticism'. There Bloom asserts that poets misread precursor poems 'even if the ephebe *never read that poem*'. How can this be? One answer can be located if we attend to Bloom's statements concerning the cultural centrality of certain original writers. In his more recent work Bloom has moved his focus towards those writers who can be said to be truly original. The author of the earliest parts of the Bible, the J-writer, along with Shakespeare and Freud, are recurrent examples in Bloom's later work of what he styles 'facticity'. We might define 'facticity' as the unavoidability of certain writers within Western cultures (see Bloom, 1988: 405–24, and Bloom, 1989).

Shakespeare, Bloom argues in *The Western Canon* and more recently in *Shakespeare: The Invention of the Human*, is the most factitious writer in history, and we live out our lives in images and figures which originated in Shakespeare's work. Thus, Shakespeare usurps the category of Nature and functions as a constant source for our emotional and psychical lives. In the recent second edition of *The Anxiety of Influence* Bloom writes: 'Shakespeare did not think one thought and one thought only; rather scandalously, he thought all thoughts, for all of us' (1997: xxvii–xxviii). Perhaps an easier example of facticity is the effect that Freud's work has on modern Western cultures. Whether people have read any work by Freud or not, they tend, nowadays, to speak of themselves in Freudian ways. We have problems with our parents, we speak of our unconscious, our drives, even our *id*, *ego* and *super-ego*. Freud is a facticity, an already-read script in modern culture, as Bloom states in his essay 'Wrestling Sigmund':

> The unconscious turns out alas not to be structured like *a* language, but to be structured like *Freud's* language, and the ego and superego, in their conscious aspects, are structured like Freud's own texts, for the very good reason that they *are* Freud's texts. We have become Freud's texts, and the *Imitatio Freudi* is the necessary pattern for the spiritual life in our time.
>
> (Bloom, 1982b: 64)

If we take this idea of facticity, we can begin to understand why a poet might be forced to misread a poet of pervasive influence even if they had not in fact read that poet themselves. Bloom frequently argues that all poetry after Milton is influenced by him, and that all lyrics after Wordsworth's 'Tintern Abbey' tend to replicate elements of that great Romantic ode.

There is, however, a major fault line in Bloom's argument here. Bloom argues that all critical reading is misreading, because its shares with literary writing an anxiety of influence. The reason reading as well as writing never brings us interpretive resolution is because, in his account, interpretive certainty is not what motivates writing or reading. The crucial motive for these activities, according to Bloom, is the recognition of having been preempted in one's words, one's sentiments, one's very experience of the world or even of one's self. The objective for poet and critical reader is identical, to persuade others to read their work, to become themselves an influence. According to Bloom, the desire to be an influence is the only motive which can explain why writing and reading still occur. To be an influence is to successfully 'lie against time', since it gives the figure who influences a sense of 'earliness' rather than of 'belatedness'.

Bloom, however, also admits that if reading is the study of intertextual relations, then there is an inevitably 'arbitrary' element in all reading. If we are not dealing with intended intertextual relations between texts, then where do we begin in our search for the text's significant inter-text? For Bloom the answer is always, 'in the poetry of the precursor'. But how do we know who the poet's precursor is? And how do we know that in certain texts other inter-texts are not also significant? We circle back to the distinction between determinate and aleatory intertextuality we observed in Riffaterre's work. To locate a *necessary* intertextual relation between a text and an inter-text or set of inter-texts can only be achieved by two processes: arguing that the text itself directs its readers to the appropriate inter-text, or, conversely, deciding arbitrarily, lacking direct textual evidence, that a particular intertextual relation is the significant and interpretively informing one. For Bloom, the significant inter-text need not even be directly linked stylistically or figuratively to the text in question. Writing of Robert Browning, Algernon Charles Swinburne, Thomas Hardy and W. B. Yeats, Bloom argues that P. B. Shelley's poetry is the significant inter-text for all four poets, even though they 'have styles antithetical to Shelley's style' (1975b: 67).

Bloom's theory of the anxiety of influence and the model of misreading he builds upon it is, then, his own act of misreading. Bloom cannot prove that all literature and all criticism is based on a desire to defend against the anxiety of influence; all he can do is to produce reading after reading which asserts this fact. Either all reading is misreading because of the anxiety of influence, or all reading is misreading because of the inability of readers to draw a verifiable frame around the intertextual domain within which texts exist and signify and to distinguish relevant from irrelevant inter-texts.

Reading Bloom's work one cannot help but come to the conclusion that the theory of misreading is actually a defence against the plurality celebrated by Barthes and Kristeva and the accompanying recognition that literature does not exist in a hermetically sealed universe. Bloom's vision refuses to accept social and cultural contexts as relevant intertextual fields of meaning for literary texts. For Bloom, literary texts can only have other specific literary texts as inter-texts. He defines his brand of literary history as 'an historicism that deliberately reduces to the interplay of personalities' (1975a: 71). Beginning with his theory of the anxiety of influence, there is nothing to stop Bloom demonstrating that poems are written by ephebes defending against their precursors. To argue that such a critical practice is circular, that it begins with a theory which can only be proved accurate by the readings Bloom then produces, is not a viable critique for Bloom himself. Bloom is a pragmatist, which is to say he is a critic for whom the relevant criteria are not accuracy and truth but persuasiveness and the gaining either of influence or of consent (1982a: 19–20).

On this pragmatist basis Bloom's theory and practice cannot be proved wrong: it can only be agreed or disagreed with. However, there is one area of his work which does seem open to clear disagreement. In order to demonstrate this we might turn to a poetic text and assess the Bloomian method's ability to account for it. The text is one of Elizabeth Barrett Browning's *Sonnets from the Portuguese*, a sonnet cycle which she addressed to her husband, the poet Robert Browning:

> The first time that the sun rose on thine oath
> To love me, I looked forward to the moon
> To slacken all those bonds which seemed too soon
> And quickly tied to make a lasting troth.
> Quick-loving hearts, I thought, may quickly loathe;
> And, looking on myself, I seemed not one
> For such man's love! – more like an out-of-tune
> Worn viol, a good singer would be wroth
> To spoil his song with, and which, snatched in haste,
> Is laid down at the first ill-sounding note.
> I did not wrong myself so, but I placed
> A wrong on *thee*. For perfect strains may float
> 'Neath master-hands, from instruments defaced, –
> And great souls, at one stroke, may do and dote.

> (Barrett Browning, 1988: 231)

This poem might be said to confirm the third revisionary ratio in Bloom's map of misreading. *Kenosis* involves a strategy whereby the poet humbles him/herself only eventually to humble the precursor more profoundly. As Bloom puts it: '*Kenosis* .... appears to be an act of self-abnegation, yet tends to make the fathers pay for their own sins, and perhaps for those of the son also' (1973: 91). A Bloomian reading of this sonnet, therefore, might begin by noting that the poetic addresser seems intent on humbling herself in relation to the addressee. The addressee is figured as a 'master-hand'; the addresser figures herself as a 'Worn viol'. The addressee seems to exist in a world of perfection and to be perfect (a 'great soul'); the addresser figures herself as a damaged person (an 'instrument defaced'). The addressee is beautiful, while the addresser is outside of beauty.

To demonstrate that a revisionary twist is occurring in this poem, and that it is dominated by *kenosis*, the reader must now move on to a reassessment of the text's figures. A Bloomian reading would take these figures of self-humbling and read them as misreadings of a precursor poem. The sonnet which might come to mind is Shakespeare's sonnet 130, 'My mistress' eyes are nothing like the sun', in which the sonneteer refuses to deploy the stock clichés for female beauty. Shakespeare's sonnet initially appears to humble its female addressee, to figure her as lacking in conventional beauty. It ultimately, however, establishes the addressee's beauty through the very act of refusing to employ stereotypical figures. Barrett Browning's sonnet might be said to perform a figurative reversal of Shakespeare's sonnet by rhetorically humbling the poetic addresser rather than the addressee. A Bloomian reading would then assess whether such a strategy achieved a reversal of canonical power: do we leave the sonnet with a sense that Barrett Browning has wrestled poetic strength and canonical authority away from Shakespeare's sonnet?

It is possible to suggest that the self-humbling going on here is more complex than it might initially appear. Is the apparently perfect addressee actually too quick to declare love? Is the love that he has declared, and the realm he appears to exist in, rather unrealistic? Barrett Browning's *Sonnets from the Portuguese* do seem to demonstrate a critique of the traditional style of amorous verse and to argue for a more realistic mode of love poetry. Does this poem stage a poetic conflict, or what Bloom calls an *'agon'* (poetry viewed as a conflict for power), in which romanticized love poetry, through a process of realistic self-assessment which appears like self-humbling, is overturned in favour of a new, modern, realistic mode of love poetry?

The answer, readers have suggested, is yes. But it is an answer which cannot be made on the basis of an approach, such as Bloom's, which focuses exclusively on an *agon* between a poetic son and a poetic father. There are two reasons why this is the case. The first concerns our need to extend the field of the intertextual. No amount of attention to the poetry of Barrett Browning and Shakespeare will fully do justice to this poem. We also need to look at the intertextual code of love poetry. Referring back to Barthes's method, we might suggest that a 'literary code' very much related to a 'cultural code' is strongly at work in this text. Love poetry tends to be idealized rather than realistic. This might be our first intertextual point, verifiable by citing any number of the numerous examples of love poems in the literary archive. The second point we might make is that in the sonnet tradition a male poet addresses a female addressee. There are, of course, exceptions, as Shakespeare's sonnets to the 'young man' prove. However, if we consider the traditional relationship between sonneteer and addressee we recognize that various intertextual codes are being overturned in Barrett Browning's sonnets. As in our example above, her sonnets are, unusually, addressed to another poet. The female poet is, again unusually, the addresser and the male poet the addressee.

The traditional relations, then, between a male poet and a female addressee are reversed by Barrett Browning – a point which seems connected to the manner in which Barrett Browning's sonnets argue for a realistic form of amatory verse. A female sonneteer, we might say, does not, like the traditional male sonneteer, idealize female beauty. The real reversal of power and authority in this sonnet might well concern what happens when women write love poetry instead of having love poetry written for them. Things change when women write and speak rather than being written about and spoken to. We cross over into issues of cultural stereotyping and of gender relations, into the very realms which Bloom, by tying literary texts to literary inter-texts, refuses to accept as a legitimate field of literary meaning: the intertextual field of social and cultural codes, stereotypes and ideological formations.

GYNOCRITICISM AND INTERTEXTUALITY

In a discussion of Bloom's theories, the US critic Annette Kolodny refers to Virginia Woolf's account of, as a woman, being barred from an Oxford library containing the manuscript of John Milton's *Lycidas* (Kolodny, 1986: 48–9). The episode acts as a symbol for the exclusion of women from the idea of the literary tradition or canon. Male critics such as Bloom may well believe that there is one singular and inescapable canon of literature, and that this is what causes the anxiety of influence; however, such monologic descriptions of the literary canon evade the fact that women writers have traditionally been excluded from it. It is not possible to conflate notions of intertextuality with notions of a monological canon without endorsing the historical practice of marginalizing certain kinds of writing, including writing by women. Yet, do we really escape from that exclusionary logic if we attempt to establish a distinctly female literary canon?

The attempt to examine previously overlooked traditions of writing by women has been a central feature of the feminist critical movement. Elaine Showalter, an influential feminist critic, describes the critical approach of gynocriticism as:

> the feminist study of women's writing, including readings of women's texts and analyses of the intertextual relations both between women writers (a female literary tradition), and between women and men.
>
> (Showalter, 1990: 189)

We get in the gynocritical approach an image of a female literary tradition which depends upon an at least implicit notion of intertextual relations between women writers. Showalter's vision here is of a set of 'images, metaphors, themes and plots' which connects women's writing across periods and national divisions and builds into something as cohesive and as intertextually rich as the traditionally sanctioned male literary canon.

Gilbert and Gubar, in their study of nineteenth-century literature by women writers, *The Madwoman in the Attic*, take up Bloom's patriarchal theory of literature and, instead of rejecting it out of hand, actually examine 'what is right' about it as a theory (Gilbert and Gubar, 1979: 47). One thing that is 'right' about Bloom's approach, they say, is that it attends to the motivations which generate writing. However, they go on to argue that the motivation of anxiety, the desire for imaginative freedom within an overpopulated literary tradition, the subsequent desire to revise (symbolically defeat or murder) the father, or precursor, are irrelevant to women writers' experience and the motivations which drive them to take up the pen, that traditional symbol of the phallus.

In societies in which women are traditionally excluded from 'serious' literature, and even from formal education, the woman writer's anxiety is concerned first and foremost with the culturally dominant images of women which would deny her access to intellectual and aesthetic achievement, which would marginalize her as an 'angel in the house' or as a dangerous 'other' (witch, madwoman, whore). As Gilbert and Gubar put it:

> precisely because a woman is denied the autonomy – the subjectivity – that the pen represents, she is not only excluded from culture (whose emblem might well be the pen) but she also becomes herself an embodiment of just those extremes of mysterious and intransigent Otherness which culture confronts with worship or fear, love or loathing.
>
> (Gilbert and Gubar, 1979: 19)

It might be objected that such statements merely collude in the patriarchal symbolic association between pen and phallus, and that women writers should define their writing in symbolic ways suitable to women's bodies. As we shall see, the notion of inter-textuality, with its connotations of webs and weaving, constitutes an opportunity for such a feminization of the symbolics of the act of writing. That the pen was traditionally associated with male authority and thus, symbolically with the phallus, remains true enough, however, and the nineteenth-century women writers discussed by Gilbert and Gubar were, it seems, deeply affected by such a cultural and symbolic association.

Gilbert and Gubar, along with other gynocritics writing from the 1970s onwards, such as Elaine Showalter (1984) and Mary Poovey (1984), demonstrate the manner in which nineteenth-century women writers avoided censure for taking up the pen by adopting various strategies in which the gendered images of patriarchal culture are accommodated on the surface level of the work. Taking male pseudonyms, or adopting the persona of what Poovey calls 'the proper lady', allowed women writers to avoid charges of unnaturalness. Yet Gilbert and Gubar's work stresses the fact that recurrent themes, images and figures – notably that of madness – mark an attempt to articulate distinctly female experience and a resistance to the dominant constructions of femininity.

The eighteenth- and nineteenth-century woman writer's experience, as Gilbert and Gubar stress, is essentially a solitary one. Lacking the sense of an inherited tradition enjoyed – or, in Bloom's account, suffered – by male writers, the woman writer also fears that writing will mark her as Other, as unfeminine. In place of Bloom's 'anxiety of influence', argue Gilbert and Gubar, the woman writer suffers from an 'anxiety of authorship': 'a radical fear that she cannot create, that because she can never become a "precursor" the act of writing will isolate and destroy her' (1979: 49). The desire for, rather than the anxiety concerning, a precursor or tradition for the woman writer makes influence and/or intertextuality, when established, a matter of legitimation rather than of emasculating belatedness.

Like Bloom before them, Gilbert and Gubar employ the term 'influence' to refer to a mode of intertextuality limited to authors within a specific literary tradition. We will keep this usage here and employ intertextuality in its poststructuralist senses. In contemplating twentieth-century women's writing, Gilbert and Gubar imply that influence is viewed differently by men and by women. There seems to be, that is, a gender difference in the writer's response to affiliations with previous writers. They write:

> The son of many fathers, today's male writer feels hopelessly belated; the daughter of too few mothers, today's female writer feels that she is helping to create a viable tradition which is at last definitively emerging.
>
> (Gilbert and Gubar, 1979: 50)

Such gendered differences might appear to connect us back to poststructuralist accounts of intertextuality. Barthes's suggestion that the marking of a text's relation to the 'cultural text' can only be made provisionally, that each reader 'writes' or partially constructs the text's intertextual dimensions, clearly allows us to recognise a space for gender and its effects on how we read within the theory of intertextuality. A woman reader, we might say, would produce a different intertextual reading of Balzac's *Sarrasine* than would a man. Barthes's homosexual position, some would argue, is clearly evident in his particular reading of that text.

Critics such as Gilbert and Gubar appear more interested in tracing the previously hidden connections between women writers than in developing a theory of a distinctly female or feminist approach to reading. The feminist theorist Toril Moi has written persuasively on the confusions such an approach can create. She argues that gynocritical and other feminist critical approaches frequently confuse the terms 'female', 'feminine', and 'feminist'. If 'female' refers to a biological state, then 'feminine' refers to a cultural ideology of womanhood, whilst 'feminist' involves a mode of social and political thought and action. On this basis, to chart previously hidden 'female' literary traditions, is not necessarily a 'feminist' activity. Moi writes:

> Gilbert and Gubar's account homogenises all female creative utterances into *feminist* self-expression: a strategy which singularly fails to

account for the ways in which women can come to take up a masculine subject position – that is to say, become solid defenders of the
patriarchal *status quo*.

(Moi, 1982: 217; see also Moi, 1985)

Gilbert and Gubar's restriction of focus allows for the recovery
of traditions and trends within a female literary tradition previously overlooked or even repressed. However, there remains a
need for a theory of feminist reading and a tension between what
we have been calling influence and intertextuality. To employ images, figures and plots concerned with madness and other states
of psychical disturbance to locate a distinctly female literary tradition is not the same thing as analysing the cultural codes which
express dominant ideological constructions of masculine and feminine identity. The cultural codes out of which female identity
and female texts are constructed might foster images of otherness,
madness, psychical disturbance. However, it seems problematic
to perceive such intertextual codes as both repressive when placed
in the context of dominant culture and liberating when placed in
the context of a developing female literary tradition. A theoretical consideration of how intertextual networks within the cultural text relate to intertextual relations within the network
(tradition) of women's writing needs to be established if this tension is not to threaten the gynocritical approach. Such a consideration will inevitably involve a focus on questions concerning the
act of reading itself: how does one read as a feminist critic? Are
concepts concerned with reading and writing, such as intertextuality, neutral, or are they gendered, and thus available for a feminist reappraisal and transformation?

A recent feminist theorist, Monika Kaup, attempts to confront
these problems by adding a poststructuralist approach to the gynocritical concern with the relations of influence within women's
writing. The association between women and madness, Kaup
writes, involves us in 'a vast cultural space, in different disciplines, such as philosophy, psychoanalysis, psychiatry and literature, feeding each other and exceeding any single textual

manifestation of that complex' (Kaup, 1993: 12). Intertextuality, or 'mad intertextuality' as Kaup terms it, gives us, then:

> an open exchange between the domain of literature and a 'universe' of intersecting scientific, cultural, ideological and literary discourses or 'voices', and, conversely, the potential rhythm, merging and overlay of those heterogeneous voices within what we usually regard as a 'single literary text'.
>
> (*ibid.*: 12–13)

Kaup's point is that the relations of influence between literary texts by women are shot through with traces of a vast cultural text or intertextuality which is itself bound up with developing disciplines and discourses. There can be no complete understanding of how individual texts relate to this vast cultural network; the reader is forced to choose various points of entrance and exit into the field of 'mad intertextuality' when coming to women's writing of the twentieth century. Kaup's approach follows that of Barthes in *S/Z*, in that it recognizes the somewhat arbitrary manner in which any reader maps out a text's intertextual relations. The challenge to the feminist reader, then, is to find constructive and illuminating ways of making entrances into the vast, heterogeneous field of mad intertextuality.

Kaup's method is firstly to employ a historically chronological approach, moving from Modernist texts of the early twentieth century, on to texts of the 1960s and then of the 1970s. Such an approach allows a recognition of the relations between a set of texts in each period, but also the ability to foreground how the cultural construction of women and madness alters in each period, and so is woven into texts of the 1960s in ways distinct from texts of the 1970s. Kaup also takes various synchronic approaches, arranging groups of texts not around historical periods but particular themes, plots and cultural configurations. Madness, for example, is a cultural construction experienced in immensely different ways by different classes and communities of women. A focus on communities and local sites disrupts a too simplistic notion of a historical development of a female literary tradition.

An example of Kaup's practice which demonstrates the above points comes in her discussion of Jean Rhys's *The Wide Sargasso Sea*, first published in 1966. Rhys's novel deals with the story of Antoinette Cosway, a Creole heiress who marries an Englishman. This man is the Mr. Rochester of Charlotte Brontë's Victorian novel, *Jane Eyre*. Antoinette is the 'madwoman in the attic', Bertha, the shadowy double of Jane, who in Brontë's text threatens the final union of Rochester and Jane and who eventually dies in the fire which ravages Thornfield Manor and cripples Rochester. Kaup cites Rachel Blau DuPlessis's *Writing Beyond the Ending* (1985) in order to establish one major intertextual revision occurring between Rhys's and Brontë's texts. Employing DuPlessis's argument, Kaup claims that:

> nineteenth-century romance 'ends', for women, in either marriage or death, which would then have to be read as the heroine's success or failure. The antithetical resolutions of the marriage plot inscribe 'the sex-gender system' ... which feeds women into heterosexual coupling while repressing their *Bildung* or quest in a way analogous to the male hero. DuPlessis's claim is that twentieth-century women authors 'write beyond' the ending of the romance plot, undoing the 'aura of the couple'.
>
> (Kaup, 1993: 81)

On the level of plot, then, Rhys's text resists the patriarchal 'ending' of marriage in its inter-text, *Jane Eyre*. This resistance can be seen in terms of both texts' relation to what Kaup calls 'mad intertextuality'. Jane Eyre is shown constantly on the verge of slipping irrevocably into social constructions which would delegitimate her as an individual; however, she finally achieves social legitimacy in marriage to Rochester. This legitimacy is achieved at the cost of Bertha/Antoinette, and Rhys's focus on the story of this woman switches our attention to the 'other' or delegitimated woman upon whom the ideal Victorian wife and mother depends. Although the bulk of Rhys's text involves a narrative, Antoinette's, which is only tangentially related to the narrative of *Jane Eyre*, the text slowly builds up to the climactic scene of the devastation through fire of Thornfield Manor. This catastrophic event, however, is experienced by the reader of Rhys's text through the viewpoint of Antoinette, and as such places us at the very centre of the dangerous 'other' who haunts the margins of Brontë's novel. The effect, as Kaup suggests, is to take the reader into the very Otherness which traditionally occupies the margins of Gothic and Gothic-inspired nineteenth-century novels. It also takes us into the point of view of a colonial subject, who is doubly or even triply 'other' to the British audience of Brontë's fiction: 'mad', a woman, a mulatto colonial subject.

Gayatri Chakravorty Spivak has captured well the intense and peculiar intertextual re-visioning at the conclusion of Rhys's novel. After a series of dreams which include snippets of events the reader will remember from Brontë's novel, Antoinette awakes with a clear sense of her role and the appropriate course of action; these, in brief, are to enter, intertextually, into the 'house' of British, imperialist fiction. As Spivak writes:

> It is now, at the very end of the book, that Anoinette/Bertha can say: 'Now at last I know why I was brought here and what I have to do' ... We can read this as her having been brought into the England of Brontë's novel: 'This cardboard house' – a book between cardboard covers – 'where I walk at night is not England' ... In this fictive England, she must play out her role, act out the transformation of her 'self' into that fictive Other, set fire to the house and kill herself, so that Jane Eyre can become the feminist individualist heroine of British fiction. I must read this as an allegory of the general colonial subject for imperialism, the construction of a self-immolating colonial subject for the glorification of the social mission of the colonizer. At least Rhys sees to it that the woman from the colonies is not sacrificed as an insane animal for her sister's consolation.

(Spivak, 1985: 250–1)

The shift in focus in Rhys's text involves, as Kaup demonstrates, immense social and cultural changes, many of which bear directly on the constructions of femininity which revolve around the oppositional network of patriarchal culture. Kaup, in her introduction, employs the famous breakdown of patriarchal binary oppositions mapped out by the French feminist theorist Hélène Cixous in her essay 'Sorties' (Cixous, 1994: 37–46). Cixous begins:

> Where is she?
> Activity/passivity
> Sun/Moon
> Culture/Nature
> Day/Night.

(Cixous, 1994: 37)

Moving through a series of cultural oppositions which figure the supposed difference between masculinity and femininity, Cixous's point is that culture depends upon a 'violent hierarchy' of binary codes, each replicating a fundamental division between men and women. In patriarchal logic, man is always what woman is not. Thus, if man is associated with culture, woman is associated with nature; if man is associated with mind and with rationality, woman is associated with body and with madness.

Whilst this kind of diagnosis of dominant patriarchal representation is crucial to feminist thinking, it does not explain how women have struggled against such hierarchies. To remain within an analysis of binary logic is to miss the crucial social and historical differences which exist between, for example, an author of Brontë's period and an author like Rhys, working from a colonial background and within the period of the 1960s.

To think of madness as simply a biological or psychical disturbance is, as Kaup suggests, merely to fall in with a patriarchal logic which argues that men are essentially rational and that women are essentially outside of rationality so defined. Michel Foucault has famously argued for a rethinking of madness as a changing historical construct which serves, at any socio-cultural moment, to silence and 'other' (marginalize) certain groups of people and certain forms of behaviour. Such a rethinking of the history of madness and its social and ideological function led, in the 1960s, to changes in the very treatment of mental disorders themselves. Elaine Showalter, in *The Female Malady*, discusses the impact of Laingian anti-psychiatry on the feminist movement. Anti-psychiatry, according to Laing's colleague, David Cooper, aimed to reverse the established power relations between doctor and patient. It represented, Showalter writes:

> an attempt to reverse the rules of the 'psychiatric game', countering 'medical power as embodied in the diagnosis ... the secret dossier ...[and] the system of compulsory detention' with 'attentive non-interference aimed at opening up of experience rather than its closing down'. According to the anti-psychiatrists, mental illness had to be examined in terms of its social contexts: the emotional dynamics of the family and the institution of psychiatry itself.
>
> (Showalter, 1987: 221)

Whilst critical of the anti-psychiatrists' actual attention to the issue of women and madness, Showalter expresses the liberatory effect of this rethinking of madness upon women patients and on women's writing. Kaup's treatment of *Wide Sargasso Sea* places that text within precisely this context, demonstrating how such social, cultural and medical transformations are intertextually reflected in the formal, rhetorical and narratological aspects of women's writing during this period. In the novels by women concerning 'mad intertextuality' during the 1960s it is no longer the female protagonist's 'double' who is mad but the protagonist herself. This transformation is immediately registered in the relationship between Brontë's and Rhys's texts. For Kaup, such a reversal of the conventions of plot and narrative voice:

> upsets narrative and ideological priorities. The sacrificial victim of *Jane Eyre* whose death by fire enables Jane Eyre's 'ascendancy' is granted the confessional first-person voice. Marginal – insane and colonial – experience is given the status of female 'heroism'.
>
> (Kaup, 1993: 93)

Kaup, then, demonstrates that only an approach which finds ways of relating the influence-relations between women writers with the intertextual spheres of social, cultural and ideological constructions of femininity, can possibly produce a method of reading which does not fall back into a binary opposition between men and women which ultimately reinforces patriarchal logic. However, we might still suggest that, dependent as she is on various combinations of gynocritical and poststructuralist theories and interpretive strategies, the question concerning the relationship between intertextuality and gender remains unresolved in her work.

The return of the female author

Nancy K. Miller's work can be placed broadly within the gynocritical approach. Miller argues that it remains important whether texts were written by men or women. Feminist criticism cannot, she argues, locate and describe gender differences within writing if it concentrates 'not [on] the productions signed by biological woman alone but [on] all productions that put the "feminine" into play – the feminine then being a modality or process accessible to both men and women' (Miller, 1988: 72). We have seen how Kristeva views writing and intertextuality in terms of a tension between phenotext and genotext. Given that the phenotext relates to dominant social discourses and structures, it can be directly related to patriarchy. As the genotext relates to the presocialized relationship between infant and mother, it is a force which seems related to the feminine. Such an opposition, which has been taken up by a host of feminist theorists, views the 'feminine' as a potential, if normally repressed, aspect of language and tends to locate its release not in texts specifically written by women but in avant-garde texts generally. Miller, however, asserts that the 'female signature' is important, and that approaches such as Kristeva's fall in with a trend within poststructuralism which implicitly collaborates with the effacement of women authors. Such poststructuralist effacement occurs, Miller argues, as part of wholesale rejection of notions of authorship.

Miller criticizes the kind of poststructuralist theory from which we have seen intertextuality emerging, since it produces a universalized vision incapable of attending to gender difference.

> The removal of the Author has not so much made room for a revision of the concept of authorship as it has, through a variety of rhetorical moves, repressed and inhibited discussion of any writing identity in favor of the (new) monolith of anonymous textuality, or, in Foucault's phrase, 'transcendental anonymity'.
>
> (Miller, 1988: 104)

Poststructuralist theories of language, textuality and intertextuality, Miller argues, deny the feminist critic the site upon which discussion of gender can be produced: that is, the authorial subject. Miller attacks the implicit universalism of poststructuralist textual theory, arguing that the woman writer's relation to language, literary tradition and the social production and reception of texts is historically different to that of men. Attention to gender, for a theorist such as Miller, disrupts any totalized description of language, textuality and, we might add, intertextuality:

> The postmodernist decision that the Author is Dead and the subject along within him does not ... necessarily hold for women, and prematurely forecloses the question of agency for them. Because women have not had the same historical relation of identity to origin, institution, production that men have had, they have not, I think, (collectively) felt burdened by *too much* Self, Ego, Cogito, etc. Because the female subject has juridically been excluded from the polis, hence decentered, 'disoriginated', deinstitutionalized, etc., her relation to integrity and textuality, desire and authority, displays structurally important differences from that universal position.
>
> (*ibid.*: 106)

Miller's position is recognizably gynocritical. Poststructural textual theory implies that it does not matter who writes and who reads; indeed, it suggests, writing and reading are the products not of human subjects but of writing and textuality themselves. However, for gynocritical theorists writing and reading are experienced and produced very differently depending on the gender of the subject who writes or reads.

Such points lead Miller, in her essay 'Arachnologies', to look with fresh eyes at the myths which stand behind the poststructuralist notions of text, textuality, and intertextuality. Citing *The Pleasure of the Text*, she reminds us of Barthes's foregrounding of the etymology of the term 'text' as connected to 'webs' and 'weaving'. Miller writes: 'Were we fond of neologisms, we might define the theory of the text as an *hyphology* (*hyphos* is the tissue and the spider's web)' (Barthes, quoted in Miller, 1988: 64).

Miller's problem with Barthes's move here is that in killing off the traditional figure of the author, not in itself a negative action, he also delegitimates 'other discussions of the writing (and reading) subject'. As she puts the point:

> This suppression is not simply the result of an arbitrary shift of emphasis: when a theory of the text called 'hyphology' chooses the spider's *web* over the spider; and the concept of textuality called the 'writerly' chooses the threads of lace over the lacemaker ... the subject is self-consciously erased by a model of text production which acts to foreclose the question of agency itself.
>
> (Miller, 1988: 80)

Theories such as those found in Barthes, according to Miller, participate in the eradication of the female subject. Taking a figure – of weaving and of spinning – culturally associated with female work and female identity, Barthes strips these figures of any signs of the female subject. In order to reverse such a trend, Miller takes her readers back to the classical myths which form the source of the etymologies utilized by Barthes. In the sixth book of Ovid's *Metamorphoses*, she reminds us, Arachne is the 'lowborn' daughter of a 'wool dyer'. So excellent is Arachne's weaving that people presume that Pallas Athena (Minerva) has taught her; but Arachne refuses to go along with such an assumption, thus implicitly challenging the authority of the goddess. Annoyed by this rebelliousness, Athena, disguised, challenges Arachne to a weaving competition. Arachne's tapestry is inflammatory in subject matter, depicting ancient heroines who were seduced or betrayed by the gods, so again she is challenging the authority of the gods. Athena punishes Arachne, mutilating her tapestry and knocking her on the head with a shuttle. When Arachne attempts suicide Athena takes pity and transforms her into a spider: Arachne becomes a virtually headless figure – sign of Athena's punishment – who is a perfect spinner of webs. Doomed to remain a spinner of webs, but now without the ability to make those webs signify, Arachne is doomed to remain, as Miller puts it, 'outside representation, to a reproduction that turns back on itself' (*ibid.*: 82). Spiders' webs may be immensely beautiful, but they are not art!

Miller's return to classical mythology and the origins of the symbolics of weaving and webs does not end here. Using, as a starting point, an essay by the deconstructive critic J. Hillis Miller, she also returns to the myth of Ariadne. We may remember that Ariadne, by holding one end of a spool of wool and giving the other to her beloved Theseus to unravel, allowed Theseus to enter the heart of the labyrinth constructed by Daedalus, to kill the Minotaur, and then to escape from the labyrinth again. Theseus later seduces Ariadne and then abandons her.

Hillis Miller's essay focuses on the relation between the two mythical female characters by way of Chaucer's conflation of their names in *Troilus and Cressida*; Chaucer there writes of: 'Ariachne's broken woof' (quoted in Hillis Miller, 1977: 91). What is the relation between Arachne and Ariadne? To simplify Miller's complex argument, Ariadne can be seen as a figure of interpretation, allowing the critic to enter into the labyrinthine web of the text and to exit from it again. Yet, as Miller goes on to suggest, Ariadne can come to stand for a female principle of interpretation, i.e. intertextual reading, which reinstates the male as critic and the female as merely a symbol or figure for reading (Miller, 1988: 93). Miller's point is that theories of intertextuality such as Barthes's have employed a whole mythology of weaving and making webs whilst, at the same moment, underplaying or even erasing those myths' connection to women's efforts to break into art. Without any attention to gender issues, theories of intertextuality threaten to consign women to figures in the position of Ariadne, who passively help male protagonists to enter and exit the labyrinth of textual meaning. Attention to the gender issues inscribed mythically within the notions of text and textuality can, Miller implies, return us to the figure of the defiant woman artist, as exemplified by Arachne. The difference between Arachne and Ariadne, Miller suggests, is that, whilst the latter is a figure of assistance to men, the former, at least before her punishment and metamorphosis, is a female artist who actually wins, in aesthetic terms, a competition or *agon* with a goddess, or 'phallic mother'.

Miller places such meditations in the context of Barthes's discussion of 'the already read'. We have seen how for Barthes intertextuality means that no text is ever read for the first time: all texts are already read. However, as Miller writes:

> Only the subject who is both self-possessed and possesses access to the library of the already read has the luxury of flirting with the escape from identity – like the loss of Arachne's 'head' – promised by an aesthetics of the decentered (decapitated, really) body.
>
> (Miller, 1988: 83)

Theories of text and intertextuality such as Barthes's, Miller argues, efface women writers and women's writing by arguing for a general de-authored textuality and for an aesthetic of the already read that historically has been available only to privileged male readers. Against such a theoretical position and rhetoric, Miller offers us Arachne, as the female artist, and an aesthetics of 'over-reading', an interpretive practice which looks for signs within the text of the female subject. As she puts it:

> the latter project involves reading women's writing not 'as if it had already been read', but as if it had never been read; *as if* for the first time. (This assumption has the added advantage of being generally true.) Overreading also involves a focus on the moments in the narrative which by their representation of writing itself might be said to figure the production of the female artist.
>
> (*ibid.*: 83)

Whilst not calling for a return to the god-like author, Miller argues for a return to a specifically female writing subject. Text and intertextuality must not be defined, that is, in a generalized way which presumes that writing and reading for women is identical to the process by which men write and read. Male critics may well be in a position to generalize about the lack of a subject in writing; such a position, however, makes little sense to feminist critics searching for adequate theories and for a retrieval of a grossly under-represented tradition.

Whilst Miller's argument here is a timely reminder of the gendered nature of the concept of intertextuality, and whilst her insistence on the need to return to the subject of writing is generally representative of recent feminist moves, it might be said that she leaves no actual room for a feminist theory of text and intertextuality itself. Reading 'for the first time' surely denies the intertextual dimension of our reading. It is difficult to understand what a 'first-time reading' might be, once we have accepted at least some of the principal theoretical moves by which the concepts of text and intertextuality enter our vocabulary. We might argue that Miller cannot move towards an 'over-reading' which eschews the notion of the 'already read', without bringing into her account a host of male critical texts which, although they may be criticized, clearly stand as mediating inter-texts for the women's writing she rightly describes as woefully under-read. It would seem that we need some additional account of the relation between women writers and the intertextual before we can begin to perform the kinds of readings which Miller proposes. Many feminist theorists have found such an account by returning to the theoretical work of Bakhtin.

THE RETURN TO BAKHTIN: FEMINISM AND POSTCOLONIALISM

At the end of her essay, 'Feminist Criticism in the Wilderness' (Showalter (ed.), 1986: 243–70), Showalter criticizes those forms of feminist criticism which seek a women's writing, an *écriture féminine*, totally outside dominant patriarchal discourse. Such a female space of discourse, a 'wild zone' of feminine utterance and writing, is, Showalter argues, unavailable and a distraction from the real task of locating and fostering women's writing and an active female subjecthood in patriarchal society. She writes:

> The concept of a woman's text in the wild zone is a playful abstraction: in the reality to which we must address ourselves as critics, women's writing is a 'double-voiced discourse' that always embodies the social, literary, and cultural heritage of both the muted and the dominant.
>
> (Showalter (ed.), 1986: 263)

The employment of Bakhtin's notion of 'double-voiced discourse' is significant here. It allows a critical focus which can capture the 'otherness' of women's writing within patriarchal culture and society. A recognition of the dialogic, double-voiced nature of discourse, allows Showalter and other feminists to cease in the exploration of a wholly 'other' tradition of writing, and to begin exploring the manner in which the writing of women, along with other marginalized groups, is always a mixture of available discursive possibilities. As she writes:

> there are muted groups other than women; a dominant structure may determine many muted structures. A black American woman poet, for example, would have her literary identity formed by the dominant (white male) tradition, by a muted women's culture, and by a muted black culture. She would be affected by both sexual and racial politics in a combination unique to her case.
>
> (*ibid.*: 254)

The desire to resist the poststructuralist effacement of the writing subject, whilst not returning to a model of authorship in which meaning is generated by a god-like, male authority figure, seems best served by a return to Bakhtinian notions. Women's lives within society, like the lives of colonial subjects, are inevitably fractured or divided. Seen as 'other', as mute, objectified and outside of discourse, the dominant male and dominant white culture, women subjects, along with colonial subjects, write within and yet against such an 'othering' process.

Whilst Bakhtin cannot be claimed as a feminist theorist, women and women's writing being conspicuously absent in his work, his concepts of the carnivalesque, of *heteroglossia*, of double-voiced discourse, and of the dialogic as opposed to the monological principle within language, are of great assistance in articulating the manner in which the 'othered' subject speaks, writes and reads. Dale M. Bauer in her *Feminist Dialogics: A Theory of Failed Community*, argues that Bakhtin can be 'an empowering model' for women writers and readers. Looking at notions of community within novels by Nathaniel Hawthorne, Henry James, Edith Wharton and Kate Chopin, Bauer takes up Bakhtin's description of the polyphonic novel and describes how characters within these novels learn to see themselves and the process of their own social construction through the language of others. Such female characters, 'othered' by the social discourse, can be linked, Bauer argues, to the carnivalesque figure of the Fool: a figure the critic Mary Russo has also discussed in terms of Bakhtin, feminism and the construction of women's identity within society (Russo, 1986). For such 'naïve' characters, Bauer argues: 'Stupidity (a form of resistance) forces the unspoken repressions into the open, thus making them vulnerable to interpretation, contradiction and dialogue' (Bauer, 1988: 11). Such female characters, finding their own identities constructed by the language of others, can be linked to the feminist reader. Both female character and feminist reader question the monological discourse dominant in society and articulated by specific characters, and thus move from a position Showalter calls 'mutedness' to an exposure of resistant, un-official, alternative discourses and subject positions. In so doing, character and reader release the dialogic play of languages previously repressed. The effect is to expose not only the fact that the self, in Bakhtin's terms, is always a product of the discourse of an other, but also to display the dialogic nature of identity itself. As Bauer argues, for those characters who are alienated and 'confused' by society, who find themselves in the position of the carnivalesque 'Fool', it becomes crucial to interpret the discourses and discursive structures which others in positions of power take as monologically unquestionable.

'Reading,' she writes, 'is an activity that by definition takes place only when one confronts the unfamiliar, the strange, the other which requires deciphering or dialogicization' (*ibid.*: 162).

Such points can be related more particularly to concepts of intertextuality, if we move to an influential essay by Patricia S. Yaeger, entitled '"Because a Fire Was in My Head", Eudora Welty and the Dialogic Imagination'. Developing an account of women writers as inevitably involved in 'plagiarism', Yaeger also turns to the Bakhtinian account of the polyphonic, dialogic novel: 'Since language,' she writes, quoting Bakhtin, 'is "over-populated with the intentions of others"', the novelist has at his or her disposal only those words that are already qualified, already inscribed by others; writing occurs within a hostile linguistic environment' (Yaeger, 1984: 957). Yaeger, in a manner she connects to the work of Showalter and Nancy K. Miller, uses Bakhtinian dialogism to explore women's writing as a resistance to patriarchal monologism. The resistance centres on a recognition of 'othering' which is clearly connected to notions of intertextuality and to double-voiced discourse. As Yaeger writes:

> Showalter is right to insist that theories of women's creativity must address the intersections of different kinds of discourse in women's writing, since the best feminocentric writing will be not only in conflict but also in dialogue with the dominant ideologies it is trying to dislodge.
>
> (Yaeger, 1984: 959)

Yaeger's example comes in Eudora Welty's appropriation of Yeats's poetry. In particular she employs Welty's collection of stories, *The Golden Apples*, to demonstrate the manner in which Yeats's poetry is intertextually inscribed but also revised, realigned and challenged by Welty's characters. Welty, she argues, uses 'Yeats's language as a form of "otherness"', only in order to expropriate it, 'to make it articulate her own point of view' (*ibid.*: 959). Bringing the work of Kristeva and Bakhtin together, Yaeger argues that Welty's use of Yeats's poetry takes the signifieds of certain Yeatsian images and reincorporates them, in *The*

Golden Apples, as new signifiers, thus establishing 'a distance between the incorporated text and its initial meaning ... [opening
the] text to another point of view' (*ibid.*: 962).

The principle inter-text for Welty's collection, Yaeger argues,
is Yeats's 'Song of the Wandering Aengus'. This poem: 'tells the
story of a man driven by the "fire" in his mind to seek an object
equal to his desire. He finds this object in "a glimmering girl/
With apple blossom in her hair/ Who called me by my name and
ran/ And faded through the brightening air"'. The poet, un-
daunted, quests after the girl's 'echoing image', and Yaeger cites
the following lines of the poem:

> Though I am old with wandering
> Through hollow lands and hilly lands,
> I will find out where she has gone,
> And kiss her lips and take her hands;
> And walk among long dappled grass,
> And pluck till time and times are done
> The silver apples of the moon
> The golden apples of the sun.

> (quoted in Yaeger, 1984: 959)

Welty's text, Yaeger argues, gives us various female figures
who not only stand for the female other as depicted in Yeats's
poem but who also, in having their own narratives and quests for
identity, challenge the patriarchal discourse in which female figures are idealized 'others' by themselves taking up the questing
role classically viewed as essentially male. By a subtle use of intertextual echo and quotation of Yeats's poem Welty challenges
the monological discourse of male quester and female other by
having her own female characters at different moments occupy
both male and female discursive positions. As Yaeger writes:

> in *The Golden Apples* [Welty] has invented a complement of [female]
> characters who replicate even as they relativize the patterns of Yeats's
> poetry. She achieves this primarily by giving the figure of Yeats's glim-
> mering girl a literary if not a social status equal to that of Yeats's

> wanderer ... she ... alters the poem's context and its meaning by in-
> sisting that Yeats's poem has two protagonists and that each protago-
> nist incarnates a different aspect of woman's story.
>
> (Yaeger, 1984: 962)

Yeats's poem, which monologically argues for a gender divide in which men are questing protagonists and women passive others symbolizing the ideal, is used by Welty to capture the double nature of her female characters, both socially 'other' and yet protagonists of their own search for identity.

Such a sense of the double nature of women's identity in society and thus of women's writing is clearly related to the social positions postcolonial theorists have sought to describe, as a reference to the title of the Frantz Fanon's classic 1950s text of postcolonial theory, *Black Skin, White Masks*, can attest. Again, in this context, a return to Bakhtin helps retain not only the notion of subjecthood, of the struggle for identity and agency, but also that of the inevitably 'double-voiced' or intertextual nature of the speech and writing of such marginalized, 'othered' subjects.

At the beginning of his book *The Location of Culture*, Homi K. Bhabha takes up the often monologic use of notions such as nationality, race, class and gender and asks a series of rhetorical questions designed to foreground the fact that modern subjects exist 'in-between' such terms:

> How are subjects formed 'in-between', or in excess of, the sum of the
> 'parts' of difference (usually intoned as race/ class/ gender, etc.)?
> How do strategies of representation or empowerment come to be for-
> mulated in the competing claims of communities where, despite
> shared histories of deprivation and discrimination, the exchange of
> values, meanings and priorities may not always be collaborative and
> dialogical, but may be profoundly antagonistic, conflictual and even
> incommensurate?
>
> (Bhabha, 1994: 2)

Bhabha's questions not only refer to the 'double' or 'in-between' position of postcolonial subjects, they also suggest that the term 'dialogue' requires to be understood in a Bakhtinian sense. Dialogism does not necessarily mean a 'conversation' between subjects equally empowered within the language game; it refers, more specifically, to a clash between languages and utterances which can foreground not only social division but a radically divided space of discursive formations within an individual subject. An African-American woman writer, as suggested earlier, may find herself the 'subject' of competing discourses which it is not possible simply to resolve. Such a subject's utterances are certainly 'double-voiced', if not 'triple-voiced', and a clash between dominant and repressed discourses may well exist within them. Bhabha's most influential term for such a radically split experience of 'being in discourse' is *hybridity*: 'a difference "within", a subject that inhabits the rim of an "in-between"' reality' (*ibid.*: 13). On this basis, beyond any possibility of a shared community or even a stand-off between mutually exclusive group positions, postcolonial criticism's focus seems highly intertextual, exploring: 'the more complex cultural and political boundaries that exist on the cusp of ... often opposed political spheres' (*ibid.*: 173). The postcolonial writer, in other words, like the woman writer we have been analysing, exists as a 'split' subject whose utterances are always 'double-voiced', their own and yet replete with an 'otherness' which we can associate with a socially oriented notion of intertextuality.

Aldon L. Nielsen, in his *Writing Between the Lines: Race and Intertextuality*, clarifies these points by returning his readers to the history of the enforced acquisition of the English language by the black slaves upon whom was built the modern United States of America. In a manner connectable to Bhabha's notion of hybridity, Nielsen demonstrates that the situation in the States presents us not simply with the African-American acquisition of English language, but equally the influence upon American English of an African-American revision, appropriation and transformation of English into new forms and styles:

> each attempt to draw borders within the language of race and to
> establish ownership of a territory encounters and is countered by the

already-in-place deterritorializing language of the other. America's mulatto past, though nearly invisible in the political discourse of the late twentieth century, is continually disseminated within its language. Each speaking subject speaks a language of racial difference and amalgamation.

(Nielsen, 1994: 78)

We find, as Nielsen suggests, that it is white American writing which lags behind the black American author's long-held recognition of the necessity to speak with what the black American theorist W. E. B. Du Bois styled 'double consciousness'. Mary O'Connor cites a pertinent passage from Du Bois's 1918 text *Souls of Black Folk*. Du Bois writes of the 'peculiar sensation' of 'double consciousness', 'always looking at one's self through the eyes of others, of measuring one's soul by the tape of a world that looks on in amused contempt and pity'. Du Bois continues: 'One ever feels his two-ness – an American, a Negro; two souls, two thoughts, two unreconciled strivings; two warring ideals in one dark body, whose dogged strength alone keeps it from being torn asunder' (quoted in O'Connor, 1991: 202).

Nielsen's argument leads not to the segregation of traditions into 'African' and 'American' but an explicit recognition that those traditions are woven into each other and that no author writes a language which does not display this intertextual, double-voiced condition. A combination of Kristeva's intertextual theory, particularly her account of a transposition of the thetic position within writing, and a return to Bakhtinian notions of double-voiced discourse and the dialogic resistance to monological positions, leads Nielsen to a positive model of reading in which 'language is at once our own and other' (Nielsen, 1994: 26). Such an intertextual approach returns us to the writing subject, now viewed as a 'palimpsestic self' always in the process of being constructed, and thus always able to form resistances to monological definitions of racial identity which would deny the dialogic, intertextual 'in-betweenness' of the writing self.

Perhaps the most impressive example of postcolonial theory's return to Bakhtin comes in the work of Henry Louis Gates, Jr. At the beginning of his seminal work *The Signifying Monkey* (1988), Gates refers to the danger for African-American theory and criticism of an unquestioning deployment of Eurocentric theoretical models. African-American criticism, indeed, has impressive theoretical antecedents of its own. Having made that point, however, Gates's work is still significantly influenced by Bakhtinian theory, although reinterpreted via the traditions of black writing his work maps out. Explaining the role of such traditional trickster figures as Esu-Elegbara originating in the Yoruba cultures of Nigeria, Benin, Brazil, Cuba and Haiti (Gates, 1988: xxi), along with the figure of the Signifying Monkey, and central black tropes such as the Talking Book, Gates develops an account of what he terms 'Signifyin(g)': 'a metaphor for formal revision, or intertextuality, within the Afro-American literary tradition' (*ibid.*: xxi). 'Signifyin(g)' represents the peculiar relation African-American writers have with regard to Standard English and the vernacular of black American speech. Like Derrida's term *différance*, 'Signifyin(g)' exemplifies the features and processes of language to which it refers. If 'signification' in Standard English, functioning on a horizontal plane of language, can be seen as a signifier pointing towards a signified, then 'Signifyin(g)' represents a vertical revision and rhetorical play with standard signifieds, turning them into new signifiers. 'Signifyin(g)', in other words, is an act which opens up supposedly closed, unquestionable significations (relations between signifiers and signifieds) to a host of associated meanings any monological view of language would wish to efface. Gates explains:

> Signifyin(g) operates and can be represented on a paradigmatic or vertical axis. Signifyin(g) concerns itself with that which is suspended, vertically: the chaos of what Saussure calls 'associative relations', which we can represent as the playful puns on a word that occupy the paradigmatic axis of language and which a speaker draws on for figurative substitutions. These substitutions in Signifyin(g) tend to be humorous or function to name a person or a situation in a telling manner. Whereas signification depends for order and coherence on the exclusion of unconscious associations which any given word

> yields at any given time, Signification [or Signifyin(g)] luxuriates in the inclusion of the freeplay of these associative rhetorical and semantic relations.
>
> (Gates, 1988: 49)

Gates spends considerable time recounting the traditions of the figure of Esu-Elegbara, who, with his two mouths, symbolizes plurality. He also explores various African-American traditions of rhetorical word play including the 'dozens' in which speakers ritually 'Signify' and make fun of each other. The result is a complex picture of a set of myths and practices which produce a notion of language, embodied by the term 'Signifyin(g)', which is essentially double-voiced in Bakhtin's sense.

The core of Gates's argument is that African-American writing is double-voiced and self-consciously intertextual in its relation to both Standard English and a black vernacular discourse which historically has been turned into 'non-speech' by Eurocentric, white cultural values. Gates demonstrates how Western Enlightenment values associate rationality with the ability to read and write. Such abilities are measured in Western culture by their performance in a standard, Western (white) manner. Western culture associates Standard Usage, whether it be English, Dutch or French, with a culture of writing and reading, whilst it associates the black vernacular with speech, a form of language outside of writing and its interpretation.

The struggle of black subjects to enter into Western literary culture is, Gates demonstrates, intensely connected to the recurring trope of the Talking Book. This trope embodies for Gates the problem facing black subjects since the arrival of slavery: 'how can the black subject posit a full and sufficient self in a language in which blackness is a sign of absence?' (*ibid.*: 169). Working through a series of slave narratives in which black characters, sometimes miraculously, learn to read Western writing, Gates demonstrates, as he puts it: 'the extent of intertextuality and presupposition at work in the first discrete period of Afro-American literary history'. Far from being isolated oddities, these early slave narratives already exhibit a highly sophisticated tradi-

tion of writing. However, this recovery of an in itself deeply intertextual tradition of black slave writing, helps to foreground a
more general issue which grounds Gates's subsequent treatment
of twentieth-century African-American literature and demonstrates:

> the curious tension between the black vernacular and the literate
> white text, between the spoken and the written word, between the oral
> and the printed form of literary discourse ... represented and thema-
> tized in black letters at least since slaves and ex-slaves met the chal-
> lenge of the Enlightenment to their humanity by literally writing
> themselves into being through carefully crafted representations in
> language of the black self.
>
> (Gates, 1988: 131)

The double-voicedness of African-American writing, according
to Gates, remains deeply rooted in the tension between standard
(English) writing and the non-standard oral traditions of black
communities. To enter (white) writing does one have to sacrifice
black speech? Gates's analysis of a number of twentieth-century
African-American authors explores the way in which such a question has been answered in dialogic, double-voiced ways.

Zora Neale Hurston's novel, *Their Eyes Were Watching God*
(1937), begins by foregrounding the difference between standard
writing and the speech of its black characters. The novel opens
with its third-person narrator writing in a manner perfectly assimilated into the literary form of Standard English:

> Ships at a distance have every man's wish on board. For some they
> come in with the tide. For others they sail forever on the horizon,
> never out of sight, never landing until the Watcher turns his eyes away
> in resignation, his dreams mocked to death by Time. That is the life of
> men.
>
> (Hurston, 1986: 9)

As soon as we move to the speech of the characters, however, we
move to the written rendition of essentially oral language:

'What she doin' coming back here in dem overalls? Can't she find no dress to put on? – Where's dat blue satin dress she left here in? – What all dat money her husband took and died and left her? – What dat ole forty year ole 'oman doin' wid her hair swingin' down her back lak some young gal? Where she left dat young lad of a boy she went off here wid? Thought she was going to marry? – Where he left *her*? – What he done wid all her money? – Betcha he off wid some gal so young she ain't even got no hairs – why she don't stay in her class? –'.

(*ibid.*: 10)

These remarks concern the return to the town of the novel's female protagonist, Janie. The first words we hear from her are also a written rendition of oral speech: 'Ah, pretty good, Ah'm tryin' to soak some uh de tiredness and de dirt outa mah feet' (*ibid.*: 14). Gates, with one eye on Barthes's categories in *S/Z*, styles Hurston's novel a 'speakerly text', which he defines as:

a text whose rhetorical strategy is designed to represent an oral literary tradition, designed 'to emulate the phonetic, grammatical, and lexical patterns of actual speech and produce the "illusion of oral narration".' The speakerly text is that text in which all other structural elements seem to be devalued, as important as they remain to the telling of the tale, because the narrative strategy signals attention to its own importance, an importance which would seem to be the privileging of oral speech and its inherent linguistic features.

(Gates, 1988: 181)

Such a 'speakerly text' exemplifies Bakhtinian notions, since the 'voice' of the novel's characters does not simply express a 'point of view' but also contains an 'otherness' within it; that is, the presence of a tradition of black speech patterns and genres. However, Hurston's novel does not simply give a written voice to black oral tradition. Gates demonstrates the manner in which, as Janie comes to self-consciousness and a more empowered state of identity, the narrator's standard 'writerly' voice and the 'speakerly' voice of the novel's protagonist begin to merge in a free indirect discourse in which we cannot always know the point of view being represented: the narrator's, or Janie's, or both? In such moments, Gates asserts: *'Their Eyes Were Watching God* resolves that implicit tension between standard English and black dialect, the two voices that function as verbal counterpoints in the text's opening paragraphs' (*ibid.*: 192). Such a blending of distinctly *writerly* and *speakerly* voices, Gates argues, produces for the first time in African-American literary tradition a resolution of the cardinal challenge facing African-American authors. The resolution is characteristically double-voiced, merging without negating white and black discourses into what might be styled a hybrid voice beyond any notion of singular or stable identity.

Gates's work, however, is concerned to do justice to the tensions and accommodations between socially recognizable discourses and to the influences and shared patterns of imagery, tropes and strategies between specific texts within that tradition. To recognize that feature of his work, we need also to refer to his analysis of Alice Walker's more recent novel, *The Color Purple*. Walker has frequently asserted the influence of Hurston on her writing, and her famous novel of 1983 mirrors Hurston's in following the passage towards self-consciousness in its female protagonist Celie. The important point for Gates is that Walker's novel, by reversing the formal strategy pursued by Hurston, 'signifies' upon Hurston's novel. Whilst Hurston, as Gates puts it, creates a 'speakerly text' in which black dialect is given a form of written life, Walker takes a 'spoken or mimetic voice' and places it within the written form of an epistolary novel. As he states:

> Whereas Hurston represents Janie's discovery of her voice as the enunciation of her own doubled self through a free indirect 'narrative of division', Walker represents Celie's growth of self-consciousness as an act of writing. Janie and her narrator speak themselves into being; Celie, in her letters, writes herself into being ... Celie ... never speaks; rather, she writes her speaking voice and that of everyone who speaks to her.

> (Gates, 1988: 243)

Celie's written voice is, as Gates shows, a complex mix of a 'dominated and undereducated adolescent' and 'a remarkably reflective and sensitive teller, or writer' capable of rendering the speech and thoughts of others within her writing voice. In this sense Walker's novel seems to evidence a growing confidence in the African-American women's literary tradition. It presents a single character with a voice capable of producing that synthesis of self and other, of dialect speech and written language, previously divided, in Hurston's work. Celie's double-voiced writing, which contains within it not only her own and all other characters' speech, but also the tradition of the African-American people's struggle to find identity between imposed and self-designed linguistic forms, is a testament to the radically intertextual nature of black American writing. It demonstrates the achievement of self-enlightenment within rather than outside of or in transcendence of a hybrid, multiracial and multivoiced environment. As Mary O'Connor states, writing of the climactic moment of the novel in which Celie asserts her independence from her husband, Celie's agency is established not simply because of her decision to speak out for herself, but also because of her friend and lover's, Shug Avery's, recognition of that speech (O'Connor, 1991: 205). As Bakhtin argues, identity is only ever achieved in relation to another, an addressee who in answering speech affirms the subject's dialogic existence:

> I'll fix her wagon! say Mr. _, and spring toward me.
>
> A dust devil flew up on the porch between us, fill my mouth with dirt. The dirt say, Anything you do to me, already done to you.
>
> Then I feel Shug shake me. Celie, she say. And I come to myself.
>
> I'm pore, I'm black, I may be ugly and can't cook, a voice say to everything listening. But I'm here.
>
> Amen, say Shug. Amen, amen.
>
> (Walker, 1983: 176)

Gates's study is a testament to the manner in which critics

have reworked the concept of intertextuality to deal with material very different from the avant-garde and classic realist texts which formed the immediate focus of the term's first theorists and practitioners. It also highlights the seminal place Bakhtin holds within such rearticulations of intertextual theory. As we move on to the non-literary arts and to discussions of Postmodernism, redefinition and the persistence of Bakhtinian theory will be confirmed as fundamental to intertextual theory and practice.

5

POSTMODERN CONCLUSIONS

INTERTEXTUALITY IN THE NON-LITERARY ARTS

Intertextuality, as a term, has not been restricted to discussions of the literary arts. It is found in discussions of cinema, painting, music, architecture, photography and in virtually all cultural and artistic productions. Despite the common-sense association between literature and the word 'text', we need only remember the connection between the early articulations of intertextual theory and the development of Saussure's notions concerning semiology to make intertextuality's use in studies of non-literary art forms understandable. In the *Course on General Linguistics*, Saussure looked forward to a new science, semiotics, which would study 'the life of signs within society' (Saussure, 1974: 16). It is possible to speak of the 'languages' of cinema, painting or architecture: languages which involve productions of complex patterns of encoding, re-encoding, allusion, echo, transposing of previous systems and codes. To interpret a painting or a building we inevitably rely on an ability to interpret that painting's or building's relationship to previous 'languages' or 'systems' of painting or architectural design. Films, symphonies, buildings, paintings, just like literary texts, constantly talk to each other as well as talking to the other arts.

Many critics welcome the availability of intertextuality as a term and argue for its positive advantage over more established terms in their field. J. Michael Allsen, for example, compares favourably the term's potentiality for musicology and prefers it to more established musicological references to 'imitation' and 'borrowing' (Allsen, 1993: 175). Robert S. Hatten takes this further by exploring the manner in which a composer's competence in particular musical styles and that same composer's strategic utilization of those styles in particular musical pieces constitute 'regulators of relevant intertextual relationships' (Hatten, 1985: 70). In this sense, whilst styles represent the available building blocks for the composer, music's version of the 'already written', strategies represent the composer's ability to transpose such styles into original compositions. As Hatten puts it:

> Strategies, to the extent they exceed complete formalization or simple predictability, assert a work's individuality even as they rely upon a style for intelligibility. Thus, a given work will typically be in and of a style, while playing with or against it strategically.
>
> (Hatten, 1985: 58)

Keith A. Reader points to the fact that intertextuality can be utilized, in the context of cinema, to examine a phenomenon like the Hollywood star system. As he writes:

> The very concept of the film *star* is an intertextual one, relying as it does on correspondences of similarity and difference from one film to the next, and sometimes too on supposed resemblances between on- and off-screen personae. Thus, Sergio Leone's *Once Upon a Time in the West* ironically inverts Henry Fonda's normal heroic role to make of him a particularly sadistic villain; Mike Nichols's *Who's Afraid of Virginia Woolf?* exploits parallels between the stormy domestic life of George and Martha on screen and that of Richard Burton and Elizabeth Taylor off it.
>
> (Reader, 1990: 176)

A recognition of the intertextuality of performance can equally be made of theatrical productions (see Carlson, 1994), and can foreground the potential intertextual connections between literary and non-literary forms; even perhaps reaffirming our sense of drama as a form lying between literary and non-literary art.

Intertextuality can often radically challenge established accounts of non-literary art forms. Wendy Steiner refers to the fact that, since painting appears to have an immediacy unavailable to other art forms more dependent upon an unfolding over time, this art form's 'a-temporality' has 'given rise to the naïve view of painting as a mirror of nature, a perfect equivalent of a visual field, a complete vision of the beautiful' (Steiner, 1985: 57). Such received ideas, Steiner goes on, can lead to assumptions that painting stands beyond semiology, or that it cannot 'mean' anything more than its own immediate appearance. Whilst the temporal arts are capable of negating or critiquing older points, or of proposing new ones, painting, so such an idea would have it, presents a pure form of representation beyond propositional or critical meaning. Intertextuality, for Steiner, offers a useful way to refute such naïve ideas. As she writes:

> It is only by viewing paintings in light of other paintings or works of literature, music, and so forth that the 'missing' semiotic power of pictorial art can be augmented – which is to say that the power is not missing at all, but merely absent in the conventional account of the structure of the art.
>
> (Steiner, 1985: 58)

As Steiner shows, the intertextual features of painting can take us from the manner in which some paintings, as in diptychs and triptychs, are completed by others, on to 'quotation' by painters of culturally recognizable styles of earlier schools or individual artists. The ability of painters to parody styles and gestures suggests a profound intertextual level to the pictorial arts. Modernist painting, with its tendency towards collage, the mixing of different media, and the use of 'found material', might extend this sense of painting's facility for intertextual expression.

Furthermore, as Steiner suggests, the tendency for paintings to be collected into exhibitions involves the pictorial arts in a kind of random intertextuality which radically affects their reception. Decisions as to what paintings are to hang together, or what paintings to reproduce within a book, set up relations between individual paintings which normally could not have been part of their original design and intention.

The idea of intertextuality can produce a similar rethinking of photography, often seen as a pure representation of reality. Recent photographic artists and critics have argued that the meaning of the photographic image depends upon its deployment of and its viewers' recognition of established codes and conventions. Cindy Sherman employs recognizable styles and specific visual inter-texts from painting, photography and film to portray her own image. Such a practice not only makes plain the intertextual nature of the photographic image but serves also to make points about the construction of female identity within culture's network of available visual codes.

Barbara Kruger's mixing of image and text exploits the tension between photography's apparent unmediated capturing of the real world and its dependence on established codes, genres and conventions. Linda Hutcheon, in her account of Postmodern photography, refers to the manner in which artists such as Kruger and Victor Burgin centre their art on an exploration of this tension. She refers to Burgin's 'Possession' with its romantic image of a man and woman kissing. In the top part of the border which surrounds the picture a text reads: 'What does possession mean to you?' A text in the bottom part of the border reads: '7% of our population own 84% of our wealth' (see Hutcheon, 1989: 122; see Walker, 1994: 113 for a reproduction). In Kruger's 'We are your circumstantial evidence', an image of a woman's face is built up in segments. The face is surrounded by other segments of photography, mainly displaying what could be seen as beads, pills or sequins. The text is laid word by word over the constructed image so that it forms a central spine from top to bottom (for a reproduction, see Wallis, 1984: 415).

Burgin and Kruger, through such combinations of text and

image, employ codes from advertising and other commercial sides of modern life to unsettle the photographic image's *doxa*, its apparent naturalness and transparency. They do this by foregrounding various culturally encoded contexts and by mixing codes, from 'high' art and from popular and commercial contexts, usually separated from each other (see Hutcheon, 1989: 135).

This practice, which brings a recognition of photography's intertextual codedness to bear on the dissemination of ideology within modern media is demonstrated by turning to Loraine Leeson's and Peter Dunn's photomurals, the most widely discussed being their 'The Changing Picture of Docklands'. Working for the East London Health Project, and backed by the Trades Council and other local political groups, Leeson and Dunn produced a series of posters on six poster sites in London's Docklands area which mixed visual images with texts styled on advertising slogans and on the more discursive form of political pamphlets (Leeson and Dunn, 1986: 102–18). The posters, which were successively changed, present a combination of image and text which 'unfold[s] an argument through time' (Hutcheon, 1989: 106). The first poster, with the banner text 'What's Going On Behind Our Backs', presents the question spray-painted onto a corrugated iron fence behind which the viewer can see an idealized cityscape of tower blocks made of coins. The next poster, 'Big Money Is Moving In', unveils more of the cityscape, the third displays it in full, complete with towering blocks of money, and the sub-text: 'Don't Let It Push Out Local People'. The next two posters develop the image, showing people being dropped into a land-fill site which rises up to obscure the tower-blocks. The last two images present the gradual shattering of these images of 'big money' by what in the last poster becomes a utopian image of local people celebrating in a municipal park.

Intertextuality is an illuminating concept to bring to a reading of this photomural series, since the work utilizes a number of culturally significant codes and conventions and also refers as a text to the environment within which it is displayed. The combination of image and texts depending on genres such as advertising and political pamphlets produces a field of signification which redeploys the principal media which the London Docklands Development Corporation also deploy: advertising, promotional literature, the sound-bite, the business slogan. The posters thus make visible the ideological messages of big business. They also transpose the 'languages' by which those messages are disseminated and do so within the very geographical sites they target. Leeson and Dunn's work is intertextual on the level of genre and code, or 'language', but it is also intertextual in its social situatedness. Their posters exposed the fact that the Docklands area of London was a text, the meaning of which was being disputed during the 1980s. Their combining of different cultural codes, visual and textual, exemplifies the manner in which modern art utilizes intertextual techniques to demonstrate the ideological nature of modes of communication which dominant culture and state power frequently assert to be neutral, transparent, and even natural. As Hutcheon argues, such practices are in tune with Barthes's association of the intertextually explicit text with a critique of what he calls *doxa* (Hutcheon, 1989: 3). They are also in tune with Bakhtinian notions of the social situatedness of art and the deployment of already existent discourses, or what he calls speech genres.

Intertextuality can also be seen as connected to a developing trend within twentieth-century art to incorporate 'real objects' into painting. The use of bits of wallpaper, string, postage stamps, within, for example, a Cubist design, incorporates segments of the physical world into the pictorial image only, paradoxically, to unsettle the notion of painting's realistic representation of the world.

Discussions of cinema have frequently explored kinds of intertextuality across artistic boundaries. T. Jefferson Kline's *Screening the Text: Intertextuality and the New Wave French Cinema*, for example, looks at the manner in which film-makers such as Jean-Luc Godard, Robert Bresson, Alain Resnais and others associated with New Wave movement, refer to and yet simultaneously repress literary inter-texts. Kline employs intertextuality in order to demonstrate how in the French New Wave we can read a specific approach to cinema's characteristic ambivalence towards the literary tradition. Literary texts, in that movement, function as ways of authorizing artistic, cultural and even ideological positions whilst at the same time being repressed or 'screened off' in the films themselves. As others have suggested, this is a recognizable element of film. As a new and popular form of artistic production, cinema has, from its earliest days, relied on the established and 'serious' form of literature to provide it with cultural value. Adapting literary texts relates the new form of cinema to a universally recognized aesthetic field. As Kline demonstrates, however, more recent 'high art' forms of cinema repress as much as they continue to rely on that intertextual connection with literature.

Kline, then, reminds us of the deeply-rooted intertextual relationship between film and literature; a relationship also inscribed, as Bruce Fleming has argued, in terms of a tension between film and original film-script (Fleming, 1994: 127–39). This is not at all to suggest that modern cinema remains subservient to literature. Many analyses of cinema demonstrate the manner in which literary traditions are radically transposed within the medium. Anne Marie Miraglia has explored how Jacques Poulin's *Volkswagen Blues* punctuates its representation of a physical journey across Canada and the United States with intertextual references to literary texts from those two countries. The film not only merges a literal and a textual journey across Canada and the United States, it also foregrounds how place is itself textualized, the places represented always already being part of a received textual map.

James Goodwin's study of the films of Akira Kurosawa draws the two strains of intertextuality together when he explores Kurosawa's place in the intertextual history of the Western film genre and the manner in which Kurosawa transposes into contemporary culture the tragedies of Shakespeare. The first instance takes us from the early Hollywood Westerns of John Ford, Howard Hawks and others, through Kurosawa's *jidai-geki* (period drama) films, with their anti-hero played by Toshiro Mifune, on to Sergio Leone's successful transpositions of Kurosawa's style in the 'Spaghetti Westerns', starring Clint Eastwood, which he made in the 1960s and 1970s. This intertextual chain demonstrates the hybridity, the crossing of Japanese and US cultures, involved in Kurosawa's and Leone's contributions to the Western. Kurosawa's later films, *Throne of Blood* and *Ran*, however, transpose Shakespearean tragedies such as *Macbeth* and *King Lear* into a modern cultural setting, by presenting his audience with tragedies denuded of any form of heroism.

Postmodernism and intertextuality

At the present time, any discussion of the place of intertextuality within the arts leads us towards the issue of Postmodernism. Ours, it appears, is a Postmodern age. Unlike poststructuralism, with which it is often compared, Postmodernism is a term which is employed by many to refer to the current historical, social and cultural epoch. Poststructuralism, in this sense, would merely be an aspect of the Postmodern era. The idea of Postmodernism is clearly a vast subject. It might be useful for us, however, to recognize the contested nature of the term. Postmodernism has been the subject of great debate over the last two decades; it is itself a dialogic word with various negative and positive connotations.

Walter Benjamin's often cited essay 'The Work of Art in the Age of Mechanical Reproduction' is a useful reference point in any discussion of these negative and positive approaches to Postmodernism (Benjamin, 1968: 217–51). Benjamin, writing in 1930s Germany, referred to the manner in which modern modes of technological production and reproduction have shattered previous ideas concerning the aesthetic value of the work of art. In particular the technological world shatters and disseminates the 'aura' of the work. In an age before the mass publication of books, possession of an individual text was extremely rare and of enormous value. The prices still paid for original classic paintings also attest a residual attachment in contemporary society to the aura of the original work of art. Technological society, however, is dominated by reproductions of original works. The signed copy of the novel may be preferable to the unsigned copy, an original painting by Van Gogh may seem priceless, attendance at a dance performance may seem preferable to viewing it on video, but in contemporary society our experience of these and all other arts are generally of their technological reproductions. New artistic media of the twentieth century, such as film, video and television, are, indeed, based on technological methods of reproduction. The aura which surrounds *The Mona Lisa* or the eighth-century *Book of Kells* in Trinity College Library, Dublin, is unavailable to, and indeed an irrelevance for, these kinds of art forms.

The new media of film, television and video also, of course, provide us with our main forms of access to local, national and global events. Reality, we might say, is something which is partially created by the media through which it is represented. This point has led many to focus on the relationship between reality and representation, fact and fiction. Benjamin, writing before the incredible increase in communications technology in the post-war period, made the point that technological processes of representation, functioning on a mass level, can be deployed by socially regressive as well as socially progressive forces. The Nazi regime in the 1930s Germany in which Benjamin lived notoriously employed film as an outlet for its propaganda.

For many theorists and critics, the Postmodern era can seem one in which reproduction takes over from authentic production. Marxist critics, such as Terry Eagleton (1986) and Fredric Jameson (1991), are of this camp, and their arguments are often augmented by reference to the work of Postmodern theorists such as Jean Baudrillard. For Baudrillard Postmodern culture is dominated by the *simulacrum*, a word taken from the work of Plato and referring to a copy which does not possess an original (see Baudrillard, 1988). Hence our experience of modern art, as we have seen, increasingly comes to us in forms of reproduction. News reports of political and social events are provided by competing television channels, often with their own political and social agendas. These reports employ processes of framing, editing and other reproductions of images and speech which the viewer, possessing only what is presented, cannot challenge. A constructed news report thus comes to substitute for any real experience of the event. The 'simulacrum', the copy, comes to replace the 'real'.

We noted earlier that for Barthes intertextuality – which for poststructuralism is usually a term denoting a radical liberation of signification – can be the cause of a certain ennui or boredom. In a culture dominated by codes so pervasive that they appear natural, the intertextual, viewed as the presence of these codes and clichés within culture, can cause a sense of repetition, a saturation of cultural stereotypes, the triumph of the *doxa* over that which would resist and disrupt it. It might seem, then, that in a Postmodern context intertextual codes and practices predominate because of a loss of any access to reality. Jameson, commenting on the manner in which Postmodern theory tends to eradicate notions of what he styles 'depth' writes: 'depth is replaced by surface, or by multiple surfaces (what is often called intertextuality is in that sense no longer a matter of depth)' (Jameson, 1991: 12). He is not merely referring to the manner in which, in Postmodernism, earlier divisions between 'serious' and 'popular' or 'high' and 'low' cultural productions are merged. Jean-François Lyotard argues that, in the culture of late capitalism, traditional notions of national identity and culture are superseded by global forms deriving from transnational corporations in control of the media, of scientific research and other technological and commercial areas of life (Lyotard, 1986). In such a situation, argues Jameson, previous modes of identity and expression, based on a shared sense of the ruling norm, give way to a heterogeneous, rootless culture in which neither norm nor a resistance to that norm seems any longer possible. Connecting such a scenario to national languages as well as to cultural styles, Jameson writes:

> If the ideas of the ruling class were once the dominant (or hegemonic) ideology of bourgeois society, the advanced capitalist countries today are now a field of stylistic and discursive heterogeneity without a norm. Faceless masters continue to inflect the economic strategies which constrain our existences, but no longer need to impose their speech (or are henceforth unable to); and the postliteracy of the late capitalist world reflects not only the absence of any great

collective project, but also the unavailability of the older national language itself.

(Jameson, 1991: 17)

In such a situation, in which there seems no longer to a be a cultural norm to resist, parody of dominant norms is impossible and gives way to what Jameson calls pastiche:

> In this situation, parody finds itself without a vocation; it has lived, and that strange new thing pastiche slowly comes to take its place. Pastiche is, like parody, the imitation of a peculiar mask, speech in a dead language: but it is a neutral practice of such mimicry, without any of parody's ulterior motives, amputated of the satiric impulse, devoid of laughter and of any conviction that, alongside the abnormal tongue you have momentarily borrowed, some healthy linguistic normality still exists. Pastiche is thus blank parody, a statue with blind eyes ... the producers of culture have nowhere to turn but to the past: the imitation of dead styles, speech through all the masks and voices stored up in the imaginary museum of a now global culture.

> (*ibid.*: 17–18)

In the culture of late capitalism, Jameson argues, a play of images and styles, with no attachment to any recognizable cultural norm or social class, pervades the way in which people speak and the art they produce or consume. Such a dialogic, double-voiced phenomenon as parody, the mixing of official with unofficial language or style, becomes impossible. Intertextual practice, no longer capable of radical double-voicedness, collapses into a kind of pointless resurrection of past styles and past voices.

John Barth's essay, 'The Literature of Exhaustion', might seem to confirm such a view of the present state of culture and cultural production. However, Barth begins his essay thus:

> By 'exhaustion' I don't mean anything so tired as the subject of physical, moral, or intellectual decadence, only the usedupness of certain forms or exhaustion of certain possibilities – by no means necessarily a cause for despair.

> (Barth, 1975: 19)

The fact that Barth went on to write a follow-up article, entitled 'The Literature of Replenishment: Postmodernist Fiction', confirms the fact that for him the perceived saturatedness of present cultural forms and styles, the sense that culture cannot (to employ the Modernist rallying cry) constantly 'Make It New', is not a cause for concern and does not mean that contemporary art is a weakened, irrelevant, and parasitic phenomenon.

Many positive accounts of Postmodernism, in fact, refer to the fact that Modernism's belief that technological innovation could be harnessed by art, and that it offered the prospect of an ideal cultural future, have proved groundless. Nowhere can this point be seen with more clarity than in the domain of architecture, many critics' choice for the origins of Postmodern theory and practice. Mary McLeod writes that Postmodern architects:

> oppose the modern movement's messianic faith in the new; no longer, they assert, can architects naïvely assume that technological innovation insures a universal aesthetic and social solution .... In contrast to the modern architects of the twenties, postmodern architects publicly acknowledge their own objectives as pluralistic and historicist. The past is neither condemned nor ignored, but warmly embraced as a vital formal and intellectual source. All period styles, whether classical or vernacular, are considered open to imitation or reinterpretation.
>
> (McLeod, 1985: 19)

Instead of architectural Modernism's call to 'Make It New', Postmodern architects practice what we can style an intertextual architecture which appropriates styles from different eras and combines them in ways which attempt to reflect the historically and socially plural contexts within which their buildings now have to exist. The Modernist architect Le Corbusier may earlier have announced that buildings are 'machines for living in', yet by the late 1960s and early 1970s the effects of Modernist innovation were being radically questioned. In his book, *What is Postmodernism?*, the Postmodern architect and theorist Charles Jencks refers to the collapse of the Ronan Point tower block in London in 1968 and the bombing of the Pruitt-Igoe Modernist building in St Louis in 1972 as significant demonstrations of the popular cultural challenge to the aesthetics of Modernism. The now famous conference, entitled the Biennale of Architecture, in Venice in 1980, which included Jencks, Paolo Portoghesi and other architects now associated with Postmodernism, is often cited as the moment in which the new aesthetic was fully articulated. Jencks refers to the slogan of that conference, and by so doing reminds us of the thoroughly intertextual nature of the Postmodern architectural movement: 'The Presence of the Past' (Jencks, 1989: 41).

For Jencks the Postmodern age is 'a time of incessant choosing ... an era when no orthodoxy can be adopted without self-consciousness and irony, because all traditions seem to have some validity' (*ibid.*: 7). Starting with the same point as Jameson's critique of the culture of pastiche, Jencks moves in a more positive direction, and views this situation as one which opens up possibilities for radical forms of intertextual practice, or what, in more Bakhtinian-sounding terms, he styles 'double-coding':

> Post-Modernism is fundamentally the eclectic mixture of any tradition with that of the immediate past: it is both the continuation of Modernism and its transcendence. Its best works are characteristically double-coded and ironic, because this heterogeneity most clearly captures our pluralism. Its hybrid style is opposed to the minimalism of Late-Modern ideology and all revivals which are based on an exclusive dogma or taste.
>
> (Jencks, 1989: 7)

Whilst Modernist architecture eschewed popular forms, Postmodernism plays with and mixes forms and styles from what were previously perceived as 'high culture' and 'popular culture'. In this way it employs an intertextual practice which seeks to reflect a building's different users. Thus it argues for:

> an architecture that [is] professionally based *and* popular as well as one that [is] based on new techniques *and* old patterns. Double coding to simplify means both elite/popular and new/old and there are compelling reasons for these opposite pairings.
>
> (*ibid.*: 14)

Jencks's discussion of James Stirling's additions to the Staatsgalerie in Stuttgart provides us with a fine example of this double-coded, intertextual practice. The 'U-shaped palazzo from the old gallery is echoed and placed on a high plinth, or "Acropolis", above the traffic' (*ibid.*: 16). At its base lies the parking area, 'one that is ironically indicated by stones which have "fallen", like ruins, to the ground'. Jencks goes on:

> The resultant holes show the real construction – not the thick marble blocks of the real Acropolis, but a steel frame holding stone cladding which allows the air ventilation required by law. One can sit on these false ruins and ponder the truth of our lost innocence: that we live in an age which can build with beautiful, expressive masonry as long as we make it skin-deep and hang it on a steel skeleton. A Modernist would of course deny himself and us this pleasure for a number of reasons: 'truth to materials', 'logical consistency', 'straightforwardness', 'simplicity' – all the values and rhetorical tropes celebrated by such Modernists as Le Corbusier and Mies van der Rohe.
>
> (*ibid.*: 18–19)

Stirling in his work at the Staatsgalerie mixes Grecian styles, references to eighteenth-century constructed ruins, Modernist monumentalism and the garish colours of the contemporary moment in the hand-rails that run along the taxi drop-off point. As Jencks says of that last area:

> the blue and red handrails and vibrant polychromy fit in with the youth that uses the museum – while the Classicism appeals more to the lovers of Schinkel .... The pluralism which is so often called on to justify Post-Modernism is here a tangible reality.
>
> (*ibid.*: 19)

Reflecting the juxtapositions of contemporary living, the plurality of cultural styles and groupings which lie around the building and are embodied by its users, Stirling's Postmodernism exemplifies the double-coded, intertextual dimension of Postmodern architecture. Far more than depthless pastiche, as Jameson's diagnosis would have it, Jencks' Postmodernism is intertextual in a manner which again seems to relate that term back to Bakhtin's insistence on the social situatedness of (here) architectural 'language'.

POSTMODERNISM AND THE RETURN OF HISTORY

Postmodernism is now a major term in the study of literature. Ihab Hassan's famous list of the key terms of Modernism and Postmodernism includes the following opposites, again making clear the relationship drawn by many between Postmodernism and poststructuralism as well as the place of intertextuality within such definitions of the former (Hassan, 1993: 152):

Modernism	Postmodernism
Purpose	Play
Design	Chance
Centering	Dispersal
Genre/Boundary	Text/Inter-text
Interpretation/Reading	Against Interpretation/Misreading
Lisible (Readerly)	*Scriptable* (Writerly)
Origin/Cause	Difference–*Différance*/Trace

The construction of such lists is somewhat of a gamble. The lists seem to posit Modernism and Postmodernism as antithetical to each other, whilst the reality, as theorists such as Jencks have suggested, is that Postmodernism remains complicit with many of the forms and theories which characterized Modernism and allows itself to utilize Modernism's major styles, genres and innovations. Linda Hutcheon, a major theorist of the relationship between Postmodernism and intertextual theory and practice, makes the same point (Hutcheon, 1988: 49) and, influenced by Postmodern architects such as Jencks, argues that what characterizes Postmodern literature is a double-codedness. This double-codedness questions the available modes of representation in culture whilst recognizing that it must still employ those modes. In such an approach Modernism can never simply be opposed to Postmodernism, since the latter movement continually relies on and exploits the former's styles, codes and approaches, just as it relies on and exploits those of other historical periods.

For Hutcheon, then, Postmodernism is contradictory and double coded, since it 'works within the very systems it attempts to subvert' (*ibid.*: 4). Contrasting the implicit nostalgia she sees in Modernism's intertextual employment of past forms with the ironic distance frequently established when Postmodern works utilize similar forms, Hutcheon writes:

> When Eliot recalled Dante or Virgil in *The Waste Land*, one sensed a kind of wishful call to continuity beneath the fragmented echoing. It is precisely this that is contested in postmodern parody where it is often ironic discontinuity that is revealed at the heart of continuity, difference at the heart of similarity .... Parody is a perfect postmodern form, in some sense, for it paradoxically both incorporates and challenges that which it parodies. It also forces a reconsideration of the idea of origin or originality that is compatible with other postmodern interrogations of liberal humanist assumptions.
>
> (Hutcheon, 1988: 11)

A statement made by Eliot concerning Joyce's use of myth in his *Ulysses*, but equally applicable to Eliot's own work, might seem to back up Hutcheon's point. Eliot's argument that Joyce's use of myth is a way of 'controlling' and 'ordering', of giving 'shape and a significance', to what he styles 'the immense panorama of futility and anarchy which is contemporary history' suggests a rather dismissive, even appalled, reaction to the present and an accompanying nostalgia for past forms and past times (Eliot, 1975: 177). In contrast to such an approach, Postmodernism's employment of the codes and forms of the past, Hutcheon argues, are best viewed in terms of the concept of parody.

Parody, the key term in Hutcheon's and other critics' work on Postmodernism, is intimately connected to notions of intertextuality. In the index to her *The Politics of Postmodernism* (Hutcheon, 1989) the entry for 'Intertextuality' simply directs the reader to the entry for 'Parody'. At times this substitution of parody for intertextuality can lead to unhelpful complications, and on occasions Hutcheon would fare better by employing the term intertextuality rather than continue to reshape and redirect notions of parody.

Whether we employ the term parody or intertextuality, it is clear that for critics such as Hutcheon Postmodern literature deploys a vast array of contemporary and historical forms. It does this to register its dependence upon established forms of representation, or what Barthes would call *doxa*. But at the same moment that it registers this fact, its juxtaposition of styles and codes, of different and sometimes apparently incompatible forms of representation, serves to question, disturb and even subvert the dominance of those established forms. At once *doxa* and *paradoxa*, Postmodern literature, like other Postmodern artistic practices, involves, or for Hutcheon *can* involve, a radical questioning of the available forms of representation and thus the available modes of knowledge within culture. Hutcheon pits such a view of Postmodernism against alternative views which understand Postmodernism as simply a playful registering of culture's current saturation of signs and sign-systems:

> parody works to foreground the *politics* of representation. Needless to say, this is not the accepted view of postmodernist parody. The prevailing interpretation is that postmodernism offers a value-free, decorative, de-historicized quotation of past forms and that this is a most apt mode for a culture like our own that is oversaturated with images. Instead, I would want to argue that postmodernist parody is a value-problematizing, de-naturalizing form of acknowledging the history (and through irony, the politics) of representations.
>
> (Hutcheon, 1989: 94)

Hutcheon's frequent focus on Postmodern novels dealing with historical subjects – she styles them 'Postmodern historiographic metafiction' – foregrounds not only how many contemporary novels intertextually integrate forms, codes and references to historically diverse texts and textual traditions, it also demonstrates the manner in which history as an idea and a practice is frequently an important part of this kind of fiction's double-coded questioning of available forms of representation. She frequently cites Salman Rushdie's *Midnight's Children* as an example of the double-coding of Postmodern historiographic fiction. As she states, the self-reflexivity of Rushdie's text:

> points in two directions at once, toward the events being represented in the narrative and toward the act of narration itself. This is precisely the same doubleness that characterizes all historical narrative. Neither form of representation can separate 'fact' from the acts of interpretation and narration that constitute them, for facts (though not events) are created in and by those acts. And what actually becomes fact depends as much as anything else on the social and cultural contexts of the historian, as feminist theorists have shown with regard to women writers of history over the centuries.
>
> (*ibid.*: 76)

Deploying the work of theorists of history such as Hayden White and Dominick LaCapra, Hutcheon argues that in such Postmodern novels as Rushdie's *Midnight's Children* we are reminded of the fact that no historical narrative of events ever directly and transparently records or represents those events. All historical narratives are themselves dependent on available modes of narrative. Hayden White, for example, utilizing the work of the literary theorist Northrop Frye, has argued that the four main genres of literature – comedy, tragedy, romance, and satire – always shape, singularly or in mixed modes, every historical narrative (White, 1973). Whether an historian narrating the events of the French Revolution or the Irish Uprising of 1798 employs an essentially comic, tragic, romantic or satiric mode of narration will depend upon that historian's own set of ideological allegiances. Historical events themselves, we might also remember, only come to the historian through what Hutcheon, following Genette, calls 'paratexts'. Whether it be newspaper accounts, diaries, military reports, parliamentary documents, private letters, or any of the vast array of historical documents the historian must depend upon, history is only available to the contemporary historian through a network of prior texts, all infused with the traces of prior authors with their own ideological agendas, presuppositions and prejudices. History exists as a vast web of subjective texts, the new historical account being one more author's struggle to negotiate a way through an intertextual network of previous forms and representations.

Writing of Postmodern historiographic metafiction, Hutcheon states:

> If the past is only known to us today through its textualized traces (which, like all texts, are always open to interpretation), then the writing of both history and historiographic metafiction becomes a form of complex intertextual cross-referencing that operates within (and does not deny) its unavoidably discursive context. There can be little doubt of the impact of poststructuralist theories of textuality on this kind of writing, for this is writing that raises basic questions about the possibilities and limits of meaning in the representation of the past.
>
> (Hutcheon, 1989: 81)

In Rushdie's novel, a contemporary narrator, Saleem Sinai, born at the moment of Pakistan's independence, tries to narrate his own life history at the same time as narrating the history of Pakistan. The historical archive, however, constantly contradicts itself, and Saleem's subjective perspective mediates and colours his narration of historical events. The personal and the social, the psychological and the cultural, with all its ideological conflicts and divisions, merge into each other in the narrative. This fact is often noted by referring to a sentence in which Saleem finds it possible to write the following: 'Aircraft, real or fictional, dropped actual or mythical bombs' (Rushdie, 1995: 341).

John Fowles's *The French Lieutenant's Woman*, first published in 1969, is another novel which clearly comes under Hutcheon's heading of Postmodern historiographic metafiction (see Hutcheon, 1985: 91–2; 1988: 45). In Fowles's novel we shuttle between a realistic narrative set in the mid-nineteenth century and a contemporary narrative voice which is able to pull into that Victorian world a host of intertextual references which disrupt the novel's historical realism. References to modern theoretical ideas, including those of Barthes, along with notes explaining aspects of Victorian society and referring to historically later ideas, mean, as Hutcheon puts it, that the reader is constantly referred to the arena of the 'extra-textual ... a world outside the novel' and to 'other *texts*, other representations' of the world being represented in the text itself.

Fowles's novel should confirm how thoroughly this form of Postmodern fiction depends upon intertextual practice. More importantly, it appears to confirm the destabilizing function of intertextuality within such fiction. Radically double-coded, such texts exploit the tension between fact and fiction, between the constructed and the real, between the *doxa* of realism and the para-doxical assertion of that realism's impossibility.

Umberto Eco's *The Name of the Rose* is perhaps the most widely discussed of all such recent Postmodern novels. The novel is set in a fourteenth-century abbey run by Benedictine monks, and involves the story of the visit of William of Baskerville and the novice Adso, their search to uncover the mysterious murder during their visit of various of the abbey's monks, and the connection those murders have with a lost or concealed text, which turns out to be Aristotle's lost work on comedy. The novel might at first appear to be an uncomplicated attempt to realistically represent the world of medieval monasticism. In his *Reflections on 'The Name of the Rose'* Eco refers to his obsession with the Middle Ages: 'I know the present,' he writes, 'only through the television screen, whereas I have direct knowledge of the Middle Ages' (Eco, 1985: 14). The reader first encounters an untitled introduction in which the history of the manuscript we are about to read is given. A note then explains the novel's division into seven days and each day into the eight religious ceremonies which order the daily life of the monks. A Prologue follows in which Adso, the novel's narrator, writes at the end of his own life of Brother William and the historical events leading up to the narrative itself. The novel finally begins with the sentence: 'It was a beautiful morning at the end of November' (Eco, 1998: 21).

It would appear that the complications involved in beginning the narrative are the traditional ones of establishing the reality of a world which, though different to the world inhabited by the author and reader, is to be, for the duration of the novel, consistently and convincingly represented. Eco writes of the need to distance the fictional world of such a novel in the current Postmodern climate of parody, irony and the deconstruction of previously unquestioned modes of narration and speech:

> Is it possible to say 'It was a beautiful morning at the end of November' without feeling like Snoopy? But what if I had Snoopy say it? If, that is, 'It was a beautiful morning ... ' were said by someone capable of saying it, because in his day it was still possible, still not shopworn? A mask: that was what I needed.
>
> I set about reading or rereading medieval chroniclers, to acquire their rhythm and their innocence. They would speak for me, and I would be freed from suspicion. Freed from suspicion, but not from the echoes of intertextuality. Thus I discovered what writers have always known (and have told us again and again): books always speak of other books, and every story tells a story that has already been told .... My story, then, could only begin with the discovered manuscript, and even this would be (naturally) a quotation. So I wrote the introduction immediately, setting my narrative on a fourth level of encasement, inside three other narratives: I am saying what Vallet said that Mabillon said that Adso said ...
>
> I was now free of every fear.
>
> (Eco, 1985: 19–20)

Eco makes plain that in writing a historically-oriented text the principal problem is intertextual: the 'already written' and 'already said' threaten to turn one's narrative and narrative voice into a mere repetition of previous utterances and previous texts. The Postmodern cultural climate, figured by Eco in terms of a loss of innocence, requires that we distance or ironize our representations and utterances if they are to be taken seriously.

Eco, however, is not describing literary techniques which finally allow for a direct and wholly serious representation of the past. On the contrary, the need to ironize historical representation means that the narrative necessarily becomes charged with intertextual traces of the past, the present and the historical periods between the two. In the place of the call to 'Make It New', the Postmodern author, Eco argues, finds that the past is unavoidable, but can only be represented and re-employed in a non-innocent, ironic or parodic fashion (*ibid.*: 67). To explain this Eco presents us with a hypothetical scenario from contemporary life:

> I think of the postmodern attitude as that of a man who loves a very cultivated woman and knows he cannot say to her, 'I love you madly', because he knows that she knows (and that she knows that he knows) that these words have already been written by Barbara Cartland. Still, there is a solution. He can say, 'As Barbara Cartland would put it, I love you madly'. At this point, having avoided false innocence, having said clearly that it is no longer possible to speak innocently, he will nevertheless have said what he wanted to say to the woman: that he loves her, but he loves her in an age of lost innocence. If the woman goes along with this, she will have received a declaration of love all the same. Neither of the two speakers will feel innocent, both will have accepted the challenge of the past, of the already said, which cannot be eliminated; both will consciously and with pleasure play the game of irony ... But both will have succeeded, once again, in speaking of love.
>
> (*ibid.*: 67–8)

To speak of love, Eco's hypothetical lovers must employ ironic or double-coded words; double-coded because they are simultaneously employed and undermined. They must do this because they exist in a self-consciously intertextual environment in which awareness of the 'already-written' and 'already-said' cancels the possibility for any direct, unironized statement or representation. Similarly, to write of the past in an historical novel means that the author enters an intertextual environment of things already written and already said so many times that it does not seem possible merely to write them or have characters utter them without at the same moment placing what the author writes at an ironic distance and thus undermining or destabilizing the very things of which the author wishes to write.

Eco achieves this double-coded practice of representation and ironization by constructing his realistic medieval world out of intertextual strands from the Middle Ages through to the present day. His protagonists, William of Baskerville and Adso are clearly based on the Sherlock Holmes and Watson of Arthur Conan Doyle's famous Victorian detective stories. William's surname directs us towards Conan Doyle's *The Hound of the Baskervilles*. The medieval world within which they live is immediately complicated, therefore, by the development of a narrative of mystery and detection through deductive logic which readers of Conan Doyle will immediately recognize as generated from that Victorian inter-text. The sinister librarian, Jorge of Burgos, directs readers to the twentieth-century Argentinian writer Jorge Luis Borges. The developing narrative centred on the mysteries contained in the Aedificium, or labyrinthine, towered structure of the library, alerts readers with a knowledge of Borges's work to texts including 'The Circular Ruins' and 'The Library of Babel' (Borges, 1970: 72–7, 78–88). Many other inter-texts also play major roles in the structuring of the narrative and the long conversations between characters. The novel is constructed from echoes, quotations and allusions to Wittgenstein's philosophical writings, medieval texts, the language and frequently the specifics of particular medieval churches and cathedrals, the paintings of Breughel, passages from the Bible, and many other examples, not all of which any one reader is likely to register in any single reading (see Hutcheon, 1985: 12; 1989: 94–5).

Interestingly for readers of this study, Bakhtin's work and ideas are frequently woven into the text, particularly in relation to the conflict between those forces, led by Jorge, that wish to repress the lost book on comedy by Aristotle, and those, like William and Adso, that search for its recovery. The glimpse which William and Adso gain of the illuminations of the ill-fated Adelmo of Otranto immediately link the narrative to Bakhtin's work on the carnivalesque:

> This was a psalter in whose margins was delineated a world reversed
> with respect to the one to which our senses have accustomed us. As
> if at the border of a discourse that is by definition the discourse of
> truth, there proceeded closely linked to it, through wondrous allu-
> sions in aenigmate, a discourse of falsehood on a topsy-turvy uni-
> verse, in which dogs flee before the hare, and deer hunt the lion.
>
> (Eco, 1998: 76)

The list of carnivalesque images which follows confirms that
Bakhtin's idea of the carnival is a significant inter-text for these
illuminations. Their placement around the border of the sacred
text serves to remind us of Bakhtin's distinction between the centripetal and centrifugal forces of language. The sacred language of
monologism, which asserts one truth and one language, is here
challenged by images of popular festivity, grotesque inversions
and the dialogic play which Bakhtin associated with the carnivalesque but equally with the polyphonic novel so important for
the ideas of double-voiced discourse, *heteroglossia* and hybridization we have seen as the basis for later work on intertextuality.

The reference to Bakhtin is useful for our reading of the novel,
since the conflict between Jorge of Burgos and William of
Baskerville seems well described as a conflict between a monologic and a dialogic attitude towards language, comedy and
laughter, and ultimately towards society itself. For Jorge there is
one God, one Law, and One Word. The duty of monks like himself is to protect the sacred books and to preach a monologic religion which effectively puts the lid on the common people, their
carnivalesque desires and heterogeneous points of view. For
William, however, 'laughter is proper to man, it is a sign of his
rationality' (*ibid.*: 131), books are not sacred unless they are read
by human beings, and the entire universe, along with the
labyrinthine library he attempts to penetrate, is a text open to interpretation.

The entire narrative, then, can be read as a commentary on
Bakhtinian ideas and other theories of intertextuality. Whilst the
novel is concerned with many other things, the intertextual nature of texts, of our interpretation of them and of the world

around us is a constant theme within Eco's novel. The whole narrative centres on the search for a lost or repressed text, yet this search merely goes to demonstrate the interconnectedness of all texts. As Adso discovers, our understanding of the world and of each individual text depends upon a vast intertextual network. He writes:

> Until then I had thought each book spoke of the things, human or divine, that lie outside of books. Now I realized that not infrequently books speak of books: it is as if they spoke among themselves. In the light of this reflection, the library seemed all the more disturbing to me. It was then the place of a long, centuries-old murmuring, a imperceptible dialogue between one parchment and another, a living thing, a receptacle of powers not to be ruled by a human mind, a treasure of secrets emanated by many minds, surviving the death of those who had produced them or had been their conveyors.
>
> (*ibid.*: 286)

Such an insight makes the destruction by fire of the library at the conclusion of the novel even more dramatic. Eco's novel, however, does not end simply with the destruction of the labyrinthine intertextual network which opens up to the mind of Adso, since it is itself constructed from and exists as a testament to that 'library of Babel', to employ Borges's phrase.

The Name of the Rose so thoroughly exemplifies the Postmodern approach to intertextuality that we can use it to repeat the kinds of distinctions between Modernism and Postmodernism made by critics such as Hutcheon, Jencks and Eco himself. Barthes, Kristeva and other poststructuralists of the 1960s and 1970s sought a text which, through intertextual practices, would go beyond the available codes and systems of the already written and already read. They remained attached to a rhetoric of textual liberation and release from conventions and even human intention which is clearly connected to a residual Modernism. Eco's novel, however, like other Postmodern novels concerned with the question of history, reads more like the Balzacian readerly text Barthes analysed in his *S/Z*. The difference, however, is that whilst it is left to Barthes as textual analyst to open Balzac's text to the writerly and the intertextual, the writerly and the intertextual are already inscribed by Eco as author into *The Name of the Rose*, and it is left for the reader to negotiate that text's paradoxical play between the readerly or realistic and the writerly or intertextual. Eco's text sharply highlights the difference between Barthes's and Kristeva's residual commitment to a Modernist aesthetic of the 'New' and the liberation from established modes of representation and the Postmodern acknowledgement of the inescapability of those modes of representation alongside a recognition of the need to submit them to parody and ironical disruption.

INTERTEXTUALITY, HYPERTEXTUALITY AND THE WORLD WIDE WEB

Eco's *The Name of the Rose* reaches its apocalyptic climax when a library which had seemed to contain the knowledge of the world is destroyed by fire. This event has its own historical inter-texts in the destruction of the ancient Alexandrian library and of the medieval library of Monte Cassino. Our new computer technologies may still be sporadically prone to physical corruption, such as that threatened by the Millennium Bug, yet they present us with a new form of textuality which is infinitely more flexible, manipulative and – given the appropriate hardware and software – accessible. One feature of the new computing technologies which has been the subject of increasing debate and theorization is its far greater capacity, compared to print culture, for interconnectedness. Digitalized computing systems such as the World Wide Web, electronic books and hypertexts present a form of intertextuality which seems to many to have finally made manifest the theoretical arguments we have analysed in this study.

Whilst theorists such as Barthes, Kristeva and Derrida attack the traditionally dominant idea of the work's isolation, individuality and authority, the new computer-based systems seem to embody such critiques. For those who write on this new form of textuality, poststructuralist and Postmodern theory seems to be merely that, a *theory* directed towards an object, books, which appear to resist notions of relationality, difference and intertextuality. What to many might seem counterintuitive in Barthes's treatment of literary books becomes obvious, inevitable and even 'natural' when dealing with hypertext systems. Such computer systems, at the same moment, seem to take us back to the medieval idea of the total library. Jay David Bolter's remarks would not have been understood by William of Baskerville, yet the spirit of such remarks has many correspondences with the ideals he expresses in *The Name of the Rose*:

> In a fully hypertextual library, readers will be able to choose any of the existing paths, or define a new path, through the materials they are reading and perhaps leave that path for other readers to follow if they choose. What we get from this speculation is a vision of the library as an encompassing hypertextual book in which everyone can read and everyone can add his or her own writing.
>
> (Bolter, 1992: 23)

As Delaney and Landow state, a hypertext is 'a variable structure, composed of blocks of text (or what Roland Barthes terms *lexias*) and the electronic links that join them' (Delaney and Landow, 1991: 3). Clearly, Genette's term 'hypertextuality' has some relevance to these new systems, but it should not be confused with the term as applied to computer-based digitalized textuality. Read on and through computer networks, web sites, or through CD-ROM disks, hypertexts can consist of one 'text' divided into *lexias* with connecting links, or can consist of a text with a range of other texts embedded within it, access to which is made by links activated by the reader on the screen. Although only one block or *lexia* may be activated at one time, readers of hypertext are assisted by 'browser' menus displaying networks of other 'links', along with the ability to link specific words to dictionary definitions or other constructed chains of explanatory or contextual *lexias*. Complex hypertext systems, like London's National Gallery system, provide us with a host of texts or images, or both, which the reader can peruse and connect through linkways. Some hypertexts, such as those described by George P.

Landow (Delaney and Landow, 1991; Landow, 1994), often educational in nature, allow not only for a main text or set of texts to be linked to numerous other related texts, but also can be added to by the reader creating new pathways and new texts within the overall hypertext system. As Delaney and Landow suggest, the use of such hypertexts challenges received ideas about reading and writing derived from an increasingly challenged 'book culture'. They write:

> Because hypertext breaks down our habitual way of understanding and experiencing texts, it radically challenges students, teachers, and theorists of literature. But it can also provide a revelation, by making visible and explicit mental processes that have always been part of the total experience of reading. For the text as the reader *imagined* it – as opposed to the physical text objectified in the book – never had to be linear, bounded or fixed.
>
> (Delaney and Landow, 1991: 30)

Landow, in his *Hypertext* (Landow, 1992), makes much of this new text's challenge to notions of linear narration and reading, the boundedness or independence of each text, and thus of traditional notions of authorial and critical authority. In doing so, he recognizes that hypertext systems and the manner in which we respond to them have many connections to textual and intertextual theories. As he writes elsewhere: 'an experience of reading hypertext or reading with hypertext greatly clarifies many of the most significant ideas of critical theory' (Landow, 1994: 3). No idea is more relevant to this new technology than that of intertextuality. Hypertextuality, the textuality generated through the new computer-based technologies, Landow states, is 'a fundamentally intertextual' phenomenon (*ibid.*: 10).

Referring to the intense intertextual references and allusions to be found in the 'Nausicaa' section of Joyce's *Ulysses*, Landow imagines a hypertext version of the novel which would be able to link the whole section to the specific inter-texts involved in Joyce's writing but also to other relevant works by Joyce. Such a hypertext would, Landow suggests, manifest far more clearly than any printed edition of *Ulysses*, no matter how annotated, the 'decenteredness' of Joyce's novel. Hypertext systems allow us to branch off from what appears to be a main text into intertextual pathways, to the extent that the main text may well be forgotten or come to seem just one more text in an intertextual, or in this case hypertextual, chain. Like the intertextual theories of Barthes, Kristeva, Derrida and others before it, hypertexts destroy the notion of the linearity of a text; we no longer read from beginning to end as if meaning were a matter of one word in a text following another. The fact that a text's significance depends upon a host of other texts is made an integral part of the reading experience of such hypertext systems and as a consequence the disturbance that intertextuality brings to notions of a text's 'inside' and 'outside' is made manifest by hypertextual reading (*ibid.*: 60).

Other key features of intertextual theory as we have studied it are also made manifest by hypertextuality. Often citing *S/Z* as a theoretical model for the hypertextual reading experience, Landow points out that the reader's ability to break the linear flow of a text by activating links, and, in some systems, to add commentaries and other *lexias* to the text being read, confirm Barthes's points about the reader's active role in the production of textual meaning. The hypertext reader can become for Landow and others an 'author-reader' who embodies poststructuralism's points about the death of the 'Author' as sole authority of meaning and the accompanying birth of the reader as 'scriptor'. As Landow states, hypertext follows Barthes in *S/Z* by making author, text and reader into joint participants of a plural, intertextual network of significations and potential significations. 'In this case, as in others,' he writes: 'hypertext embodies many of the ideas and attitudes proposed by Barthes, Derrida, Foucault, and others' (*ibid.*: 72–3).

We might take two examples to back up our sense of the manner in which hypertextuality can be said to embody the notions of intertextuality we have studied so far. The first concerns Landow's own hypertext system at Brown University, the *In Memoriam* web. Tennyson's *In Memoriam*, written over many years to mark the death of his friend Arthur Hallam, consists of 131 lyric sections plus a Prologue and an Epilogue. The poem, as Landow states, is highly intra- and intertextual. Its intratextuality fundamentally concerns the manner in which different lyrics or groups of lyrics relate to others, sometimes spaced far apart in the text's overall arrangement. Thus, for example, lyric sections 28, 78, 104 and 105 can be grouped together as the 'Christmas lyrics', a grouping which alerts the reader to the passing of time. In this way *In Memoriam* employs intratextual links to combine lyric intensity with a sense of narrative movement. Whilst the reader of a book-based version of the poem has difficulty in marking and exploring the many intratextual links which operate within the text as a whole, the reader of the *In Memoriam* web has no trouble in activating links between lyrics displayed visually on the computer screen. Many of the intratextual connections between lyrics within the series work on the level of shared or complementary imagery, and the hypertext version allows readers to make searches throughout the text of particular images and words. In an example of a 'typical screen' Landow shows us an 'Imagery Overview' within which are a number of keywords relating to section 7 of the poem. Words such as 'dark, darkness', 'veil', 'wind', 'ice, frost, cold', and many others exist as *lexias* available for the reader to activate and thus make searches throughout the entire text (*ibid.*: 39).

In Memoriam is also intertextual in that a great part of its significance comes from its engagement with social, political, historical and scientific issues of Tennyson's own time. It is also a highly intertextual text on the level of literary allusion, echo and citation. The *In Memoriam* web allows readers to call up a vast array of contextual material, including other literary texts as well as texts concerning the poem's scientific, religious and philosophical concerns. An overview entitled 'Cultural Context: Victorianism' displays link pathways concerning, amongst others, 'Artistic Relations', 'Political and Social Background', 'Religion and Philosophy', 'Science and Technology' (*ibid.*).

The reader of the web can also call up student essays and other comments on the 'Web View'. The same reader is able to contribute to discussion by adding his or her own comments, essays, and suggestions for further links. Such hypertexts, moving beyond strict 'read-only' systems to active systems which turn the reader into not only a potential 'reader-author' but also a collaborative 'worker' are compared by Landow to the kind of Bakhtinian ideas we have seen as so important to intertextual theory. Placing the reader in a dialogue with other readers of the same text, hypertext systems such as the *In Memoriam* web also serve to dramatically demonstrate the intertextual place of such a text; that is, hypertext disallows any notion that the text is singular, independent and thus monologic in nature. Starred and punctured by numerous links, as Landow puts it: 'hypertext does not permit a tyrannical, univocal voice' (*ibid.*: 11).

The second example moves us to an example of hypertext's potential for literary writing. Michael Joyce's *Afternoon, a story* is a much-discussed hypertext fiction consisting of 538 *lexias* and around 950 links. The reader reads one *lexia* at a time, and the first one ends with the question: 'Do you want to hear about it?' (see Bolter, 1992: 25). The reader can answer this question by typing either 'Yes' or 'No' in the space provided. Typing 'Yes' moves the reader onto the next *lexia*. The reader can then choose to answer 'yes' every time, which will take him or her through 36 *lexias*. At the end of these the reader will have been presented with an incomplete story concerning a narrator, his missing son, the question of whether he saw a car accident on the way to work in the morning and various other details concerning the narrator's life. To continue, the reader must access other parts of the hypertext by clicking on 'yield words' which each *lexia* contains. Although some 'yield words' cannot be accessed unless others earlier in the series have also been followed, it becomes clear that each reader will 'read' a somewhat different text, and that each time the same reader 'reads' the text s/he can choose to select the same path or branch out into new ones. Commenting on the manner in which the nature of the experience of reading *Afternoon* reflects its status as a 'mystery story', Bolter writes:

> The father's quest also becomes the reader's – to establish what really happened to the son. The episodes the reader visits will deter-

mine the answer he or she receives. In that sense, 'Afternoon' becomes an allegory of the act of reading. The reader's own participation in the story becomes the story.

(Bolter, 1992: 29)

There is no 'ending' to Joyce's text, since, as Terence Harpold
states, every conclusion will be a 'contingent conclusion', the
product of the reader's selection of some links and avoidance or
sheer ignorance of others (Harpold, 1994: 192–3). Joyce's text is
not simply intratextual; it contains various intertextual connections to cultural and literary inter-texts, notably the *Ulysses* by
Afternoon's author's namesake, James Joyce. The main point derived by Landow and others from Joyce's hypertext, however, is
that the emphasis which poststructuralist theories of intertextuality placed on the 'reversibility' of texts, on the fact that no text
can ever fully be 'consumed' or 'finished', is made manifest and
embodied by such hypertextual texts.

It seems, then, that the new hypertextuality unarguably fulfils
the textual and intertextual vision of poststructuralists such as
Barthes, Kristeva and Derrida, along with the theoretical stress
on dialogism inherited from the work of Bakhtin. Landow's work
certainly appears to confirm such a response. David Coughlan
also compares literary intertextuality and the Net or World Wide
Web. The term 'Net', he reminds us, refers both to the connection between millions of computer terminals world-wide and also
to the concept of 'cyberspace': the mass of 'words, images, and
sounds' which those connected computers contain. Remarking on
the spatial dimension of 'cyberspace', Coughlan writes:

> Perhaps intertextual space exists in the same way, flowing between
> the texts which form it, each text acting now as a terminal through
> which to access this network, quotations and references serving as
> hypertext, transporting the reader to another page on the web, to an-
> other part of the textual space.
>
> If the computer is the point of intersection between physical space
> and cyberspace, then the text is the porthole to the space of intertex-
> tuality, each text simply one exposed section of a limitless network of

> other texts which are, some would say, already present within that one
> text.
>
> (Coughlan, 1997: 116)

Despite these clear connections between intertextuality and new computer systems, it remains difficult to imagine that technological changes by themselves will produce more active and productive 'author-readers' and an increased 'democratization' of language, reading and the communication and possession of information. At times Landow and others seem rather too easily to take the basic theories of poststructuralism without considering the deeper motivations which produced those theories. We might, for instance, wonder whether systems which are said to increase the capacity of readers to 'download', process and then utilize 'information', or systems which immensely speed up and facilitate 'communication', actually fit as well as they appear to do with the kind of arguments against notions of 'information', the 'consumption' of literature, and the 'clear' and 'transparent' conveyance of meaning we have seen at the heart of *Tel Quel* theory. When we remember that in Kristeva and Barthes 'text' and 'intertextuality' are terms meant to highlight a resistance to notions of reading, direct and full communication, and the capitalist exchange or consumption of texts, then 'hypertextuality' can seem less obviously connected to poststructural theory.

Landow's references to Bakhtin are also at times more questionable than they might appear. We can see this most clearly when we remind ourselves, as Landow does near the conclusion of his *Hypertext*, that not all members of society are currently able to deploy the new computer technology. Landow states: 'Technology always empowers someone, some group in society, and it does so at a certain cost' (Landow, 1994: 171). As he goes on to remark: 'The vision of hypertext as a means of democratic empowerment depends ultimately upon the individual reader-author's access to these networks' (*ibid.*: 187). Landow's remarks have direct links to what has become a recognizable debate within the Western world: whilst great claims are made for the democratizing power of the World Wide Web, the fact remains that the majority of the world's population remain without access to that mode of communication.

In discussing the issue of access Landow makes two central points. Using historical examples, he argues that it is never possible to determine whether a new technology will be a force for democratization or will merely shore up existing power groups, or even create new dominant classes and groups. He then argues, contradicting his first point, that the new 'information technology' will necessarily produce an increase in 'democratization' (*ibid.*: 174). Attempting to substantiate this second point, Landow takes the example of print technology and the seventeenth-century French Academy Dictionary:

> This dictionary is one of the most obvious instances of the way print technology sponsors nationalism, the vernacular, and relative democratization. It standardizes the language in ways that empower particular classes and geographical areas, inevitably at the expense of others. Nonetheless, it also permits the eventual homogenization of language and a corollary, if long-in-coming, possibility of democratization.
>
> (Landow, 1994: 175)

As we have observed, however, intertextual theories have argued that the 'homogenization' of language establishes or supports monologic power. Democracy, for Bakhtin and the theories of intertextuality he helped to inspire, stems from the release of plurality and multivocality, the dialogic and hybrid play of different languages, dialects, registers and/or speech genres. It remains open to question whether hypertextuality will incorporate such a dialogic play of voices and languages or will in fact be a medium through which monologism exerts its centripetal force in society. Can hypertext incorporate the differences between gendered or nationally or racially specific languages, or between other social classes or other minority dialects and points of view? Can it produce the kind of double-voiced discourse described within feminist and postcolonial criticism? or the kind of resistance to dominant discourse described within poststructuralist theory?

If the answers hypertextuality provides prove to be negative, it will not be the fault of the new digitalized computing technology itself. Rather, the fault will lie in the producers, designers, programmers, authors and readers of that new medium. Intertextual theory, far from being seamlessly incorporated within the new hypertextual systems, has much to offer and perhaps to teach the new information technologies and their users.

CONCLUSION

In this study we have observed the manner in which intertextuality is increasingly assimilated into literary theory and into theories of cultural, artistic and even technological production and reproduction. In the work of Genette, Riffaterre and Bloom we have seen ways in which the term is employed to draw limits around the relations between texts and the field of critical enquiry and interpretation. However, the two main strands which dominate theories of intertextuality have constantly reasserted themselves and proved their interconnectedness as we have moved from the term's origins to its later adaptations. Whether it be based in poststructuralist or Bakhtinian theories, or in both, intertextuality reminds us that all texts are potentially plural, reversible, open to the reader's own presuppositions, lacking in clear and defined boundaries, and always involved in the expression or repression of the dialogic 'voices' which exist within society. A term which continually refers to the impossibility of singularity, unity, and thus of unquestionable authority, intertextuality remains a potent tool within any reader's theoretical vocabulary. By that same logic, however, it also remains a tool which cannot be employed by readers wishing to produce stability and order, or wishing to claim authority over the text or other critics. This is perhaps the reason, since cultural debate never ceases, that intertextuality promises to be as vital and productive a concept in the future as it has been in the recent past.

GLOSSARY

Key: Fr. = French; Gr. = Greek; L. = Latin; OED = *The Oxford English Dictionary*.
Where a term is associated with a particular theorist, his or her name appears, bracketed, at the beginning of the explanation.

addressivity (Bakhtin) Refers to the fact that any utterance is directed towards an addressee (listener, potential respondent).

agency term used in literary theory and criticism to retain notions of human participation in the production of meaning without suggesting more absolute notions such as originality, genius or uniqueness.

anagram 'a transposition of the letters of a word, name, or phrase, whereby a new one is formed' (OED); Samuel Butler's *Erewhon* is an *anagram* for 'nowhere'. Explored by Saussure in the context of classical poetry.

architextuality (Genette) 'the entire set of general or transcendent categories – types of discourse, modes of enunciation, literary genres – from which emerges each singular text' (Genette, 1997a: 1). If literature is conceived as a formally defined system filled with categories such as the realist novel, tragedy, and so on, then architextuality is the study of literature in terms of these formal categories.

carnival for Bakhtin, 'carnivalesque' forces in society are connected to popular forms of literature and language which disrupt the dominant order and monologic view of society and language promoted by dominant power groups. 'Carnivalization' relates to his term, 'dialogicism', and is opposed to notions of single meaning and unquestionable authority.

deconstruction a movement associated with poststructuralism, and with the work of Derrida in particular. Deconstruction can be said to be generally critical of ideas of stable and authoritative meaning. It attempts to demonstrate how a reliance on the unstable phenomenon of language unravels dominant ideas and structures from within.

descriptive system (Riffaterre) 'the network of words, phrases and stereotyped sentences associated with one another in ... relation to a kernel word to which they are subordinate' (Riffaterre, 1990b: 126–7). Centrally important words in texts suggest a series of associated words and concepts which the text then manipulates to create its specific overall meaning.

diachrony   a diachronic study in linguistics is the study of language over time.

dialectics   (Hegel, Marx) Can refer to argument where a final position is achieved via dialogue, or can simply refer to the main argument or tendency of a work or a body of work (see Cuddon, 1992: 238–9). *Hegelian* dialectics is the clash between 'thesis' and 'antithesis', resolved by their 'synthesis'. Hegel sought to demonstrate that distinctions between say science and art or mind and body could be resolved by the emergence of a 'higher truth'. Marx recast this onto the conflict between the owners of capital and the workers who produced that capital.

dialogic   (Bakhtin) refers to the idea that all utterances respond to previous utterances and are always addressed to other potential speakers, rather than occurring independently or in isolation. Language always occurs in specific social situations between specific human agents. Words always contain a dialogic quality, embodying a dialogue between different meanings and applications. Bakhtin's dialogism undermines any argument for final and unquestionable positions, since every position within language is a space of dialogic forces rather than monologic truth.

différance   (Derrida) combines Fr. 'to defer, postpone, delay' and 'to differ, to be different from'. The word itself illustrates Derrida's point that writing does not copy or follow speech. The distinction between the two different meanings does not 'correspond to any distinction in their spoken form' (Cuddon, 1992: 246). It makes no difference if we write or speak the word *différance*, we cannot help but invoke notions of both difference and deferral. The word thus illustrates that language involves at one and the same time the differences between and the deferral of meanings.

discourse   term used in distinct contexts in different disciplines. In the study of narrative the term 'narrative' is used to refer to the recounting of events without attention being paid to the person doing the recounting, e.g. 'The King is dead'. In contrast, 'discourse' directs attention to the speaker or writer and the situation from which they speak or write, e.g. 'He told them the sad news that the King was dead'. 'Discourse' has gained a more general sense of language in its social and ideological contexts. Culture and society can be seen as built up of recognizable 'discursive practices', such as those used in educational, legal, religious or political contexts. 'Discourse' points to the fact that language always occurs in specific social contexts and always reflects specific codes, expectations, ideological pressures and presuppositions.

double-voiced discourse   (Bakhtin) refers to the idea that language is always *double-voiced*. No word has a single, independent meaning. All language is shot through with prior utterances, prior uses of the same words, and is always addressed towards other speakers. Bakhtin's vision of double-voiced discourse is essentially intertextual, in that it recognizes that all utterances contain within them the dialogic force of competing interpretations, definitions, social and ideological inflections and so on.

doxa   (Barthes) '-doxy' or '-*doxa*' mean 'opinion'. Barthes uses this suffix as a term for anything which constitutes general opinion, or is at any one moment in society considered unquestionable or natural.

ego   (Freud) a term only explainable in relation to the id and the superego. The *id* is that part of the unconscious which contains a subject's desires, including frequently repressed sexual (libidinal) desires. The *superego* is that part of the conscious mind which, echoing received morality and ideology, strives to police the desires emanating from the id. The ego is the part of the psyche 'which tries as best as it can to negotiate the conflicts between the insatiable demands of the *id*, the impossibly stringent requirements of the *superego*, and the limited possibilities of gratification offered by the world of "reality"' (Abrams, 1993: 265).

epitext   (Genette) refers to 'outside' elements which help us interpret a text (letters, interviews and so on). Genette contrasts 'epitextual' features with what he calls the *peritext*, which consists of all the features which literally frame a text, such as prefaces, covers, titles and so on.

facticity   (Bloom) term based on 'fact', also punning on 'fictitious', and perhaps 'factive' ('causative'). Refers to the unavoidable influence of certain canonical writers. Shakespeare's plays may have been fictitious, but their influence on every subsequent writer gives them the status of facts, or *facticity*.

filiation   'filial' relations are family relations. The traditional notion of authorship views the author as a kind of parent giving life to a text. This 'myth of filiation' is attacked by poststructuralists such as Barthes.

free indirect discourse   refers to the manner in which 'the reports of what a character says and thinks shift in pronouns, adverbs, tense, and grammatical mode, as we move – or sometimes hover – between the direct narrated reproduction of such events by the narrator. Thus, a direct representation, "He thought, 'I will see her home now, and may then stop at my mother's'," might shift, in an indirect representation, to: "He would see her home then, and might afterwards stop at his mother's'" (Abrams, 1993: 169). Allows a narrator to merge their own voice with the inner thoughts or the speech of a particular character.

genotext (Kristeva) refers to elements of a text which unleash or signal semiotic forces which derive from the earliest stages of a subject's existence, when drives and desires are not controlled and channelled into the 'Symbolic Order' (the social categories and divisions of language). Texts which unleash the genotext are resistant to social standards of communication, breaking stylistic and linguistic conventions, and tend to be those of avant-garde and experimental writers. In contrast, Kristeva refers to the *phenotext*, which can be described as 'the language of communication and ... the object of [traditional] linguistic analysis' (Roudiez in Kristeva, 1980: 7). Texts which attempt to produce clear and unequivocal meaning will be almost totally describable in terms of the phenotext.

gynocriticism 'criticism concerned with writings by women ... and all aspects of their production and interpretation' (Cuddon, 1992: 340); 'the branch of modern feminist literary studies that focuses on women as writers, as distinct from the feminist critique of male authors' (Baldick, 1990: 93).

hegemony the OED defines that which is 'hegemonic' as 'the ruling part, the master-principle'. Often used to refer to power which is so dominant that it appears unquestionable, even natural.

heteroglossia, *heteroglot* (Bakhtin) *hetero*, Gr. 'other' + *glossia* Gr. 'tongue': 'other-tongued', 'other-voiced'. Defined by Graham Roberts thus: '*heteroglossia* ... refers to the conflict between "centripetal" and "centrifugal", "official" and "unofficial" discourses within the same national language'. The term also has a smaller-scale application: 'every utterance contains within it the trace of other utterances, both in the past and in the future' (Roberts in Morris, 1994: 248–9). If we call an utterance 'heteroglot' we refer to the presence within it of other utterances, past utterances and future responses or redeployments. A heteroglot utterance would openly attest to the dialogic nature of language, and could be contrasted to an utterance which concealed such features and presented itself as *monoglot*. As dialogism is contrasted to monologism, so *heteroglossia* is contrasted to *monoglossia*.

hybridization (Bakhtin) 'the mixing, within a single concrete utterance, of two or more different linguistic consciousnesses, often widely separated in time and social space' (Clark and Holquist, 1984: 429).

hypertextuality (Genette) 'any relationship uniting a text B (... the *hypertext*) to an earlier text A (.... the *hypotext*), upon which it is grafted in a manner that is not that of commentary' (Genette, 1997a: 5). Genette tends to limit his analysis to satire and intentional relations of this kind.

hypogram (Riffaterre) 'the text imagined in its pretransformational state' (Riffaterre 1978: 63). Since, for Riffaterre, all texts are transformations of small units of meaning, the hypogram is the series of basic units upon which the text is built: 'The *hypogram* may be made out of clichés, or it may be a quotation from another text, or a *descriptive system*' (*ibid.*: 63–4).

hypotext see **hypertextuality**.

id see **ego**.

ideologeme (Kristeva) Fredric Jameson defines this as 'the smallest intelligible unit of the essentially antagonistic collective discourses of social classes' (Hawthorne, 1992: 80). Kristeva employs the term in the context of her work on Bakhtin and relates it to the manner in which texts do not simply reflect but contain elements of society's ideological structures and struggles.

idiolect see **sociolect**.

invariant see **matrix**.

jouissance Fr. 'bliss', often in the sense of sexual climax. Used in poststructuralist theory, notably in Barthes's *The Pleasure of the Text*. He distinguishes between the text which gives *plaisir* (pleasure) and the text which gives *jouissance* (bliss). The former he associates with the kind of text which he had previously called *lisible* (readerly), the latter with the kind of text he had called *scriptible* (writerly).

langage see *langue*.

langue (Saussure) refers to language in its synchronic state, as it is shared by every member of a speaking community. It involves the rules of combination, definitions and distinctions which operate in language at any moment in time. *Parole* concerns the activation of such rules in particular utterances. Thus *parole* can be seen as each specific utterance or utilization of the system of *langue*. Saussure also uses the term *langage*. Since *langue* is an abstract system of rules and codes, it is not simply the accumulation of all acts of utterance, *parole*. Even if we could group all utterances together, we would not describe the full extent of *langue*. *Langage* stands for that sum total of all acts of *parole*, and so is to be distinguished from the abstract system, *langue*.

lisible (Barthes) Fr. 'legible'. A lisible or 'readerly text' encourages readers to view themselves as passive decipherers of meanings already existent in the text itself. Contrasted with the *scriptible* text.

matrix (Riffaterre) refers to a word, phrase or sentence upon which the whole semiotic structure of a text is built. The matrix might not be linguistically present in the text, but would be the basis for the text's *invariants*, its recognizable patterns and structures, all of which will be transformations of that matrix. The word *model* is also employed by Riffaterre to refer to this idea of texts as constructed through transformations of basic elements of meaning.

metafiction 'fiction about fiction; or more especially a kind of fiction that openly comments on its own fictional status ... the term is normally used for works that involve a significant degree of self-consciousness about themselves as fictions' (Baldick, 1990: 133).

metatextuality (Genette) 'the relationship most often labelled "commentary". It unites a given text to another of which it speaks without necessarily citing it ... sometimes even without naming it' (Genette, 1997a: 4).

mimesis from Gr. 'imitation'. The idea that art directly represents external reality. Mimetic views of art are severely challenged by theories of intertextuality, which argue that art works, or 'texts', refer not directly to external reality but to other texts.

model see **matrix**.

Modernism a period of cultural and aesthetic practice usually dated from the beginning of the twentieth century. Not to be confused with 'modernity', which is often used as a term for ideas concerning human and social progress stemming from the eighteenth century. Many movements called Modernist argued that an increase in technological sophistication would liberate society, or at least art, from the shackles of tradition and conformity to established rules and norms.

monoglossia; monoglot   see *heteroglossia*.

monologic   see dialogic.

paradigmatic   the associative aspect of language. 'The *paradigmatic* relationship entails a consideration of the fact that each word in [a sentence] has a relationship with other words that are *not* used but are *capable of being used* – and by being capable are thus associated' (Cuddon, 1992: 946).

paradoxa   (Barthes) Represents anything which is contrary to common opinion and to that which is considered 'natural'.

paratextuality   (Genette) relates to all the elements which stand on the 'threshold' of a text.

parody   'a mocking imitation of the style of a literary work or works, ridiculing the stylistic habits of an author or school by exaggerated mimicry. *Parody* is related to *burlesque* in its application of serious styles to ridiculous subjects, to *satire* in its punishment of eccentricities, and even to criticism in its analysis of style' (Baldick, 1990: 161).

parole   see *langue*.

pastiche   'a literary work composed from elements borrowed either from various other writers or from a particular earlier author. The term can be used in a derogatory sense to indicate lack of originality, or more neutrally to refer to works that involve a deliberate and playful imitative tribute to other writers. Pastiche differs from *parody* in using imitation as a form of flattery rather than mockery, and from *plagiarism* in its lack of deceptive intent' (Baldick, 1990: 162).

peritext   see epitext.

phenotext   see genotext.

polyphony   (Bakhtin) (from Gr. 'many-voicedness'). 'A *polyphonic novel* is one in which several different voices or points of view interact on more or less equal terms' (Baldick, 1990: 173). It demonstrates and celebrates the dialogic nature of society by presenting a vision of human society dominated by the dialogue and play between voices and utterances.

polysemy *poly*, from Gr. 'much', 'many' + *semeio*, 'sign' or 'signal'. That which is polysemous has many meanings or significations. Employed within poststructuralist theory as a way of resisting traditional notions of the singularity of meaning and thus of texts and signs.

Postmodernism a term which has emerged since the 1970s, suggesting a break from Modernism or from the notion of 'modernity'. Since it attempts to represent contemporary trends, Postmodernism is a particularly debated term. However, there are recurrent themes in these debates. Firstly, the idea that national limits for social and cultural identity have been superseded by a global environment in which multinational companies are now more important than national governments in directing social and cultural tendencies. Secondly, such a transnational system is characterized by 'empty signifiers', or representations and signs which have no base in a recognizable, lived reality. Many descriptions of Postmodernism depict a transnational cultural situation in which pastiche and parody of earlier forms and styles predominate. Postmodern art, many argue, rejects notions of originality and Modernism's desire to 'Make it New', and cultivates a wilfully derivative, mixed and thoroughly intertextual approach which attempts to capture a new age in which old certainties about historical knowledge, social progress and even the ability to represent the external world have collapsed.

poststructuralism poststructuralist theorists argued that Saussurean structuralism did not provide scientific objectivity and methodological stability but, rather, demonstrated the unstable nature of language and of meaning. Poststructuralists deny any claims for a scientific study of texts or cultural sign systems and insist that all texts are polysemous.

readerly see *lisible*.

revisionary ratios (Bloom) in historical and political studies 'revisionism' concerns the rewriting of the standard accounts of historical events, often for contemporary ideological purposes or to expose the ideological purposes of prior, established and apparently 'neutral' accounts. Bloom uses revisionary ratios to refer to the different ways in which poets seek to rewrite the works of previous poets.

satire a text which ridicules or ironically comments on socially recognizable tendencies or the style or form of another text or author. Close to the concept of parody, but traditionally has a more moralistic intention.

scriptible see *lisible*.

semianalysis Kristeva's term to characterize her approach to semiotics. She defines it as a 'critique of meaning, of its elements and its laws' (Kristeva, 1980: 4).

semiology see **semiotics**.

semiotic, the (Kristeva) 'the flow of pre-linguistic rhythms or "pulsions" that is broken up by the child's entry into the *Symbolic order* of language. The unconscious energies of the *semiotic* are repressed and marginalized by patriarchal logic and rationality but they may still disrupt the *Symbolic order*, transgressing its rigid categories (including those of identity and sexual difference)' (Baldick, 1990: 201). Kristeva at times refers to language in its 'semiotic phase' (the language of pre-linguistic subjectivity), as opposed to language in its 'thetic phase' (the language of the subject after entry into the Symbolic order).

semiotics, semiology (Saussure, C. S. Pierce) 'the systematic study of *signs*, or, more precisely, of the production of meanings from *sign-systems*, linguistic or non-linguistic' (Baldick, 1990: 201). The relationship between sign and system is particularly important. Sign-systems can be any recognizable field of human communication. Clothing might signify within the cultural 'fashion system', for example. Semiotics and semiology as developed in structuralism and poststructuralism can treat anything emanating from a signifying system as a text to be read.

sign (Saussure) a linguistic or non-linguistic element of communication. Saussure divides the sign into two parts: the *signifier* and the *signified*. The signifier is the material 'sound pattern', a written or spoken word, whilst the signified is the 'concept' associated with that particular signifier. For Saussure signs do not refer directly to things in the external world but have their meaning in terms of the relation between signifiers and signifieds, depending upon the synchronic system of language and its rules and codes of association, combination, definition and distinction.

signifiance (Kristeva, Barthes, poststructuralists) as opposed to the term 'signification' and its association with clear communication of meaning, *signifiance* is used to refer to a kind of language 'that enables a text to signify what representative and communicative speech does not say' (Roudiez in Kristeva, 1980: 18). *Signifiance* also refers to the 'production of meaning' which the reader is involved in when reading such radical forms of language. *Signification* implies the creation of meaning before the act of reading; *signifiance* implies that meaning is only ever produced in the act of reading.

signification   see **signifiance**.

signified   see **sign**.

signifier   see **sign**.

signifyin(g)   (Gates) refers to traditions in African-American culture which play upon conventional 'white' modes of signification. The bracketed '(g)' marks the division between standard written language (associated with dominant 'white' culture) and the spoken dialects of African-Americans.

sociolect   'used to denote language ... which is specific to a particular social group, and which carries with it the values and status of the same group. The social group in question can be defined in terms of class ..., age, or gender – or a permutation of all three' (Hawthorne, 1992: 167). Often paired with *idiolect*, or 'the features of a particular person's language which mark out him or her *individually* from others' (*ibid*.: 80).

speech genre   (Bakhtin) denotes a particular kind of language-use associated with specific social situations.

split subject, the   (Kristeva) the idea that the human subject is divided. In psychoanalysis the split is between the conscious and the unconscious, while for theorists such as Kristeva there are other interesting divisions, such as the split between semiotic and symbolic modes of language.

structuralism   a movement which stems particularly from Saussure's vision of semiology, the study of all the sign-systems operative in culture. Structuralism took texts, from works of literature to aspects of everyday communication, and accounted for them in terms of the system from which they were produced.

subject of enunciation   distinguished in linguistics from the *subject of utterance*, which can be said to be the actual person who performs an act of communication. When that subject refers to itself as an 'I', however, it has become a subject of enunciation. This difference involves 'the particular, time-bound *act* of making a statement, and the *verbal result* of that act, a result which escapes from the moment of time and from the possession of the person responsible for the act' (Hawthorne, 1992: 57). A particular subject (of utterance) might write the words 'I love you' on a card. Years later, when this card is found by someone else, that subject has become merely a first-person pronoun in a conventional and depersonalized statement (subject of enunciation). The same process occurs in any act of writing or repeatable linguistic utterance.

subject of utterance   see **subject of enunciation**.

superego   see **ego**.

Symbolic Order, the   see **semiotic, the**.

synchrony   a synchronic study in linguistics involves the study of how language functions at any one moment in time.

syntagmatic   the combinatory aspect of language. Concerns the sequential placing of words together to form sentences and the relationship of those words when thus combined.

Tel Quel   a school of theory and writing formed in the 1960s and associated with many leading poststructuralist theorists of the period, including Kristeva, Derrida and Barthes. *Tel Quel* sought to theorize and unleash the revolutionary power of language and to celebrate writers who were seen as having performed a similar action.

text   from L. *texere, textum* 'to weave', 'woven' (Cuddon, 1992: 963). Traditionally, a text was the actual words or signs which made up a work of literature. It gave permanence to the work. In structuralist and poststructuralist theory the 'text' comes to stand for whatever meaning is generated by the intertextual relations between one text and another and the activation of those relations by a reader. 'Text' becomes a term associated with the absence of stable and permanent meaning, while 'work' is now associated with the idea of a stable and self-contained meaning.

thetic   see **semiotic, the**.

trace   According to Derrida, 'every sign .... contains a *trace* of other signs which differ from itself .... No sign is complete in itself. One sign leads to another via the *trace* – indefinitely' (Cuddon, 1992: 981).

transcendental signified   (Derrida) a sign which provides a centre for a particular linguistic system. As a centre, it promotes stability, presence and singular, transparent meaning, because its own meaning is not dependent upon any other sign. The signs 'God', 'Justice' or 'Truth' function in this way. Without these 'transcendental signs' the traditional notion of the discursive systems of religion, law and philosophy would collapse due to a lack of cohesion and the lack of a central term. Derrida argues that no sign can ever attain such a position, since every sign has its meaning in relation to other signs. Demonstrating this forms a large part of his deconstruction of the traditional fields of Western thought.

transposition (Kristeva) used to reinforce the notion that intertextual processes have nothing to do with traditional notions concerning 'influence'. Far from an author-to-author transmission of ideas and styles, Kristeva argues that intertextuality, or what she renames transposition, concerns the way in which one 'sign system' is incorporated into another 'sign system' and the semiotic changes this transposition entails.

transtextuality (Genette) 'the textual transcendence of the text .... defined roughly as "all that sets the text in a relationship, whether obvious or concealed, with other texts"' (Genette, 1997a: 1). Genette's term transtextuality is his particular variation on the idea most other critics call intertextuality. He reduces the term intertextuality to 'a relationship of copresence between two texts or among several texts .... the actual presence of one text within another' (Genette, 1997a: 1–2).

trope a figure, where language is not used literally.

ungrammaticality (Riffaterre) refers to anything within a text which alerts the reader to a meaning or structural pattern beyond or below that of the referential or mimetic level of a text. A poem, for example, might have a title which does not seem in any way to relate to the text of the poem itself. The ungrammaticality may well be resolved, however, if the reader shifts from a mimetic to a semiotic level of reading.

work see **text**.

writerly see *lisible*.

BIBLIOGRAPHY

Abrams, M. H. (1993) *A Glossary of Literary Terms*, Harcourt Brace Jovanovich, Fort Worth TX.

Allen, Graham (1994) *Harold Bloom: a poetics of conflict*, Harvester Wheatsheaf, Hemel Hempstead.

Allsen, J. Michael (1993) 'Intertextuality and compositional process in two cantilena motets by Hugo de Lantis' in *Journal of Musciology* 11 (2), 174–202.

Bakhtin, M. M. (1981) *The Dialogic Imagination: four essays*, C. Emerson and M. Holquist (trans.), M. Holquist (ed.), University of Texas Press, Austin TX.

——(1984a) *Problems of Dostoevsky's Poetics*, C. Emerson (trans. and ed.), University of Minnesota Press, Minneapolis MN.

——(1984b) *Rabelais and His World*, Hélène Iswolsky (trans.), Indiana University Press, Bloomington IN.

——(1986) *Speech Genres and Other Late Essays*, V. W. McGee (trans.), C. Emerson and M. Holquist (eds), University of Texas Press, Austin TX.

Bakhtin, M. M./ P. N. Medvedev (1978) *The Formal Method in Literary Scholarship: a critical introduction to sociological poetics*, Albert J. Wehrle (trans.), Johns Hopkins University Press, Baltimore MD and London.

Bakhtin, M. M./ V. N. Volosinov (1986) *Marxism and the Philosophy of Language*, L. Matejka and I. R. Titunik (trans.), Harvard University Press, Cambridge MA and London.

——(1987) *Freudianism: a critical sketch*, I. R. Titunik (trans.), I. R. Titunik with N. H. Bruss (eds), Indiana University Press, Indianapolis IN.

Baldick, Chris (1990) *The Concise Oxford Dictionary of Literary Terms*, Oxford University Press, Oxford and New York.

Barth, John (1975) 'The literature of exhaustion' in Federman (ed.), 19–33.

——(1980) 'The literature of replenishment: postmodernist fiction' in *The Atlantic*, 245 (1), 65–71.

Barthes, Roland (1974) *S/Z*, Richard Howard (trans.), Hill and Wang, New York.

——(1975) *The Pleasure of the Text*, Richard Miller (trans.), Hill and Wang, New York.

——(1977a) *Image – Music – Text*, Stephen Heath (trans.), Fontana, London.

——(1977b) *Roland Barthes by Roland Barthes*, Richard Howard (trans.), Hill and Wang, New York.

——(1979) *A Lover's Discourse: fragments*, Richard Howard (trans.), London, Jonathan Cape.

——(1981a) 'Theory of the text' in Young (ed.) (1981), 31–47.

——(1981b) 'Textual analysis of Poe's "Valdemar"' in Young (ed.) (1981), 133–61.

——(1983) *Barthes: selected writings*, Susan Sontag (ed.), Fontana, London.

——(1984) *Elements of Semiology*, Annette Lavers and Colin Smith (trans.), Jonathan Cape, London.

——(1986) *The Rustle of Language*, Richard Howard (trans.), Basil Blackwell, Oxford.

——(1987) *Sollers Writer*, Philip Thody (trans.), Athlone Press, London.

Baudelaire, Charles (1989) *Baudelaire, Vol. 2: The Poems in Prose and La Fanfarlo*, Francis Scarfe (trans.), Anvil Press, London.

Baudrillard, Jean (1988) *Selected Writings*, Mark Poster (ed.), Stanford University Press, Stanford CA.

Bauer, Dale M. (1988) *Feminist Dialogics: a theory of failed community*, State University of New York Press, Albany NY.

Benjamin, Walter (1968) 'The work of art in the age of mechanical reproduction' in *Illuminations: essays and reflections*, Hannah Arendt (ed.), Schocken Books, New York, 217–51.

Bhabha, Homi K. (1994) *The Location of Culture*, Routledge, London and New York.

Bloom, Harold (1973) *The Anxiety of Influence: a theory of poetry*, Oxford University Press, Oxford.

——(1975a) *A Map of Misreading*, Oxford University Press, Oxford.

——(1975b) *Kabbalah and Criticism*, Seabury Press, New York.

——(1976) *Poetry and Repression: revisionism from Blake to Stevens*, Yale University Press, New Haven CT and London.

——(1982a) *Agon: towards a theory of revisionism*, Oxford University Press, New York and Oxford.

——(1982b) *Breaking the Vessels*, University of Chicago Press, Chicago IL and London.

——(1988) *Poetics of Influence: new and selected criticism*, Henry R. Schwab, New Haven CT.

——(1989) *Ruin the Sacred Truth: poetry and belief from the Bible to the present*, Harvard University Press, Cambridge MA and London.

——(1995) *The Western Canon: the books and schools of the ages*, Macmillan, London.

——(1997) 'Preface: the anguish of contamination' in *The Anxiety of Influence: a theory of poetry*, 2nd ed., Oxford University Press, New York and Oxford, xi–xlvii.

——(1999) *Shakespeare: the invention of the human*, Fourth Estate, London.

Bloom, Harold (ed.) (1979) *et al.*, *Deconstruction and Criticism*, Seabury Press, New York.

Bolter, Jay David (1992) 'Literature in the electronic writing space' in *Literacy Online: the promise [and peril] of reading and writing with computers*, Myron C. Tuman (ed.), University of Pittsburgh Press, Pittsburgh PA and London, 19–42.

Borges, Jorge Luis (1970) *Labyrinths: selected stories and other writings*, Donald A. Yates and James E. Irby (eds), Penguin, Harmondsworth.

Browning, Elizabeth Barrett (1988) *Selected Poems*, Chatto and Windus, London.

Burns, Robert (1969) *Poems and Songs*, James Kinsley (ed.), Oxford University Press, London.

Cancalon, Elaine D. and Antoine Spacagna (eds) (1994) *Intertextuality in Literature and Film: selected papers from the 13th State University of Florida Conference on Literature and Film*, University of Florida Press, Gainesville FL.

Carlson, Marvin (1994) 'Invisible presences: performance intertextuality' in *Theatre Research International* 9 (2), 111–17.

Cixous, Hélène (1994) *The Hélène Cixous Reader*, Susan Sellers (ed.), Routledge, New York and London.

Clark, Katerina and Michael Holquist (1984) *Mikhail Bakhtin*, Belknap Press, Cambridge MA and London.

Clayton, Jay and Eric Rothstein (eds) (1991) *Influence and Intertextuality in Literary History*, University of Wisconsin Press, Wisconsin.

Coughlan, David (1997) *Writing on Society: Henri Lefebvre and the space of literature*, M.Phil. diss. University College, Cork.

Cuddon, J. A. (1992) *Dictionary of Literary Terms and Literary Theory*, Penguin, Harmondsworth.

Culler, Jonathan (1975) *Structuralist Poetics: structuralism, linguistics and the study of literature*, Routledge and Kegan Paul, London.

——(1981) *The Pursuit of Signs: semiotics, literature, deconstruction*, Routledge and Kegan Paul, London.

Delaney, Paul and George P. Landow (eds) (1991) *Hypermedia and Literary Studies*, MIT Press, Cambridge MA and London.

Dentith, Simon (1995) *Bakhtinian Thought: an introductory reader*, Routledge, London.

Derrida, Jacques (1973) *Speech and Phenomena, and Other Essays on Husserl's Theory of Signs*, David B. Allison (trans.), Northwestern University Press, Evanston.

——(1976) *Of Grammatology* Gayatri Chakravorty Spivak (trans.), Johns Hopkins University Press, Baltimore MD and London.

——(1978) *Writing and Difference*, Alan Bass (trans.), Routledge and Kegan Paul, London.

——(1987a) *Positions*, Alan Bass (trans.), Athlone Press, London.

——(1987b) *The Truth in Painting*, Geoff Bennington and Ian McLeod (trans.), University of Chicago Press, Chicago and London.

Duff, David (1997) 'Intertextuality and the Theory of Genre', paper delivered to the *Influence and Intertexuality* conference at the University of Bristol.

DuPlessis, Rachel Blau (1985) *Writing Beyond the Ending: narrative strategies of twentieth-century women writers*, Indiana University Press, Bloomington IN.

Durey, Jill Felicity (1991) 'The state of play and interplay in intertextuality' in *Style* 25 (4), 616–35.

Eagleton, Terry (1986) 'Capitalism, modernism and postmodernism' in *Against the Grain: essays 1975–1985*, Verso, London and New York, 131–47.

Eco, Umberto (1985) *Reflections on 'The Name of the Rose'*, Secker and Warburg, London.

——(1998) *The Name of the Rose*, Vintage, London.

Eliot, T. S. (1974) *Collected Poems: 1909–1962*, Faber and Faber, London.

——(1975) *Selected Prose of T. S. Eliot*, Frank Kermode (ed.), Faber and Faber, London.

Fanon, Frantz (1986) *Black Skin, White Masks*, Charles Lam Markmann (trans.), Pluto Press, London.

Federman, Raymond (ed.) (1975) *Surfiction: fiction now ... and tomorrow*, Swallow Press, Chicago.

Ffrench, Patrick (1995) *The Time of Theory: a history of 'Tel Quel' (1960–1983)*, Clarendon Press, Oxford.

Ffrench, Patrick and Roland-François Lack (eds) (1998) *The Tel Quel Reader*, Routledge, New York and London.

Fleming, Bruce (1994) 'Pictures of pictures: reference and reality in two script versions of *Potemkin*' in Cancalon and Spacagna (eds) (1994), 127–39.

Foucault, Michel (1977) *Language, Counter-Memory, Practice: selected essays and interviews*, Donald F. Bouchard and Sherry Simon (trans.), Donald F. Bouchard (ed.), Cornell University Press, Ithaca NY.

——(1979) 'What is an author?' in Josué V. Harari (ed.) *Textual Strategies: perspectives in post-structuralist criticism*, Cornell University Press, Ithaca NY, 141–60.

Fowles, John (1977) *The French Lieutenant's Woman*, Triad Panther, London.

Freud, Anna (1948) *The Ego and the Mechanisms of Defense*, Cecil Baines (trans.), Hogarth Press, London.

Frow, John (1986) *Marxism and Literary History*, Harvard University Press, Cambridge MA.

Gaskell, Elizabeth (1966) *The Letters of Elizabeth Gaskell*, J. A. V. Chapple and Arthur Pollard (eds), Manchester University Press, Manchester.

Gates, Henry Louis, jr. (1988) *The Signifying Monkey: a theory of Afro-American literary criticism*, Oxford University Press, New York and Oxford.

Genette, Gérard (1982) *Figures of Literary Discourse*, Alan Sheridan (trans.), Columbia University Press, New York.

——(1988) 'The Proustian paratext' in *SubStance: a review of theory and literary criticism* 17 (2), 63–77.

——(1992) *The Architext: an introduction*, Jane E. Lewin (trans.), University of California Press, Berkeley CA and Oxford.

——(1997a) *Palimpsests: literature in the second degree*, Channa Newman and Claude Doubinsky (trans.), University of Nebraska Press, Lincoln NE and London.

——(1997b) *Paratexts: thresholds of interpretation*, Jane E. Lewin (trans.), Richard Macksey (foreword), Cambridge University Press, Cambridge.

Gilbert, Sandra M. and Susan Gubar (1979) *The Madwoman in the Attic: the woman writer and the nineteenth-century literary imagination*, Yale University Press, New Haven CT and London.

Goodwin, James (1994) *Akira Kurosawa and Intertextual Cinema*, Johns Hopkins University Press, Baltimore MD and London.

Hardy, Thomas (1978) *Tess of the D'Urbervilles*, Penguin, Harmondsworth.

Harpold, Terence (1994) 'Conclusions' in Landow (ed.) (1994), 189–222.

Hartman, Geoffrey H. (1987) 'The use and abuse of structural analysis' in G. H. Hartman, *The Unremarkable Wordsworth*, Methuen, London, 129–51.

Hassan, Ihab (1993) 'Toward a concept of Postmodernism' in *Postmodernism: a reader*, Thomas Docherty (ed.), Harvester Wheatsheaf, New York and London, 146–56.

Hatten, Robert S. (1985) 'The place of intertextuality in music studies' in *American Journal of Semiotics*, 3 (4), 69–82.

Hawthorn, Jeremy (1992) *A Concise Glossary of Contemporary Literary Theory*, Edward Arnold, London and New York.

Hermerén, Göran (1992) 'Allusions and intentions' in *Intention and Interpretation*, Gary Iseminger (ed.), Temple University Press, Philadelphia PA.

Hillis Miller, J. (1977) 'Ariachne's broken woof' in *The Georgia Review* 31 (1), 36–48.

——(1979) 'The critic as host' in *Deconstruction and Criticism*, Bloom (ed.) (1979), 217–53.

Hollander, John (1981) *The Figure of Echo: a mode of allusion in Milton and after*, University of California Press, Berkeley, Los Angeles, and London.

Hurston, Zora Neale (1986) *Their Eyes Were Watching God*, Virago, London.

Hutcheon, Linda (1985) *A Theory of Parody: the teachings of twentieth-century art forms*, Methuen, New York and London.

——(1986) 'Literary borrowing ... and stealing: plagiarism, sources, influences, and intertexts' in *English Studies in Canada* 12 (2), 229–39.

——(1988) *A Poetics of Postmodernism: history, theory, fiction*, Routledge, New York and London.

——(1989) *The Politics of Postmodernism*, Routledge, New York and London.

——(1991) 'The politics of Postmodern parody' in Plett (ed.) (1991), 225–36.

Jameson, Fredric (1991) *Postmodernism, or, The Cultural Logic of Late Capitalism*, Verso, London and New York.

Jencks, Charles (1989) *What is Post-Modernism?*, Academy, New York.

Jenny, Laurent (1982) 'The strategy of forms' in *French Literary Theory*

Today: a reader, T. Todorov (ed.), Cambridge University Press, Cambridge, 34–63.

Joyce, James (1971) *Ulysses*, Penguin, Harmondsworth.

Kaup, Monika (1993) *Mad Intertextuality: madness in twentieth-century women's writing*, WVT, Trier.

Kline, T. Jefferson (1992) *Screening the Text: intertextuality in the new wave French cinema*, Johns Hopkins University Press, Baltimore MD and London.

Kolodny, Annette (1986) 'A map for rereading: gender and the interpretation of literary texts' in Showalter (ed.) (1986), 46–62.

Kristeva, Julia (1973) 'The ruin of a poetics' in *Russian Formalism: a collection of articles and texts in translation*, Stephen Bann and John E. Bowlt (eds), Scottish Academic Press, Edinburgh, 102–19.

——(1980) *Desire in Language: a semiotic approach to literature and art*, Thomas Gora, Alice Jardine and Leon S. Roudiez (trans.), Leon S. Roudiez (ed.), Columbia University Press, New York.

——(1984a) *Revolution in Poetic Language*, Margaret Waller (trans.), Leon S. Roudiez (intro.), Columbia University Press, New York.

——(1984b) 'My memory's hyperbole', Athena Viscusi (trans.), in *The Female Autograph*, Domna C. Stanton and Jeanine Parisier Plottel (eds), New York Literary Forum, New York, 261–76.

——(1986) *The Kristeva Reader*, Toril Moi (ed.), Blackwell, Oxford.

——(1989) 'An interview with Julia Kristeva' by Margaret Waller, Richard Macksey (trans.), in O'Donnell and Davis (eds) (1989), 280–93.

——(1998a) 'Towards a semiology of paragrams' in Ffrench and Lack (eds) (1998), 25–49.

——(1998b) 'The samurais "tel quels"' in *Parallax*, 4 (1), special issue (ed. Patrick Ffrench), 'from tel quel to l'infini', 7–11.

Landow, George P. (1992) *Hypertext: the convergence of contemporary critical theory and technology*, Johns Hopkins University Press, Baltimore MD and London.

Landow, George P. (ed.) (1994) *Hyper/Text/Theory*, Johns Hopkins University Press, Baltimore MD and London.

Lavers, Annette (1982) *Roland Barthes: structuralism and after*, Methuen, London.

Leeson, Loraine and Peter Dunn (1986) 'The changing picture' in *Philosophy/Politics: two*, Patricia Holland, Jo Spence and Simon Watney (eds), Comedia Publishing, London, 102–18.

Lotman, Jurij (1971) *The Structure of the Artistic Text*, Gail Lenhoff and Ronald Vroon (trans.), University of Michigan, Ann Arbor MI.

Lyotard, Jean-François (1986) *The Postmodern Condition: a report on knowledge*, Geoff Bennington and Brian Massumi (trans.), Manchester University Press, Manchester.

McLeod, Mary (1985) 'Architecture' in *The Postmodern Moment: a handbook of contemporary innovation in the arts*, Stanley Trachtenberg (ed.), Greenwood Press, Westport CT and London, 19–52.

Mallarmé, Stéphane (1994) *Collected Poems*, Henry Weinfield (trans.), University of California Press, Berkeley, Los Angeles CA and London.

Man, Paul de (1986) *The Resistance to Theory*, Manchester University Press, Manchester.

Miller, Nancy K. (1988) *Subject to Change: reading feminist writing*, Columbia University Press, New York.

Miraglia, Anne Marie (1994) 'Texts engendering texts: a Québecois rewriting of American novels' in Cancalon and Spacagna (eds) (1994), 49–60.

Moi, Toril (1982) 'Feminist literary criticism' in *Modern Literary Theory: a comparative introduction*, Ann Jefferson and David Robey (eds), Batsford, London, 204–21.

——(1985) *Sexual/Textual Politics: feminist literary theory*, Routledge, New York and London.

Morgan, Thaïs (1985) 'Is there an intertext in this text?: literary and interdisciplinary approaches to intertextuality' in *American Journal of Semiotics* 3 (4), 1–40.

Moriarty, Michael (1991) *Roland Barthes*, Polity Press, Oxford.

Morris, Pam (ed.) (1994) *The Bakhtin Reader: selected writings of Bakhtin, Medvedev, Voloshinov*, Edward Arnold, London.

Nielsen, Aldon L. (1994) *Writing Between the Lines: race and intertextuality*, University of Georgia Press, Athens GA and London.

Norris, Christopher (1982) *Deconstruction: theory and practice*, Methuen, London and New York.

O'Connor, Mary (1991) 'Subject, voice, and women in some contemporary black American women's writing' in *Feminism, Bakhtin, and the Dialogic*, Dale M. Bauer and S. Jaret McKinsky (eds), State University of New York Press, Albany NY, 199–217.

O'Donnell, Patrick and Robert Con Davis (eds) (1989) *Intertextuality and Contemporary American Fiction*, Johns Hopkins University Press, Baltimore MD and London.

Pearce, Lynn (1994) *Reading Dialogics*, Edward Arnold, London.

Pfister, Manfred (1991) 'How Postmodern is intertextuality?' in Plett (ed.) (1991), 207–24.

Plath, Sylvia (1981) *Collected Poems*, Ted Hughes (ed.), Faber and Faber, London.

Plett, Heinrich F. (ed.) (1991) *Intertextuality*, Walter de Gruyter, Berlin and New York.

Plottel, Jeanine Parisier and Hanna Charney (eds) (1978) *Intertextuality: new perspectives in criticism*, New York Literary Forum, New York.

Poe, Edgar Allan (1986) *'The Fall of the House of Usher' and Other Writings*, David Galloway (ed.), Penguin, Harmondsworth.

Poovey, Mary (1984) *The Proper Lady and the Woman Writer: ideology as style in the works of Mary Wollstonecraft, Mary Shelley and Jane Austen*, University of Chicago Press, Chicago IL and London.

Quirk, Tom (1995) 'Sources, influences, and intertexts' in *Resources for American Literary Study* 21 (2), 240–57.

Reader, Keith A. (1990) 'Literature/cinema/television: intertextuality in Jean Renoir's *Le Testament du docteur Cordelier*' in Worton and Still (eds) (1990), 176–89.

Rhys, Jean (1968) *Wide Sargasso Sea*, Penguin, Harmondsworth.

Riffaterre, Michael (1973a) 'The self-sufficient text' in *Diacritics* 3 (3), 39–45.

——(1973b) 'Interpretation and descriptive poetry: a reading of Wordsworth's "Yew-Trees"' in Young (ed.) (1981), 103–32.

——(1977) 'Semantic overdetermination in poetry' in *PTL: a journal for descriptive poetics and theory of literature* 2, 1–19.

——(1978) *Semiotics of Poetry*, Indiana University Press, Bloomington IN.

——(1980a) 'Syllepsis' in *Critical Inquiry* 6 (4), 625–38.

——(1980b) 'Interpretation and undecidability' in *New Literary History* 12 (2), 227–42.

——(1983) *Text Production*, Terese Lyons (trans.), Columbia University Press, New York.

——(1984) 'Intertextual representation: on mimesis as interpretive discourse' in *Critical Inquiry* 11 (1), 141–62.

——(1985) 'The interpretant in literary semiotics' in *American Journal of Semiotics* 3 (4), 41–55.

——(1990a) 'Compulsory reader response: the intertextual drive' in Worton and Still (eds) (1990), 56–78.

——(1990b) *Fictional Truth*, Johns Hopkins University Press, Baltimore MD and London.

Rushdie, Salman (1995) *Midnight's Children*, Vintage, London.

Russo, Mary (1986) 'Female grotesques: carnival and theory' in *Feminist Studies: critical studies*, Teresa de Laurentis (ed.), Indiana University Press, Bloomington IN, 213–29.

Rylance, Rick (1994) *Roland Barthes*, Harvester Wheatsheaf, Hemel Hempstead.

Saussure, Ferdinand de (1974) *Course in General Linguistics*, Wade Baskin (trans.), Jonathan Culler (intro.), Charles Bally, Albert Sechehaye, in collaboration with Albert Reidlinger (eds), Fontana, London.

Shelley, Mary (1994) *The Last Man*, Morton D. Paley (ed.), Oxford University Press, Oxford and New York.

——(1996) *Frankenstein*, J. Paul Hunter (ed.), W. W. Norton, New York and London.

Showalter, Elaine (1984) *A Literature of Their Own: British women novelists from Brontë to Lessing*, Virago, London.

——(1987) *The Female Malady: women, madness and English culture, 1830–1980*, Virago, London.

——(1990) 'Feminism and literature' in *Literary Theory Today*, Peter Collier and Helga Geyer-Ryan (eds), Polity Press, Oxford, 179–202.

Showalter, Elaine (ed.) (1986) *The New Feminist Criticism: essays on women, literature and theory*, Virago, London.

Sollers, Philippe (1975) 'The novel and the experience of limits' in Federman (ed.), 59–74.

Spivak, Gayatri Chakravorty (1985) 'Three women's texts and a critique of imperialism' in *Critical Inquiry* 12 (1), 243–61.

Starobinski, J. (1979) *Words upon Words: the anagrams of Ferdinand de Saussure*, Olivia Emmet (trans.), Yale University Press, New Haven CT.

Steiner, Wendy (1985) 'Intertextuality in painting' in *American Journal of Semiotics* 3 (4), 57–67.

Todorov, Tzvetan (1984) *Mikhail Bakhtin: the dialogical principle*, Wlad Godzich (trans.), Manchester University Press, Manchester and New York.

Vice, Sue (1997) *Introducing Bakhtin*, Manchester University Press, Manchester and New York.

Walker, Alice (1983) *The Color Purple*, Women's Press, London.

Walker, John A. (1994) *Art in the Age of Mass Media*, Pluto Press, London.

Wallis, Brian (ed.) (1984) *Art after Modernism: rethinking representation*, New Museum of Contemporary Art, New York.

White, Hayden (1973) *Metahistory: the historical imagination in nineteenth-*

century Europe, Johns Hopkins University Press, Baltimore MD and London.

Worton, Michael and Judith Still (eds) (1990) *Intertextuality: theories and practices*, Manchester University Press, Manchester and New York.

Yaeger, Patricia S. (1984) '"Because a Fire Was in My Head": Eudora Welty and the dialogic imagination' in *PMLA* 99, 955–73.

Young, Robert (ed.) (1981) *Untying the Text: a post-structuralist reader*, Routledge and Kegan Paul, London.

INDEX